# A YEAR OF WATERCOLOUR

## A SEASONAL GUIDE TO BOTANICAL WATERCOLOUR PAINTING

### HARRIET DE WINTON

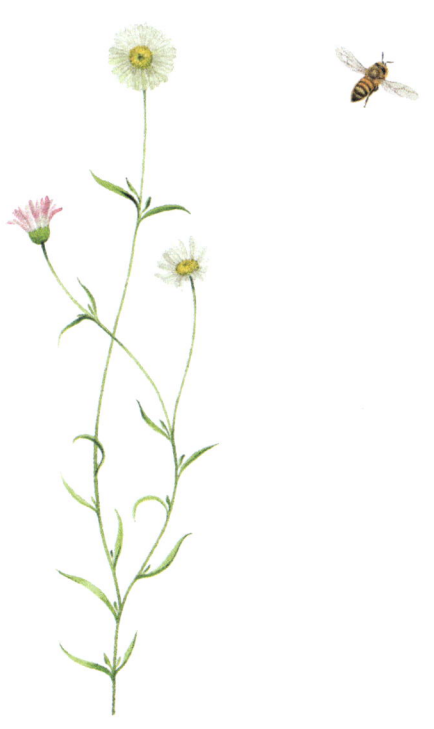

**ilex**

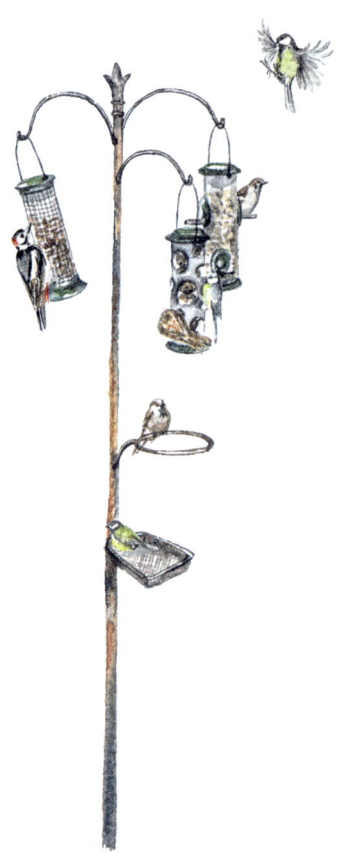

# CONTENTS

# INTRODUCTION

I've spent the last ten years working as a watercolour artist
on wedding stationery, teaching workshops and a few private
commissions. I love my job. I normally work from photo references
provided by clients of houses, wedding bouquets, pet portraits,
all sorts of things. Despite feeling lucky to be doing this every
day, painting from photos rather than real life subjects led to an
inevitable disconnect with my work. Something needed to change.

In March 2020 the wedding work evaporated as lockdown hit.
Weddings all over the world were being cancelled or postponed and
I had little more to do than make a long list of worries and take the
dog for a walk. An enforced slowdown allowed my brain to notice the
changes in nature: the cherry blossom trees' gradual bud and blossom
in the spring months, the changing colours as summer became
autumn and the seedpods' paper thin transformation as we greeted
winter. Along the way I foraged wild garlic and elderflower, stared
quizzically at mushrooms and left them well alone. I observed the
natural world in a way I never had before.

It wasn't until we were well into autumn that I thought to take a
sketch book out and document some of this. I'm a novice nature
journaller, with much to learn but what I can show you in this book is
how my paintings and general approach to creating were enhanced
through observing the changing world around me.

The world seems quite different a few years on and it feels more
important than ever to prioritize the simple pleasures of quiet
observation on daily dog walks.

Before, I would paint a single flower floating on the page; now I'm
more inclined to include the fields and skies that are its natural
backdrop. With the travel restrictions of 2020 I was amazed to
find so many of this book's subjects literally on my doorstep; the
hedgerow along our lane reinvented itself each season, animals
came and went from our garden, and I could watch flocks of birds
and sheep from my studio window. The daily dive into nature
with our dog Crumble provided a few new sights and sounds but
the contents of this book were largely observed within a square
mile of our house. I would never have believed I would see so
much had I not slowed down to look.

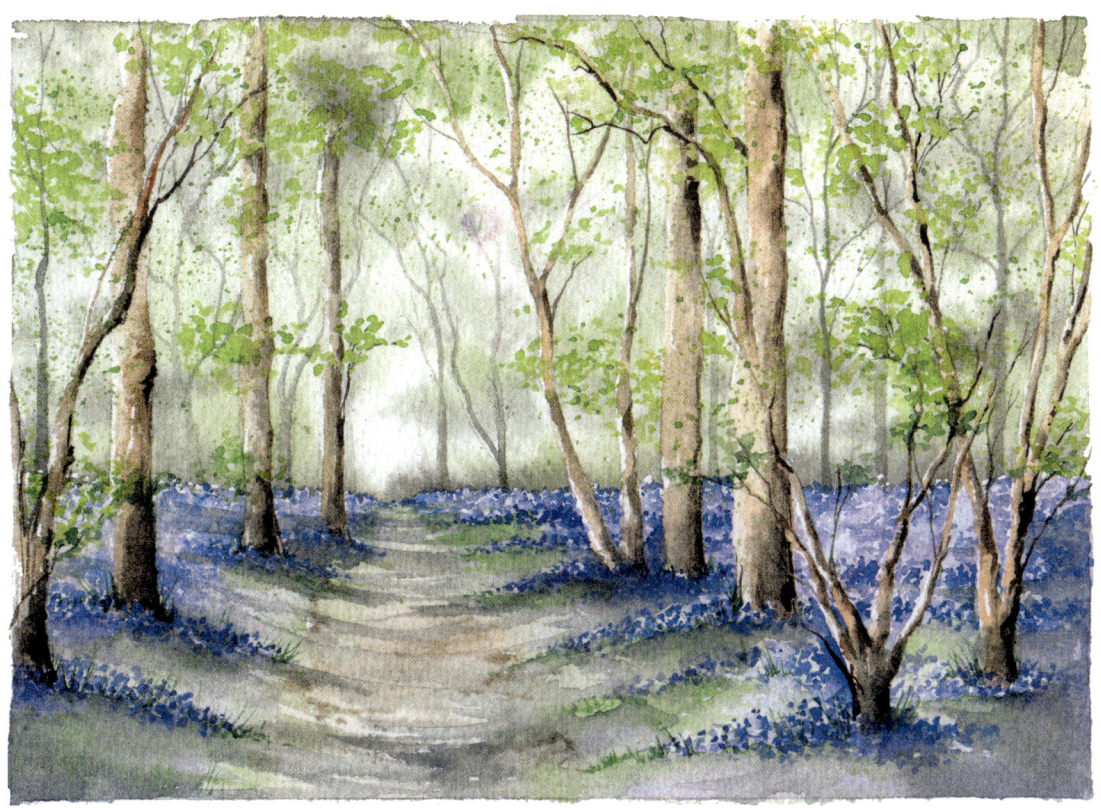

Throughout the book I've given occasional examples of the sketches and quick loose paintings that I did when nature journalling as well as the fully formed, detailed painting tutorials that were my previous hallmark.

I've loved forcing myself out of the comfort of my studio to paint and scribble in the great outdoors and I would encourage you to take a sketch book out with you on your next walk. I walked many times with painting materials in my bag and never got them out; I had to unlearn years of painting 'perfect' pieces in the studio and see the journalling process as the ultimate experimentation phase that could only improve my pieces back at my desk.

So be brave, put pencil and paint to page wherever you are and see what happens!

# MATERIALS

Watercolour painting requires a relatively simple and affordable kit list. The joy of painting in the great outdoors is seeing how to get the best from a streamlined field kit and a simplified list of colours. If you have favourite pencils, brushes and other tools it is worth getting duplicates for your field kit and studio setup.

### Paint

In the studio I use tubes of watercolour. I've got a Loxley foldable plastic palette with all the colours squeezed out into wells. Over time these paints dry and act just like pans (dry, concentrate blocks of watercolour) so would be easy to transport. However, my studio palette is large and cumbersome.

For nature journalling I've used ready-made half-pan travel kits with up to 12 colours and even created my own little homemade travel set by using a hinged metal tin that used to carry sweets and filled some empty half-pan cases with colours of my choice. A very clever friend taught me to stick little flat magnets to the bottom of each pan which helps keep it securely in place. In both instances the lid of the paint set doubles up as a mixing palette.

I've always been very happy with Daler-Rowney and Winsor & Newton's professional range. They also have a lower-quality, more affordable 'student range' which is perfectly good for beginners, but I always encourage students to buy the best quality they can afford.

### Brushes

In addition to the wonderfully versatile pointed round brushes I've used for years (I use sizes 8, 6, 4, 2, 0, ⅖, ⅙ in this book) I've introduced a few new shapes. My brand of choice with all these brushes is Pro Arte. The pointed rounds are the Masterstroke Series 60 range: synthetic brushes with a great snap.

The rigger brush has long slender bristles which have revolutionized painting fine stems, leaf detail and animal whiskers.

The mop brush can put down a quick and even wash and is a brilliant addition to any kit when painting landscapes and larger areas of colour.

If you enjoy nature journalling you will love a water brush: a synthetic bristled brush with a channel to hold water in the thick handle, doing away with the need to balance a water jar on your painting station. I love using the Pentel Aquash, which comes with a screw on lid to ensure the bristles remain protected while you're moving around.

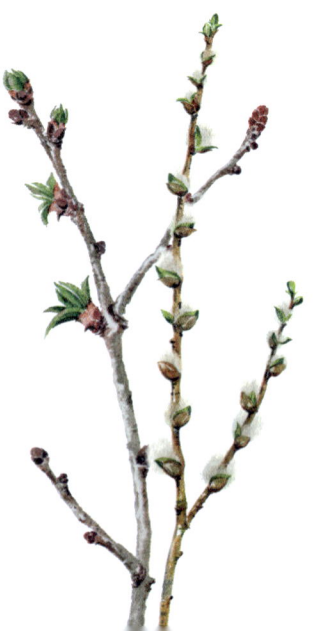

Your brushes will last longer if you clean them thoroughly after use and never leave them bristles down in a jar of water. The paint will flake off the handle of a brush left in water making it uncomfortable to hold, not to mention that the poor bristles will be bent out of shape.

## Paper

The projects in this book are done entirely on cold pressed paper. It has a slightly mottled texture and soaks up paint and water in an even manner. The worst thing you can do is get too precious about your paper and fear 'ruining' it. Every mark you make, however unsteady, is contributing to your improvement as a painter.

Paper quality depends on two things: the paper's content and thickness. When painting in the studio I use the Langton Prestige by Daler-Rowney: a relatively affordable cotton pulp 300gsm paper. A more affordable option is paper made from wood pulp.

For nature journalling, I recommend a journal. The paper tends to be thinner and can warp with lots of water so look for thicker, cold pressed pages if you enjoy wet, expansive landscapes. For me the most important feature of a journal is whether it can lie flat on an open page spread. Head to your nearest art store and have a good look at all the journals on offer and find the right one for you.

## Palette

When using paint tubes, a ceramic plate works just fine as a palette. If you are working with plenty of wet colour, it is wise to buy a palette with wells that compartmentalize the paint. You can buy plastic, ceramic and enamel metal palettes. Ceramic is best for mixing watercolours (which is why I often end up on a plate).

My Loxley folding plastic palette is the best-sized palette I've found for holding plenty of colours with lots of space for mixing. To prep the plastic, I scrubbed it with wire wool to rough up the surfaces. If I could get an equivalent in ceramic that would be the ultimate palette.

### Masking fluid

Art masking fluid is a yellow-tinted latex mix which can be painted on paper and over dry washes of watercolour to preserve layers, which can be revealed later. I use Winsor & Newton art masking fluid. I suggest allocating a brush just for applying masking fluid as it won't be fit for purpose afterwards. Alternatively, you can buy masking fluid applicators.

### Water jar

In the studio any low-ball glass, mug or plastic container will do as long as its sides aren't too high. I prefer a clear vessel so I can see when to replenish the water. Painting with swamp water will inevitably affect the colours on your page. I work with two jars of water: one to clean off the brush and the other to dip the newly clean brush into.

For nature journalling I've been known to use a little Tupperware and a big piece of Blu Tack (reusable adhesive) to keep it in place. See also the water brush.

### Pencil and erasers

You can buy water soluble graphite pencils that dissolve when wet. I choose to use a regular HB pencil working as lightly as possible because I like to keep an eye on the guidelines for as long as possible. If my drawings are too heavy, rubbing lightly with a Faber-Castell kneadable art eraser (before applying paint) leaves a faint pencil line. Once the pencil is painted over, I use a regular hard eraser for one last rub-out of any visible pencil.

### Pens

On occasion I've enjoyed scribbling a pen sketch and adding a loose wash of watercolour to quickly document a subject matter's colours and movement. I love to use the water-resistant Winsor & Newton fineliner pens.

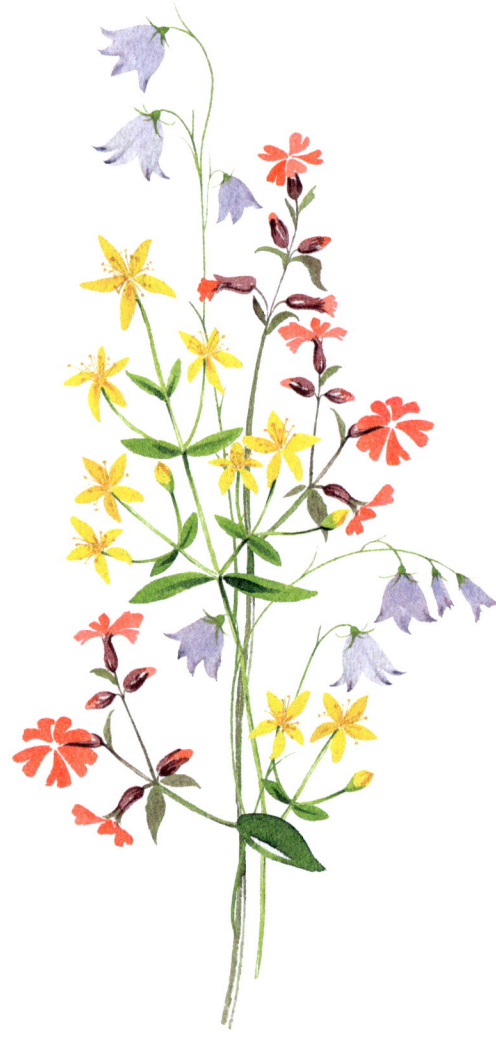

### Compass
If you don't have a compass for the birds' nest project you can draw around something round.

### Ruler
Every now and then we need to draw a horizon line for a landscape.

### Washi tape
This is useful either to mark out a crisp area for painting or to keep a piece of paper anchored to the desk.

### Bull dog clips
Use these to keep your journal pages anchored flat while you are nature journalling.

### Kitchen roll
In the studio I always place my palette on the edge of a piece of kitchen roll to stop it from sliding about and also to blot my brush dry. When blotting it like this you will find hidden paint lingering in the seemingly clean bristles, warranting another swish in the jar of water.

### Your workspace
When painting at home seat yourself at a table in a space with as much natural light as possible. I am lucky enough to have a studio with a rural view that constantly revitalizes my energy. Feeling good in your environment both mentally and physically is so important.

When in the great outdoors, find a sheltered spot with a good view of your subject matter. I've always been OK sitting on the ground, but you could take a little camping chair if it's not too heavy to carry. Painting with a journal on your knees can be a little awkward and I've experimented with taking a piece of board to rest the book on. It's large enough to Blu Tack my paint set and water jar onto. Some might find it cumbersome, but I've found it suits me!

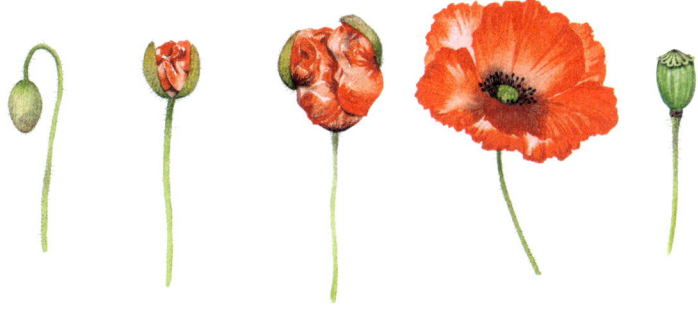

# PAINTING TECHNIQUES

If you've followed along with one of my books before, then this section will be familiar to you, but it's always worth coming back to the very basics of watercolour.

Watercolour pigment is intensely concentrated – you only need the tiniest bit. Water is the vehicle for the colour to travel and it does most of the work, so the golden rule of watercolour is that your brush should always be wet. I don't mean waterlogged at all times, but the bristles need to be damp enough to hold paint even you are when working on precise detail. Swish the brush around in your water jar and wipe the bristles on the rim a few times. This allows paint to flow from brush to page as smoothly as a felt tip pen.

Throughout this book I will refer to the paint as wet, diluted and concentrated.

**Wet:** plenty of water on the brush with plenty of colour, allowing for broad coverage and bright, seamless blending.

**Dilute:** plenty of water and very little colour to achieve a pale, translucent quality.

**Concentrate:** used most often for precise detail in the final stages of a painting; a good coverage of colour on the brush with minimal water.

**Wash:** a watercolour wash is an area of transparent, diluted colour.

The following painting techniques are all carried out with a size 4 rounded point brush.

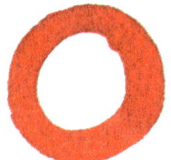

**Dry on dry**
Applying concentrated paint to a dry surface: either a dry page or a painted page that has dried fully.

Your brush should never be bone dry: the term 'dry on dry' refers to watercolour in its most concentrated form.

Paint a concentrated circle on a dry page; not very exciting, but the colour is opaque and going nowhere on a dry page.

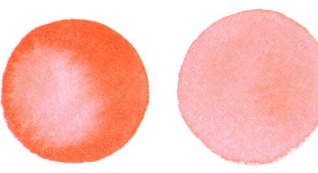

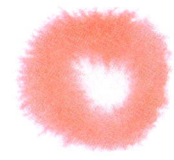

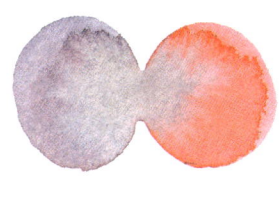

### Wet on dry

Applying wet paint to a dry surface: either a dry page or a painted page that has dried fully.

Clean your brush off and wet it again. Fill in that dry on dry circle with water, stroking the brush to pick up colour from the inner edge of the circle and watch the colour blend inwards. An initial sweep round will bring in a paler colour to fill the circle. A few more strokes will intensify the colour to make a solid colour circle. The outer edge of the circle is still crisp on the dry paper.

Alternatively, painting a new circle in a more diluted colour will result in an even, translucent shape.

### Wet on wet

Applying wet paint to a wet surface when you want to create a soft, diffused edge and a seamless blend.

With a clean brush, wet a section of page (don't leave puddles of standing water but just make the surface evenly damp), approximately 5cm (2in) square. Paint that same red circle with your wet brush and watch the paint feather out. The more soaked your page is, the more unruly your watercolour will be in its travels. It is tempting to prod and poke the watercolour tendrils, but this technique is always more effective when you let the paint do its thing, undisturbed.

### Standing water vs an even blend

If you are left with puddles of standing water having wet your page, you've gone too far. Colour that is applied to puddles struggles to reach the page and results in an uncontrollable and erratic blend. It can be saved by gently blotting your puddles with kitchen roll. A piece of paper that has been wetted evenly with no puddles allows for smooth and even blends.

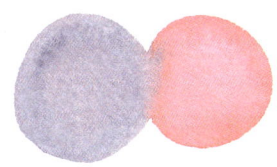

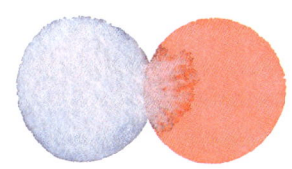

### Blending and layering

When working on a composition, you add colour either by blending (wet on wet) or layering (wet on dry, dry on dry).

Blending colours involves a little restraint. Refrain from prodding the two colours into each other with your brush. This can lead to over-mixing which nearly always results in a dull, flat colour.

Paint a wet circle, then choose a different wet colour and paint a second, just overlapping circle. As long as you are using enough water in your colour mix the paint will do its thing unaided.

Try to balance the wetness of each shape. If one colour holds more water than the other, you will get a bloom effect.

**Layering**

Once a layer of paint is bone dry, you can add additional layers of colour and detail with no fear of it bleeding.

It is far easier to add a darker/more concentrated colour to a lighter/more diluted one than the other way around. In the projects I will always start with a light wash and build it up in intensity, layer by layer. When it comes to the compositions in Winter (see page 120), you need to keep this in mind when you choose what to paint first.

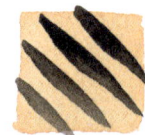

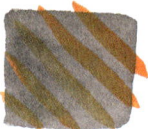

## BASIC BRUSHSTROKES

Now you've tested the paint and water, it's time to see what the brushes can do

**Lines: thin to thick**

Thin line

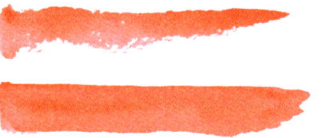

Thick line

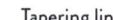

Tapering line

### 1.

You wouldn't think a size 8 rounded point would be the best brush for fine detail but try painting the thinnest line you can. You might be surprised. Wet the brush and coat the tip with paint and paint a line just using the point of the tip. If your paintbrush has a blob of paint on the end, twist the tip of the bristles in the palette to regain the fine tip.

### 2.

Now coat the full length of the bristles first in water and then paint. Angling the brush low against the page so the full length of the bristles is touching the paper, sweep the brush sideways and see how thick a line you can paint. You will find the paint dries out fairly quickly. Wet your brush and smooth the clean wet bristles over the colour and it will travel much further. You don't need to add any more paint.

### 3.

The combination stroke to create a tapered line is the first of the three key watercolour brush strokes. Starting with the tip of the brush, paint that fine line and as you move the brush across the paper, press down so the full thickness of the bristles creates a gradual thickening line. Keep going and smoothly lift the brush back to just the tip touching the page. You will have created an elongated eye shape. Play around with this stroke and see what different shapes you can make. This will be referred to as a tapered line throughout the book.

## Curves: C

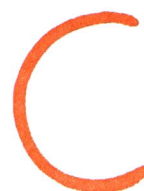  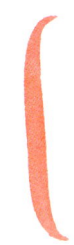

### 1.

Now you have mastered strokes in a straight line, it is time to add some shape. Paint a curve that resembles the letter 'C' with the tip of your brush. You are aiming for a line that maintains a consistent thickness.

### 2.

Keep each end of the C thin, and the middle as thick as possible; you are essentially painting a tapered line in the shape of a C. Start with the tip of the brush and press the full thickness of the bristles down as the brush travels down around in a curve, finishing with the tip in a controlled manner so that the bristles don't flick out of control.

### 3.

The C-curve may not always closely resemble the letter C, but it still follows the premise. Try a long, elongated stroke that curves in at both ends.

## Curves: S

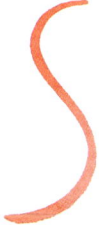 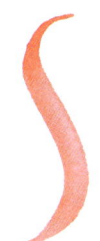 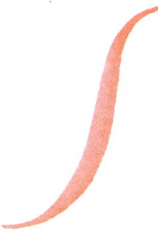

### 1.

The S-curve is the third watercolour stroke that dominates these projects. With the tip of your brush, paint an elongated S, maintaining a consistent thickness.

### 2.

Start the S with the tip of the brush and press it down as you reach the middle, finishing with the tip in a controlled manner so that the bristles don't flick out of control. The angle of your brush should stay in line with the direction of the curve.

### 3.

An S-curve may not always resemble the letter S, but it still follows the premise. This third version of the S-curve is commonly used when painting leaves. Angling your brush at 90 degrees to the S-curve, paint a thick S-curve but keep the brush low to the page to fill out the thicker section, creating a fuller line before lifting the brush to finish at the tip.

# LEAVES

We paint leaves and petals of all shapes and sizes in this book. The common rule throughout is to use the largest brush with which you're able to maintain good control as the fewer the brush strokes the better-looking the leaf or petal.

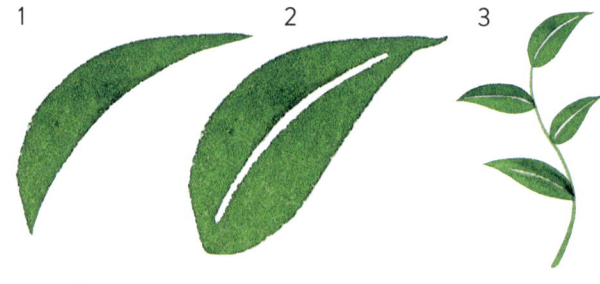

### Smooth-sided leaves
Example project: Wild Garlic
(see page 30)

## 1.

Draw a pencil curve, which will act as the central line of your leaf. Load up your brush with wet sap green. If you have a blob of water on the tip, tap it gently in your palette to get a fine tip. Starting with the tip of the brush at one end of the pencil line, paint a fine line and move the brush along one side of the pencil line, pressing down so the full thickness of the bristles creates a gradual thickening line. Keep going and smoothly lift the brush back to just the tip touching the page at the other end of the pencil line. Your leaf should have a finer tip and rounded bottom. If you're left with a blob of paint on the leaf, clean and dry off your brush and carefully lift off this blob while the leaf is still wet.

## 2.

Load up your brush again and start from the same starting point with a mirrored stroke leaving a tiny sliver of unpainted space down the middle. If your pencil line is curved, your second paint stroke will have to accommodate this curve. Play around with leaves bending in all different directions until you feel confident enough to paint them onto a stem.

## 3.

For many people these leaves don't make much sense until they're on a stem. Draw a faint pencil curved stem and numerous curves branching off. These aren't branches, they are central leaf lines. Paint the stem with a size 0 brush and then proceed to paint in each leaf with your size 4 brush.

### Serrated-edge leaves
Example project: Blackthorn
(see page 112)

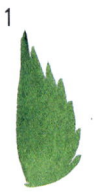 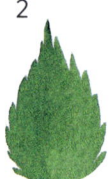

## 1.

Paint a tapered line in wet sap green. Paint another, slightly smaller line by its side with the tip curving out but coming down into the central base point. Add another slightly smaller line and repeat until you've created one half of a serrated leaf.

## 2.

Repeat on the other side.

### Scalloped edge leaves
Example project: Wild Violets
(see page 54)

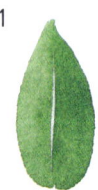 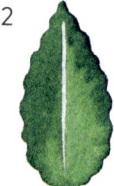

## 1.

Paint your smooth-sided leaf shape with wet sap green.

## 2.

While still wet, use your size 0 brush to paint a wet sap green scalloped edge around the leaf. Work quickly and this will blend into the body of the leaf.

# PETALS

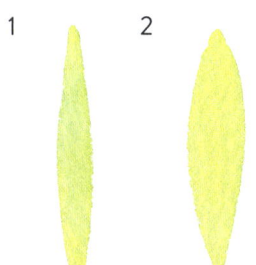

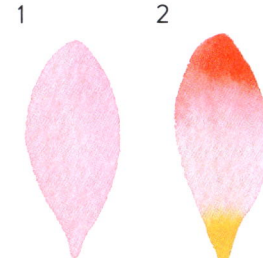

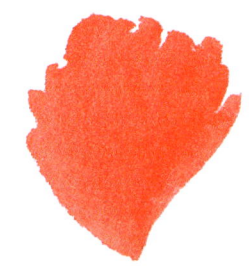

### Smooth one-colour petals
Example project: Dandelions (see page 56)

## 1.
Mix plenty of wet/diluted colour in the palette ready to go, then load up your brush with paint, making sure to avoid a blob of water on the tip. Paint a tapered line (this might make your perfect petal shape and you can stop there).

## 2.
Fill out the shape by painting smooth mirrored C-curves either side of the central stroke. If you're left with a blob of paint on the petal, clean and dry off your brush and carefully dab the blob and lift it off while the petal is still wet.

### Smooth colour blend petals
Example project: Dog Rose (see page 94)

## 1.
Paint a smooth-sided petal with a diluted base colour. Start with the fine point of your brush and add pressure to fan out the bristles as you paint outwards. The amount of water in this petal shape should be a smooth, even wetness with no puddles.

## 2.
While still wet, edge the petal with more concentrated colour and a dab of colour at the central point of the flower.

### Frilled edge petals
Example project: Field Poppy (see page 88)

## 1.
Start with the fine point of your brush at the flower centre and add pressure to fan out the bristles as you paint outwards. Lift the brush with some immediacy leaving the edges rough and frilled. You will need a few brush strokes to create each petal.

# CHOOSING COLOURS

The colours you choose will depend on whether you use this book as a guide for painting at home or as an introduction to nature journalling. While I have space for multiple palettes on my desk, one of my favourite experiences of nature journalling was seeing just how many colours I could produce from a very limited colour palette.

## HOW TO MIX COLOURS

To mix colours most effectively you will need a large brush (size 8 pointed round). 'Wake up' the colours you're mixing by adding a little water to them in the palette well. Find a clean area of your palette and deposit one of the wet, woken up colours into it. Clean off your brush and add a tiny amount of the second colour (you can always add more but it's hard to remove it from the mix). Mix together with your brush and see what colour you're left with. Consider how much of this colour you will need and whether you need it concentrated or diluted. Add water or further colour to make a large enough batch.

### Primary colour mixing

Unsurprisingly the three primary colours are the main foundations of colour mixing. Adding in sap green broadens the mixing potential even further.

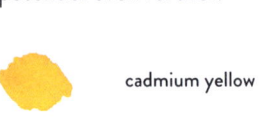

cadmium yellow

cadmium red

French ultramarine blue

sap green

Mix cadmium yellow and cadmium red to make a range of oranges and ochres.

Mix French ultramarine blue and sap green to make teals and forest greens.

Mix cadmium yellow and sap green to make green golds.

Mix cadmium red and French ultramarine blue to make purple and burgundy.

Mix cadmium yellow and French ultramarine blue to make turquoise and greens.

Mix cadmium yellow, cadmium red and French ultramarine blue for browns.

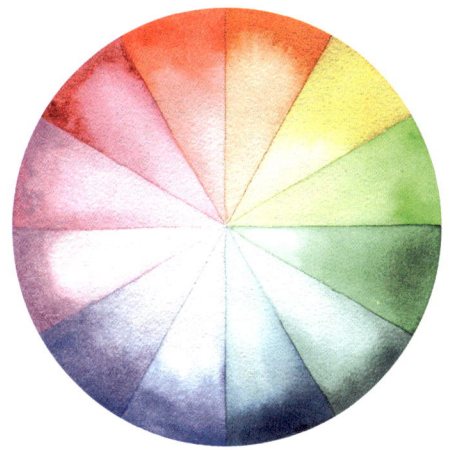

## Complementary colours

Complementary colours appear opposite each other on the colour wheel. Mixing equal parts of complementary colours results in brown but a tiny addition of the complementary colour creates a wonderfully muted palette, great for autumn and winter scenes.

## Complementary pairs

red and green
orange and blue
yellow and purple

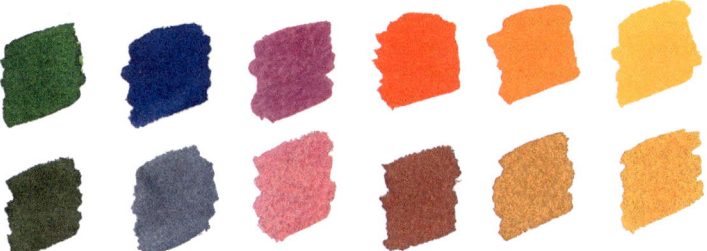

**Unmixed colours**

**Mixed with small amount of complementary colours**

## Listed colours

This book's projects feature 20 colours, which can be categorized into warm, cold and earth tones. For each project I've listed the colours and mixes used but you will also find corresponding colour swatches which are a great resource to colour match with if you're using a more limited colour palette.

### Warm

sap green
green gold
French ultramarine blue
cobalt blue
cobalt blue deep
cobalt turquoise
cadmium red
cadmium orange
cadmium yellow
Mars black

### Cold

Payne's grey
Winsor blue
Prussian blue
permanent rose
alizarin crimson
lemon yellow

### Earth

yellow ochre
burnt sienna
raw umber
burnt umber

## Value (light and dark)

A colour's value refers to its lightness or darkness. Watercolour becomes lighter with dilution. White watercolour paint is used more as a thickener than a lightener. To explore the value range of any colour, paint a filled in wet circle of concentrated colour. Clean off your brush and paint a filled-in circle of water that just overlaps the edge of the previous circle. Watch the paint bloom into the wet space. Repeat this step multiple times until the colour has faded entirely.

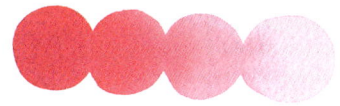

# LABELLED DIAGRAMS

I don't expect you to be fluent in the anatomy of plants and animals so these labelled diagrams offer a reference to some of the words I use in the painting projects.

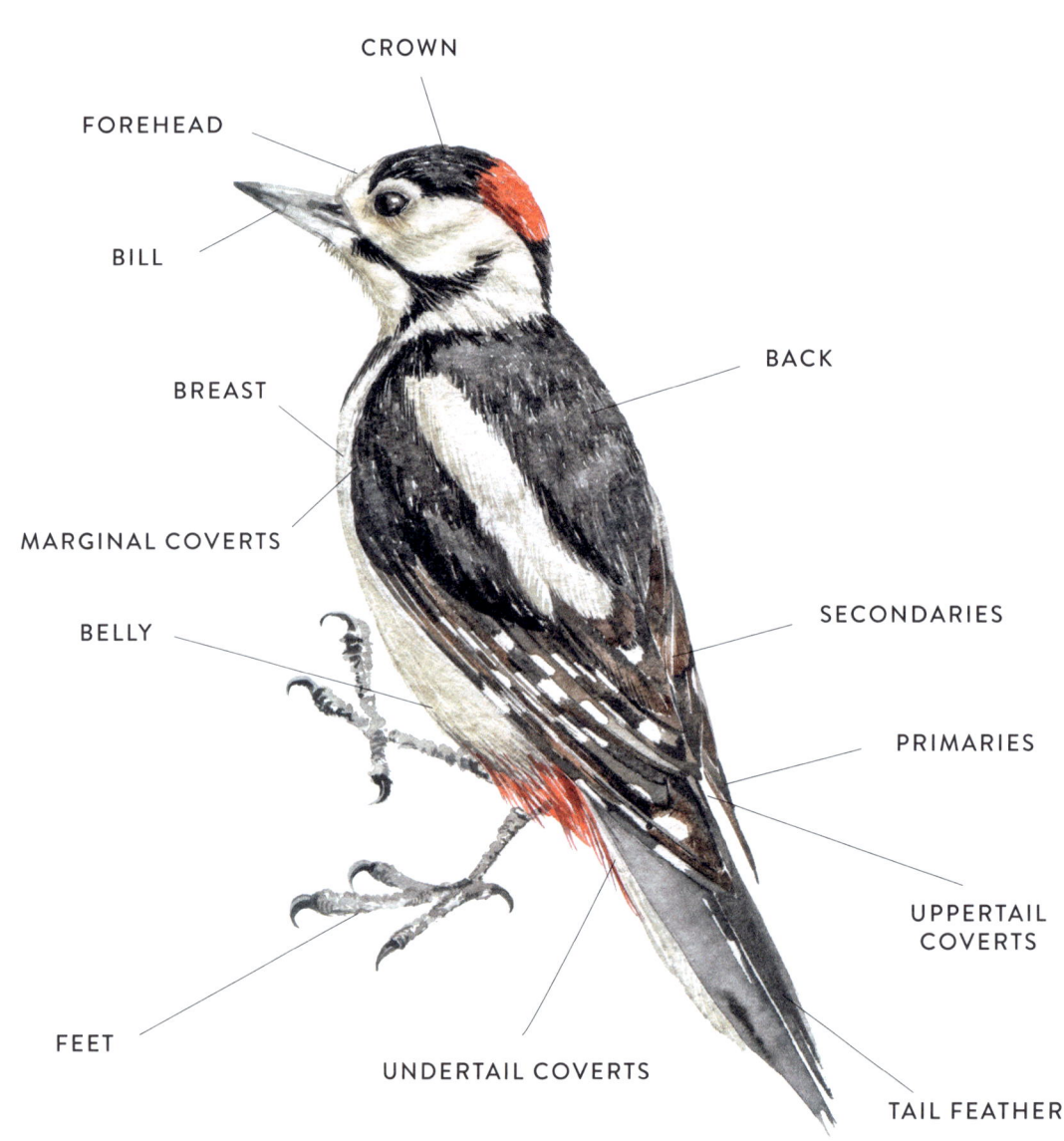

CROWN

FOREHEAD

BILL

BREAST

MARGINAL COVERTS

BELLY

BACK

SECONDARIES

PRIMARIES

UPPERTAIL COVERTS

FEET

UNDERTAIL COVERTS

TAIL FEATHER

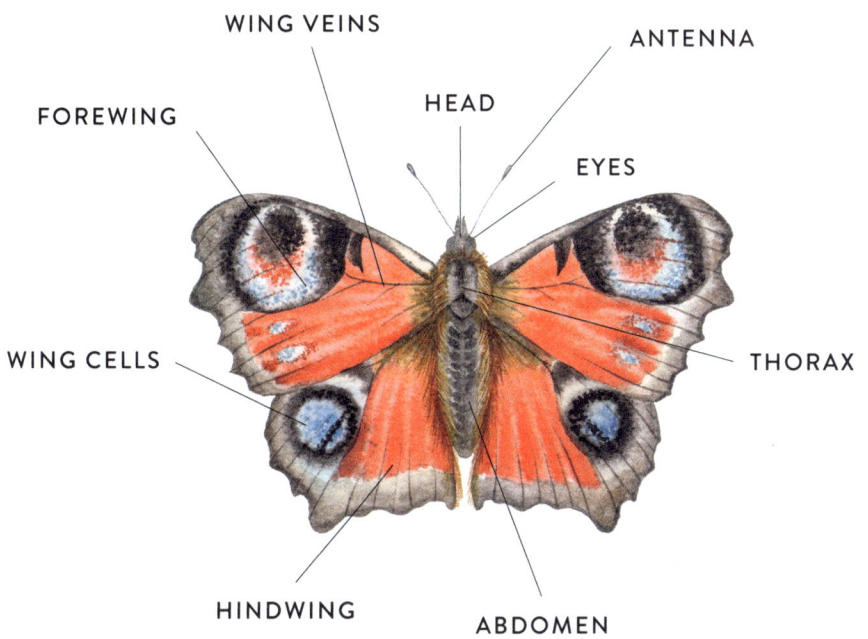

WING VEINS

ANTENNA

FOREWING

HEAD

EYES

WING CELLS

THORAX

HINDWING

ABDOMEN

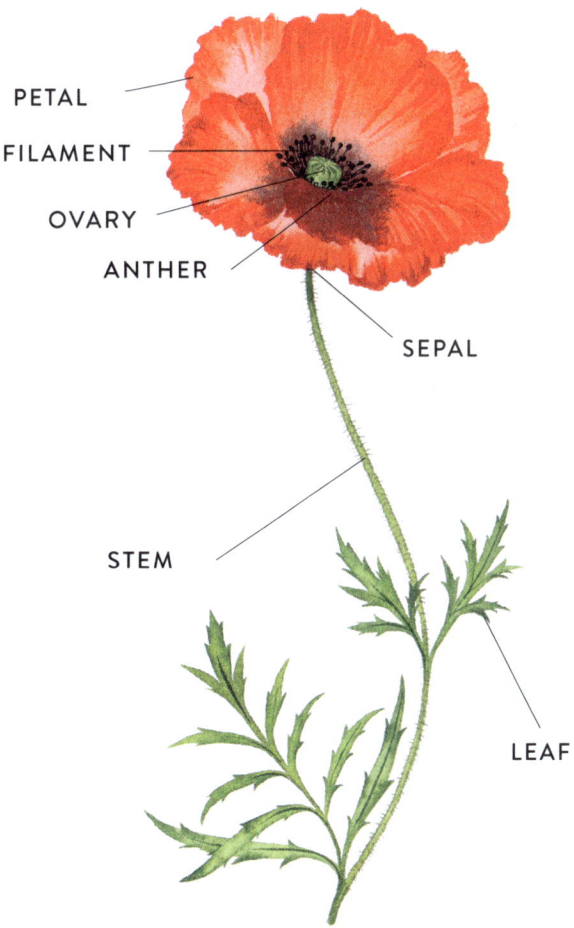

PETAL

FILAMENT

OVARY

ANTHER

SEPAL

STEM

LEAF

19 LABELLED DIAGRAMS

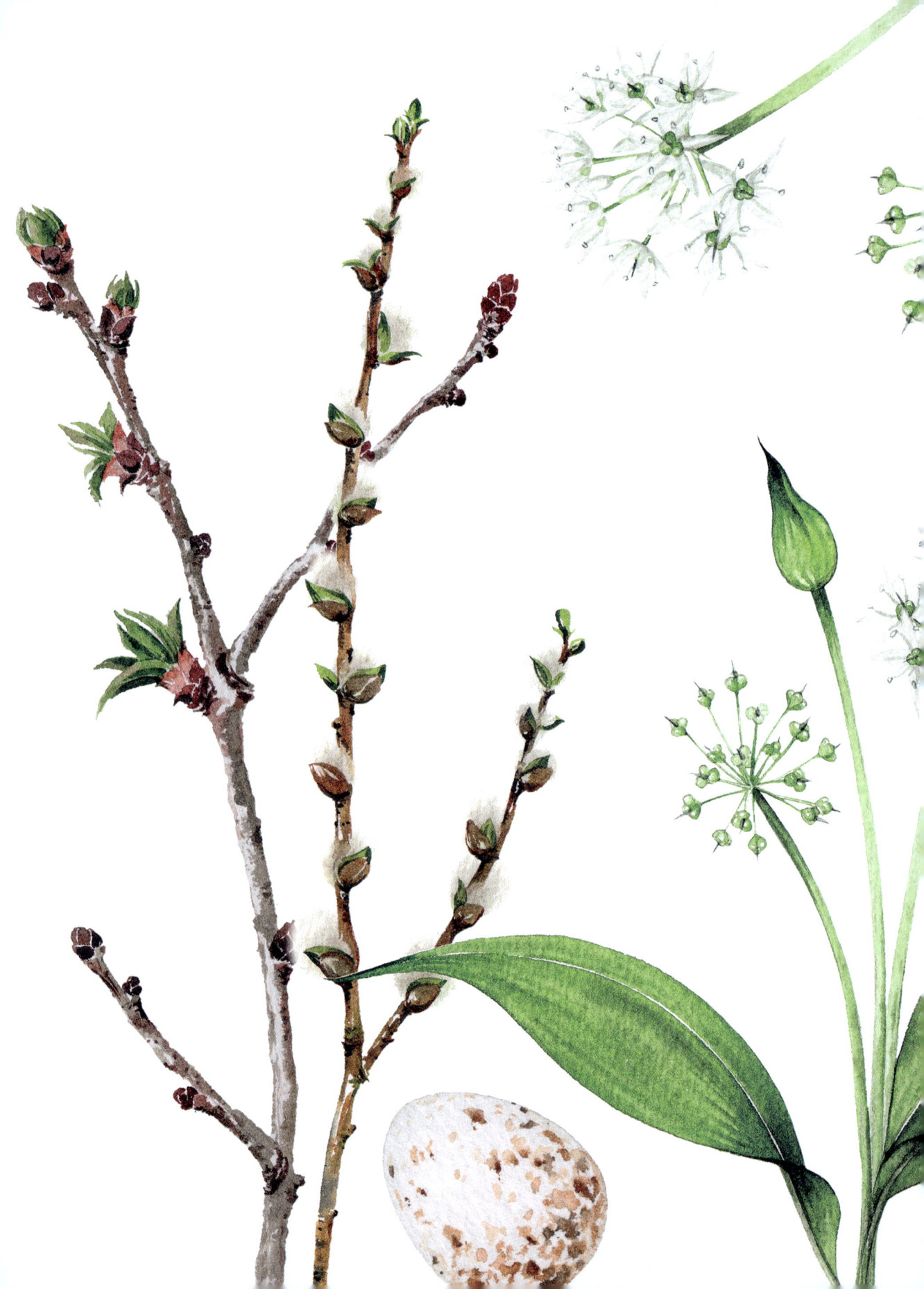

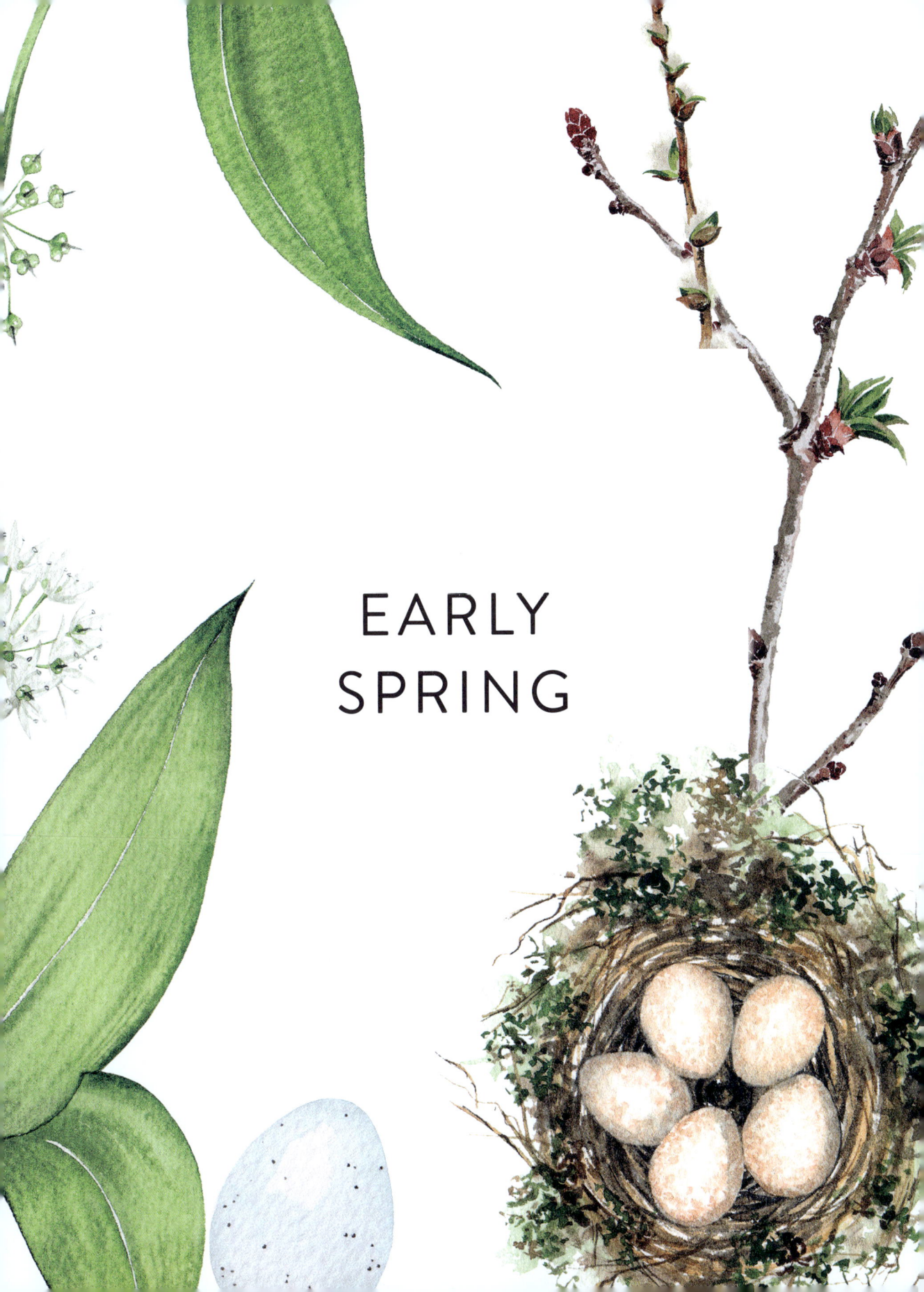

EARLY
SPRING

# BIRDS' NEST & EGGS

The bare trees of winter and early spring offer a rare opportunity to spot some of last year's birds' nests. Each bird has its own method of building and it's possible to tell the species just from looking at an empty nest. You may also come across fragments of eggshells on the ground, which make a wonderful watercolour painting subject, with delicate colours and patterns that can keep you occupied for hours.

Take care when investigating nests; it is an offence to disturb nesting birds (the breeding season tends to be spring to late summer).

## EGGS

**Brushes**
Pointed round size 2, 0, ⁴⁄₀

**Paper**
Cold pressed (textured)

Approximate size of the egg painting 3 x 2.5cm (1⅕ x 1in).

**Colours for the example egg (see opposite for individual egg colours)**

 Payne's grey

 burnt sienna

 cobalt turquoise

**Mix**

 **Shadow mix:** burnt sienna and Payne's grey

Once you've mastered these steps, try out different colour and pattern combinations to create all sorts of eggs.

## 1.

I find it much easier to paint individual eggs without attempting it in pencil first. This example egg uses a diluted mix of cobalt turquoise, Payne's grey and burnt sienna. Hold your size 2 brush vertically above the page, loaded with diluted colour, and try painting the egg shape in one fluid motion. This will certainly take a bit of practice but sketching it in pencil is even trickier in my opinion.

1     2     3     4

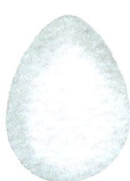 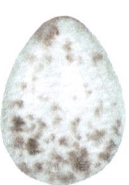 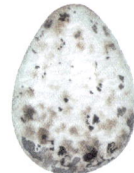

## 2.

While the outline is still wet, clean and wet your size 2 brush and use it to draw the colour in from the outside edge in concentric ovals. The colour will naturally dilute and appear paler. Keep dipping your brush in your jar of water if the brush gets too dry to spread the paint smoothly. Leave a tiny area of unpainted space to achieve a 'shine' on the egg.

## 3.

Some egg patterns resemble the wet on wet technique in watercolour. While the egg is still damp dab marks of shadow mix with your size 0 brush and watch them spread and bleed into the egg.

## 4.

If your egg's patterns are more defined, allow the base layer to dry fully before layering patterns and detail with more concentrated shadow mix with your size ⁴⁄₀ brush.

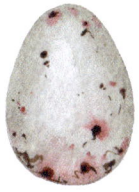

### CHAFFINCH EGG

**Egg base:** diluted mix of cobalt turquoise, Payne's grey, burnt sienna.
**Wet on wet:** alizarin crimson.
**Wet on dry:** concentrated mix of alizarin crimson and burnt sienna.

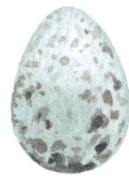

### JACKDAW EGG

**Egg base:** diluted mix of cobalt turquoise, Payne's grey, burnt sienna.
**Wet on dry:** mix of majority Payne's grey, burnt sienna, two layers at different concentrations.

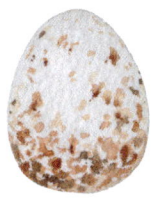

### HOUSE SPARROW EGG

**Egg base:** diluted mix of Payne's grey, burnt sienna.
**Wet on dry:** mix of Payne's grey, burnt sienna, two layers at different concentrations.

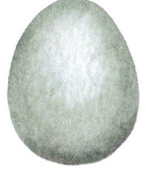

### PHEASANT EGG

**Egg base:** mix of cobalt turquoise, Payne's grey, burnt sienna.

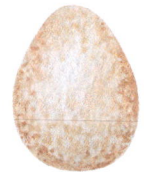

### ROBIN EGG

**Egg base:** diluted mix of yellow ochre, permanent rose and raw umber.
**Wet on wet:** mix of burnt sienna and raw umber.
**Wet on dry:** concentrated mix of burnt sienna and raw umber.

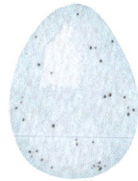

### STARLING EGG

**Egg base:** diluted mix of cobalt turquoise, Prussian blue
**Wet on dry:** fine dots of Mars black.

# ROBIN'S NEST

A robin nested in a raised bank of tree roots in my mum's garden. We watched from afar as the parents flew in and out in spring, feeding their young. Months later when the surrounding greenery and the birds were long gone, I was able to have a look at the nest's construction.

This is one of a few projects where I recommend using masking fluid. Masking the eggs allows you to paint the nest freely. It's not vital but does make life easier.

## WHAT YOU WILL NEED

**Brushes**
Pointed round size 2, 0, ⁴⁄₀
Rigger size 0

**Paper**
Cold pressed (textured)

**HB Pencil**
**Eraser**
**Masking fluid**
**Compass**

**Colours**

 yellow ochre

 sap green

 Payne's grey

 burnt sienna

 permanent rose

 raw umber

**Mix**

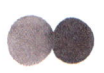 **Brown shadow mix:** majority burnt sienna and Payne's grey

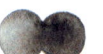 **Shadow mix:** burnt sienna and Payne's grey

1

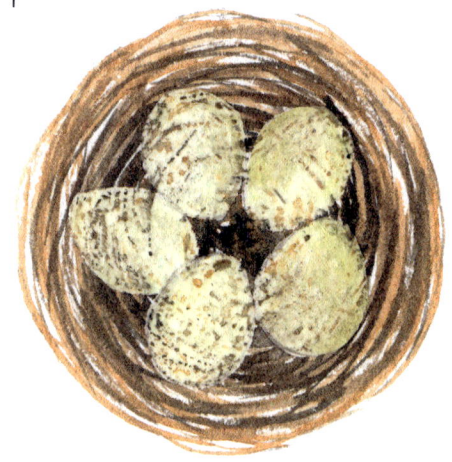

**Robin Egg**
**Egg base:** diluted mix of yellow ochre, permanent rose and raw umber.
**Wet on wet:** mix of burnt sienna and raw umber.
**Wet on dry:** concentrated mix of burnt sienna and raw umber.

Approximate size of the nest painting 8 x 8cm (3 x 3in).

## 1.

Draw a pencil circle and five eggs in the middle. Paint each egg in masking fluid and allow to dry. Do not try to speed up the process with heat, just be patient.

Once the masking fluid is dry, paint a nest of tangled fine-line curves in a circular motion using the tip of your size 2 brush. First paint in yellow ochre curves, then add some burnt sienna. Leave tiny slivers of unpainted space. Add some shadow mix lines in the centre of the nest.

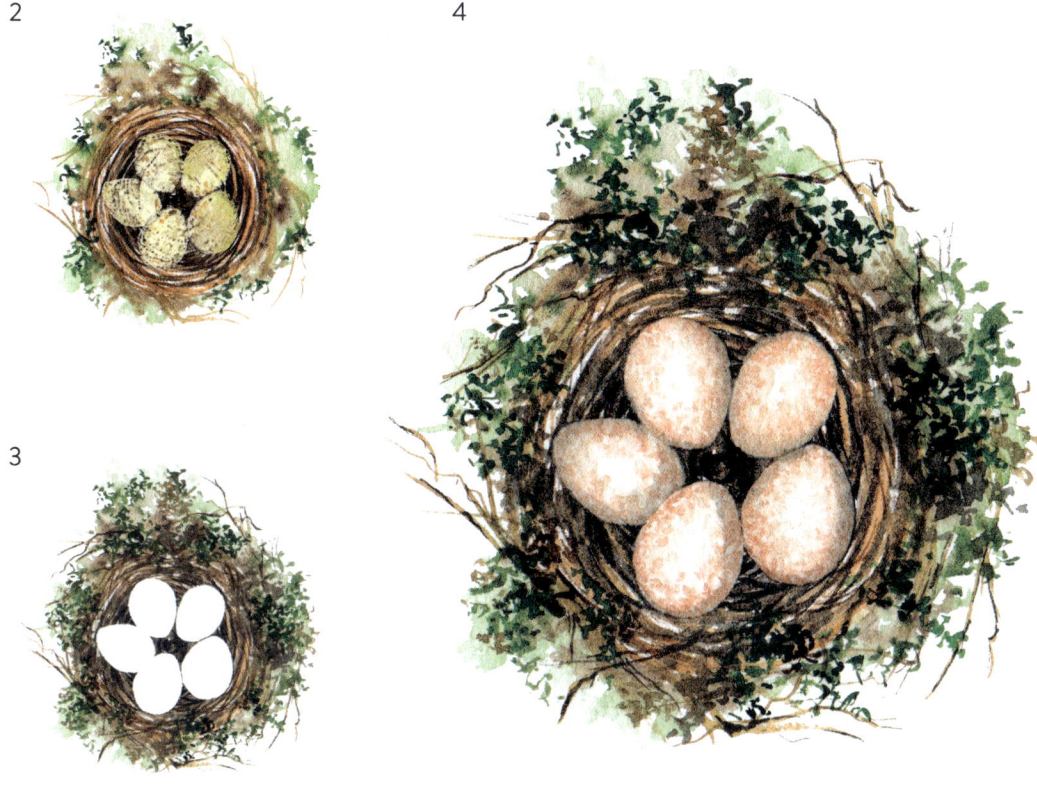

## 2.

Paint diluted dabs of sap green around the edge to create mossy sections with your size 2 brush. Drop in diluted dabs of yellow ochre and burnt sienna. Once dry add a few more wayward lines of straw and twigs in yellow ochre and some more concentrated dabs of sap green to the mossy areas. Allow to dry.

## 3.

Paint in extra burnt sienna and shadow mix twigs protruding from all angles with your rigger brush. Add a little shadow mix to the sap green and build up darker areas of textured moss. Once you have added more shadow mix to the centre of the nest and all the paint has dried, gently rub the masking fluid off the eggs. Do this with your fingertip and it will come away after a few nudges. Rub out any visible pencil lines.

## 4.

Use the robin egg colours to paint in the eggs, adding a little bit of diluted shadow mix to the edges. This will help place the eggs in the nest.

# BLUEBELL WOOD

Discovering a carpet of bluebells in nearby ancient woodland was my first dose of spring in glorious technicolour following the cold dark winter. It was just what the doctor ordered!

## WHAT YOU WILL NEED

**Brushes**
Pointed round size 8, 2, ²⁄₀, ⁴⁄₀
Rigger size 0

**Paper**
Cold pressed (textured)

**HB Pencil**
**Eraser**
**Masking fluid**
**Washi tape**

Approximate size of the bluebell wood painting: 18 x 13cm (7 x 5in)

### Colours

Payne's grey

burnt sienna

green gold

cadmium yellow

yellow ochre

sap green

permanent rose

cobalt blue deep

### Mix

**Leaf mix:** sap green and green gold

**Ground mix:** green gold, Payne's grey, yellow ochre

**Brown shadow mix:** majority burnt sienna and Payne's grey

**Bluebell mix:** cobalt blue deep and permanent rose

**Warm sky mix:** cadmium yellow, Payne's grey, yellow ochre

**Shadow mix:** burnt sienna and Payne's grey

## 1.

When working with washes, I like to tape my paper down around the edges with washi tape to keep it flat. It's not officially stretching the watercolour paper but it minimizes warping while painting. In this instance I also masked-off the painting area to protect the paper from the splattering technique.

Draw a horizon line, the path and the tree trunks in the foreground in pencil. Paint the trees and area just below the horizon in masking fluid and allow to dry

naturally. Paint a diluted warm sky mix wash above the horizon line and dab in 'clouds' of shadow mix and ground mix to create a distant forest canopy with your size 8 brush. Also make sure to paint shadow mix along the horizon line. As the page slowly dries, paint diluted shadow mix trees in the distance with your rigger brush. Some will bleed into the wet page, others will remain intact. This variation helps create a sense of perspective. Allow to dry fully and keep the masking fluid in place.

## 2.

Paint the path in diluted yellow ochre and add curves of burnt sienna and shadow mix with your size 2 brush.

With the same brush, paint the ground with diluted washes of ground mix and bluebell mix. Allow to fully dry and then carefully peel off the masking fluid.

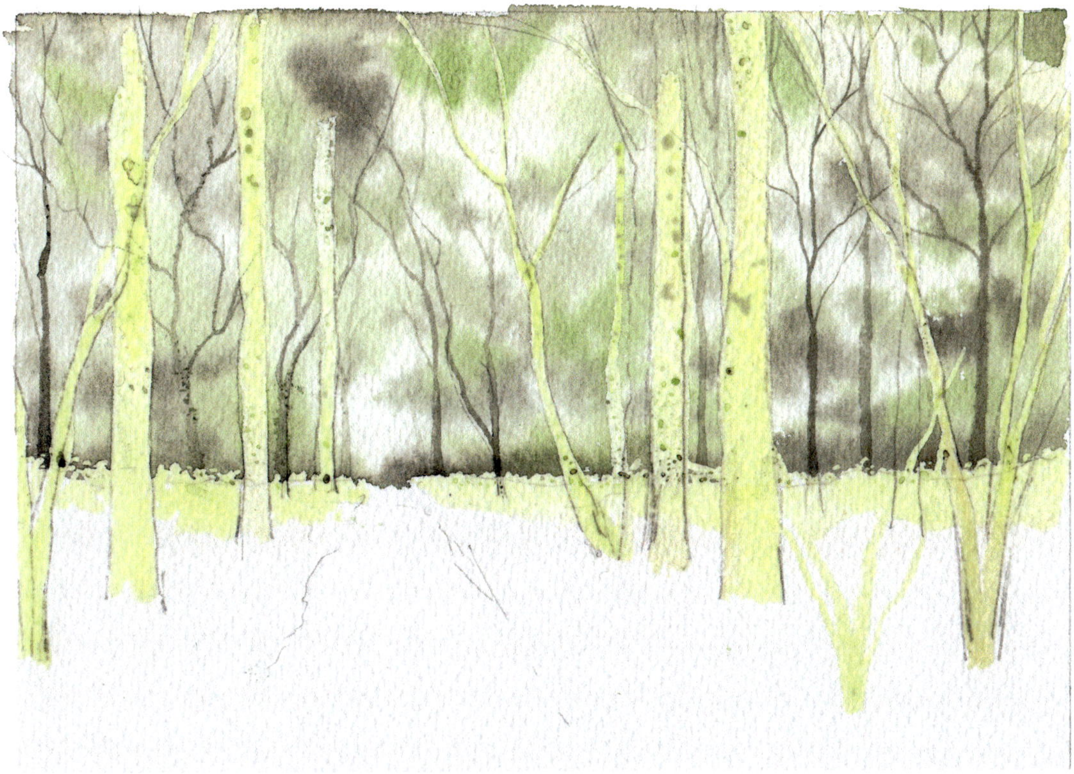

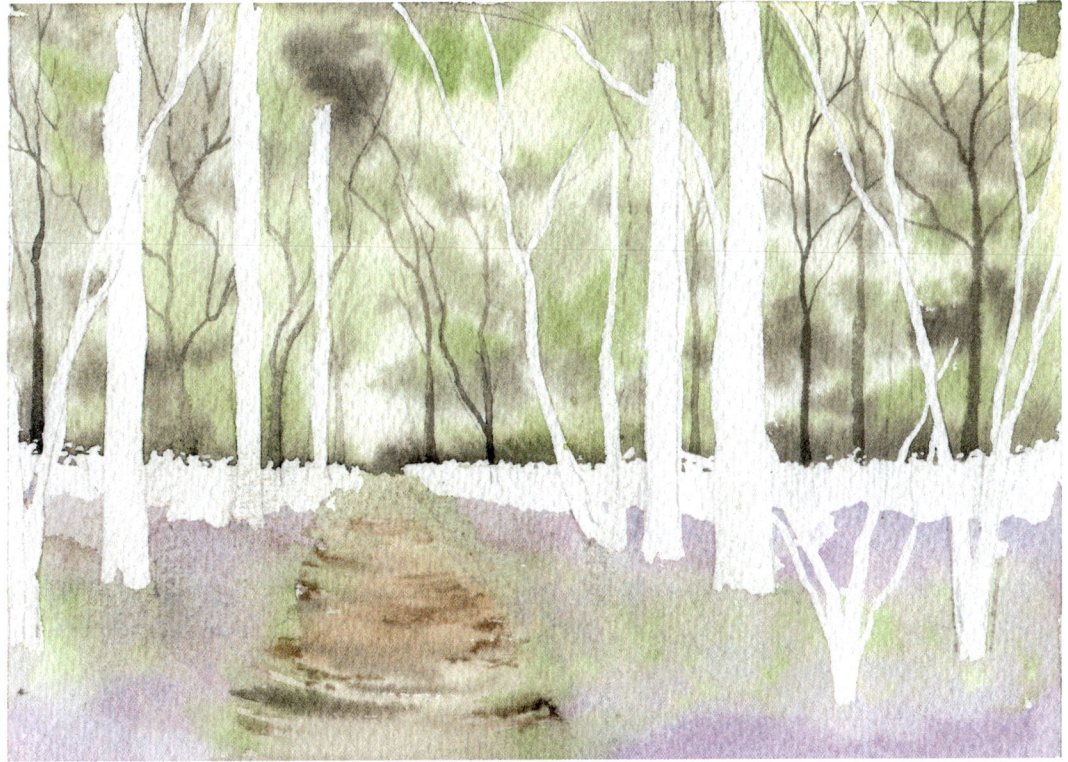

1

2

27 BLUEBELL WOOD

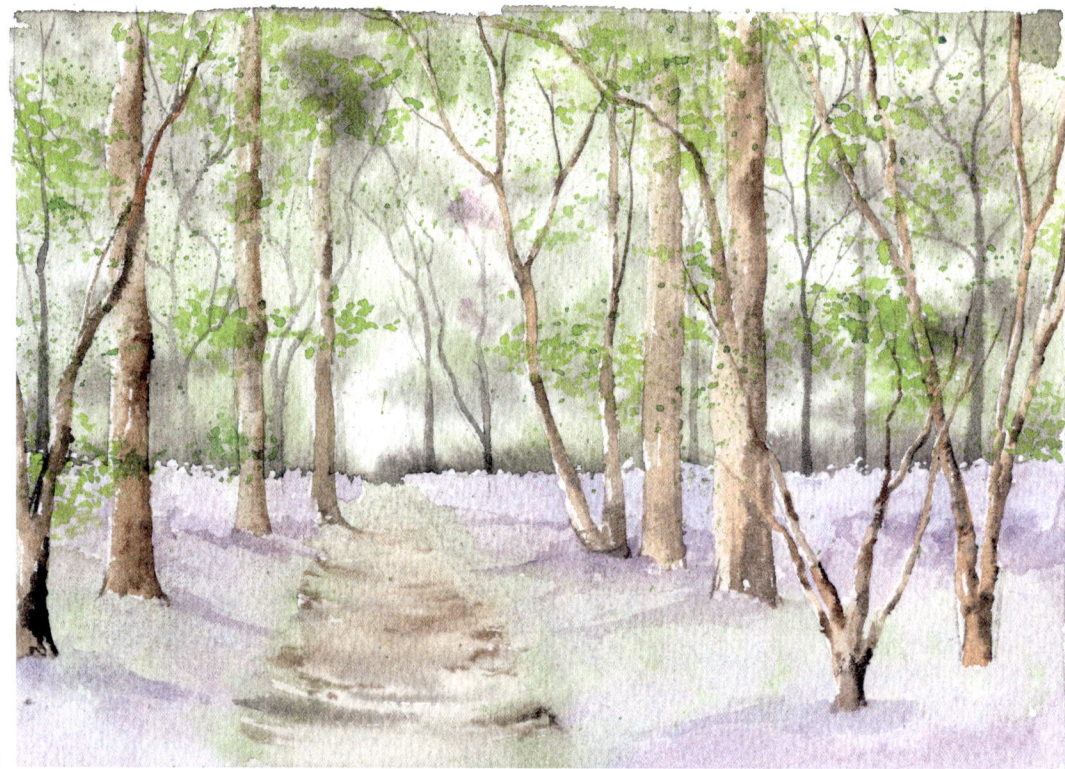

3

### 3.

Paint in the trees with diluted washes of burnt sienna and brown shadow mix with your size 2 brush and a smaller brush for the slender branches. Decide where your light source is coming from and which part of the trees is in shadow. Add shadow mix to the shadowy side but keep your paint light so you can layer up easily later on. Allow to dry. Paint tree foliage by splattering leaf mix across the top half of the painting with a size 8 brush and dabbing clusters of leaf mix dots with a size 0 rigger brush. Just make sure your surrounding paper is protected if you're splattering.

Paint diluted sweeps of bluebell mix beneath each tree with your size 2 brush, curving down to the path.

### 4.

Starting in the distance paint diluted dots of bluebell mix with your size ⁰⁄₀ brush to create the bluebell carpet. Increase the concentration of the paint at the base of each tree. Once you've painted a cluster, clean off your brush and use the wet bristles to dab and spread the colour further along the ground.

Add some more brown shadow mix branches and lowlights to trees in the foreground with your size ⁴⁄₀ brush. Allow to dry fully.

### 5.

Add diluted sap green to the clearer patches on the ground and build up even more bluebell dots with your size ⁰⁄₀ brush. With the same brush, paint sap green lowlights to the tree foliage in the foreground. Once dry, paint sweeps of diluted shadow mix down the tree trunks and across the forest floor with your size 2 brush.

Finish with sap green tufts of grass around the base of the trees and either side of the path with your rigger brush.

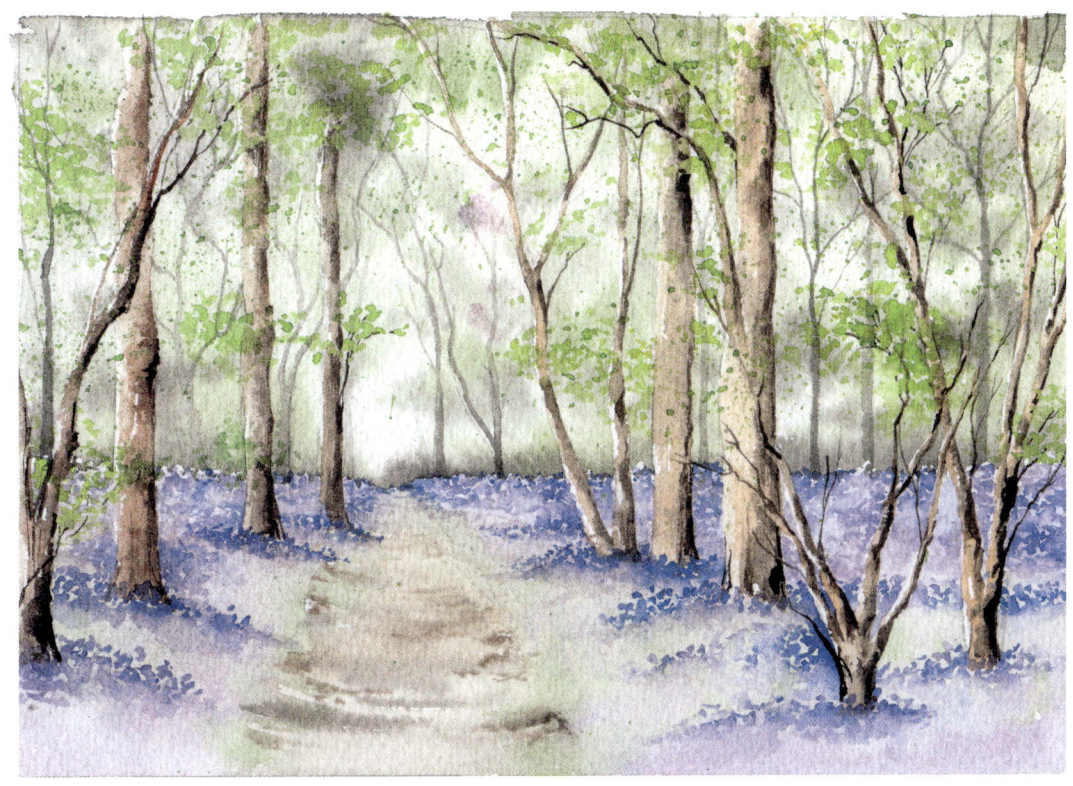

4

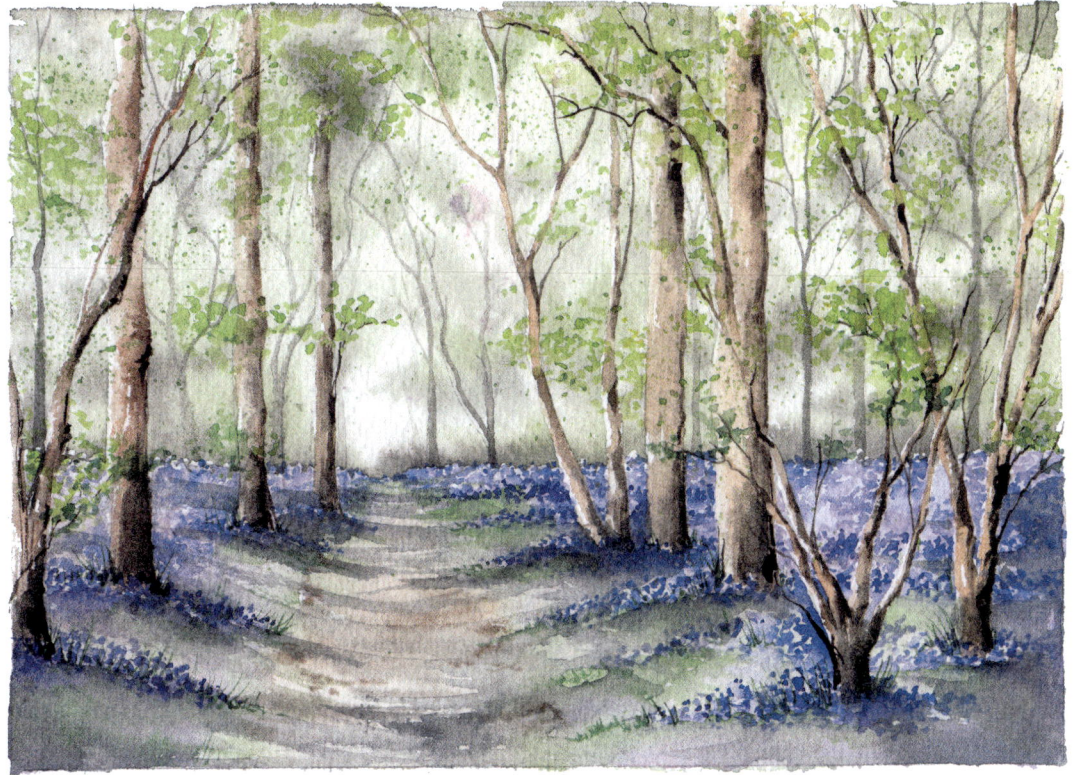

5

29 BLUEBELL WOOD

# WILD GARLIC

This white starry flower forms a woodland carpet from mid-spring onwards. Its distinct smell and the volume of bulbs growing together make it an easy find for novice foragers like myself. As well as providing a brilliant flavour in cooking, it's been credited as a traditional remedy too.

Although at first glance this feels like a relatively simple plant, it's got plenty of little elements – each stem can hold up to 20 flowering branches. Draw in each flower and bud to help with the detailed flower painting process later on.

## WHAT YOU WILL NEED

**Brushes**
Pointed round size 8, 2, 0, ⁴⁄₀
Rigger size 0

**Paper**
Cold pressed (textured)

**HB Pencil**
**Eraser**

## Colours

Payne's grey

sap green

green gold

burnt sienna

yellow ochre

lemon yellow

## Mix

**Stem mix:** green gold, sap green, lemon yellow

**Shadow mix:** burnt sienna and Payne's grey

**Petal mix:** yellow ochre, green gold, Payne's grey

## 1.

From a central point, draw three curving pencil stems. At the top of the flowering stems, it can be helpful to draw a circle as a boundary for the branches, then draw a starburst of branches from that central point. Follow the drawing guide to place in your six-petal flowers or little bulbous seeds. The bud stem has a large teardrop shape at the top of the stem. For the leaves, draw in long, curving lines for the central vein of each leaf and then create the leaf shape around it.

Approximate size of the wild garlic painting: 14 x 15cm (5½ x 6in).

2

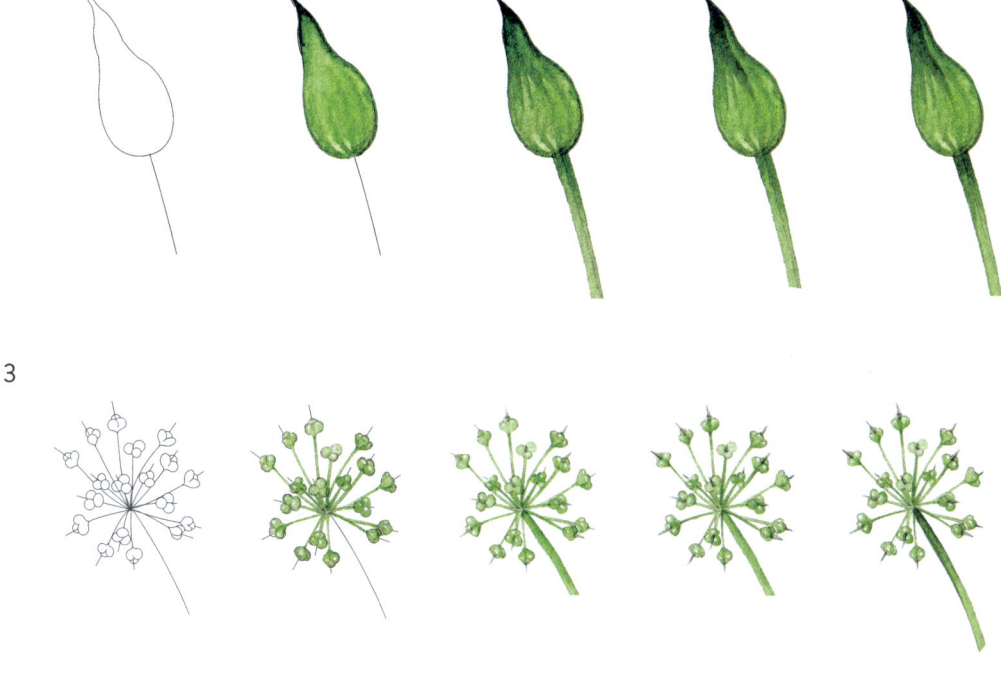

3

## 2.

To paint the leaves with your size 2 brush, paint a wash of green gold on the bud. While still wet, outline with stem mix and paint curved streaks from the base, upwards. Outline the tip with sap green.

Once dry, add a few more streaks of diluted sap green from the top, downwards and paint a stem mix stem with your size 2 brush. Add a streak of diluted Payne's grey from the bud tip, downwards.

## 3.

To paint the bulblets (the rounded shapes), with your ⅕ brush outline each one in wet stem mix leaving a tiny bit of unpainted 'shine' and paint fine line branches back to the central stem.

Paint a tiny shadow mix stamen protruding from the centre of each bulblet with your ⅕ brush and paint a stem mix stem with your size 2 brush.

Paint in a few sap green lowlights on the undersides of the bulblets and branches, then paint shadow mix lowlights on the filament with your size ⅕ brush.

4

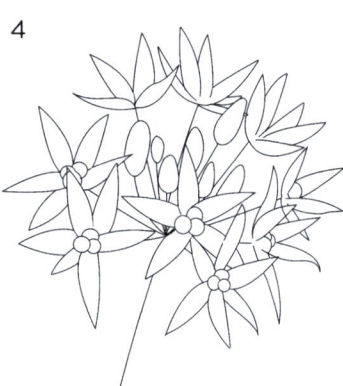

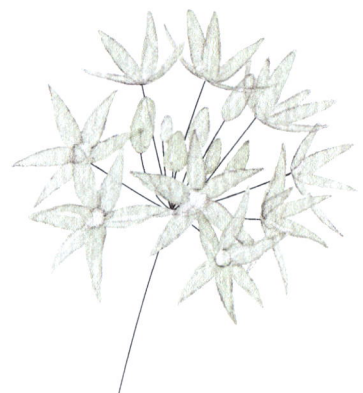

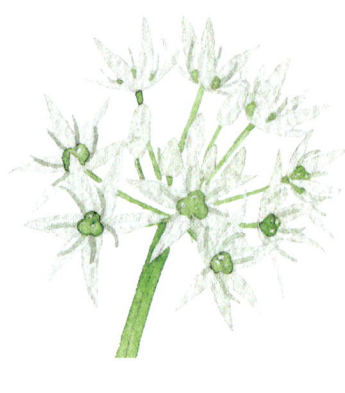

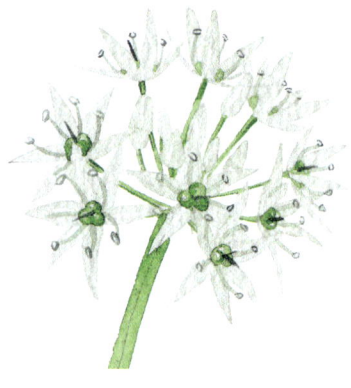

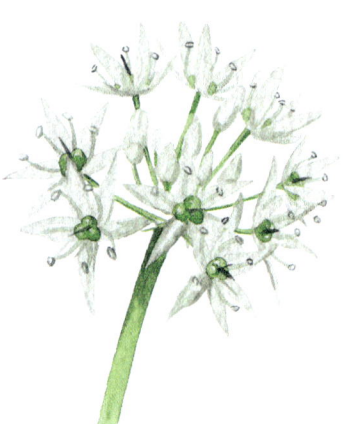

## 4.

To paint the flowers, paint diluted petal mix petals with your size 0 brush. Allow the petals to dry before painting ones immediately next to them.

Among the petals, outline each bulblet in wet stem mix (⅜ brush), leaving a tiny bit of unpainted 'shine' and fine line branches back to the central stem, as you did for the bulblets in step 3.

Paint in six shadow mix filaments as well as the central stamen with your ⅜ brush. Once dry, add tiny looped anthers in concentrated shadow mix.

Paint in a few sap green lowlights on the undersides of the bulblets and branches, then paint shadow mix lowlights on the petals.

## 5.

With your stems painted, you can now form the leaves around them. Load your size 8 brush with wet stem mix (you will need a lot) and paint one leaf section. While still wet, paint streaks of sap green that follow the curve of the leaves with the point of your size 2 brush. Add more concentrated sap green to the tip of the leaves with a small brush. Repeat this for each section leaving an unpainted sliver down the middle of each leaf. Add a few streaks of shadow mix for the smaller underside sections of the leaves. Once dry, paint in the leaf stems with diluted stem mix and a little shadow mix.

5

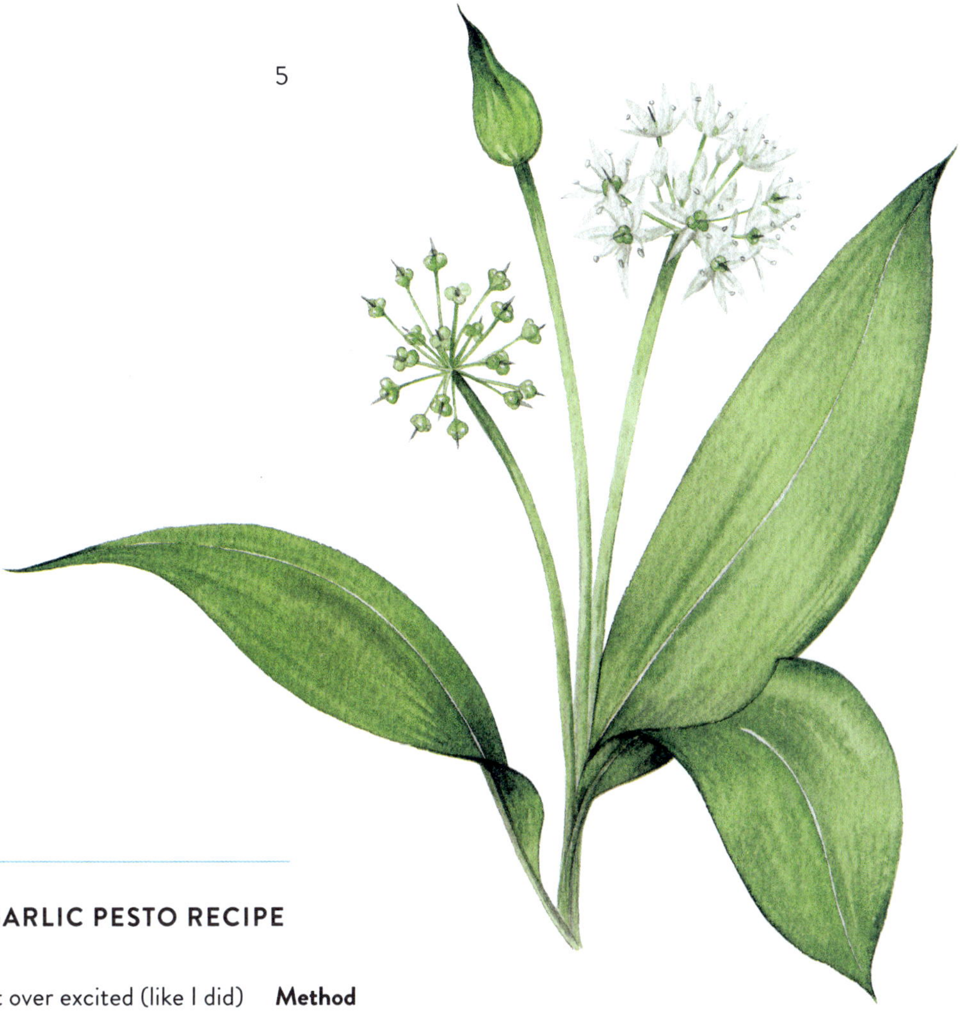

## WILD GARLIC PESTO RECIPE

Don't get over excited (like I did) and make vast quantities; while delicious, the flavour is strong and even the biggest wild garlic fans will want a change after a few weeks.

### Ingredients
300g (10oz) wild garlic leaves
100g (3oz) Parmesan or hard
    cheese alternative, grated
juice of 1 lemon
2 garlic cloves, crushed
100g (1½oz) pine nuts or any
    nut/seed alternative (I like to
    use hazelnuts)
300ml (10fl oz) olive oil
salt and pepper

### Method
Rinse the wild garlic leaves and tear into halves.

Place the leaves, cheese, garlic, lemon juice, nuts and seasoning into a food processor and pulse until it resembles a paste.

Add the oil and blitz for 30 seconds. Season to taste.

Spoon into a sterilized jar. It will keep chilled in the fridge for up to two weeks.

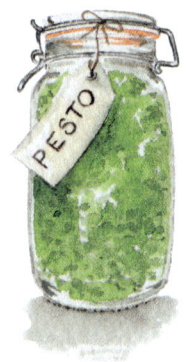

# SPRING LAMBS

We live in an area where sheep easily outnumber people. The arrival of spring tips the balance further in their favour when we welcome a chorus of bleating lambs in the neighbouring field. Walking up on Dartmoor in Devon you can come face to face with ancient breeds whose shaggy coats withstand the harsh, windswept landscape. I've chosen to paint one of these traditional longwool sheep native to Devon, the Greyface Dartmoor.

## WHAT YOU WILL NEED

**Brushes**
Pointed round size 2, 0, ⁰⁄₀
Rigger size 0

**Paper**
Cold pressed (textured)

**HB Pencil**
**Eraser**

### Colours

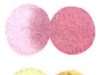 permanent rose

 yellow ochre

 sap green

 Payne's grey

 burnt sienna

 Mars black

### Mix

 **Light wool mix:** yellow ochre with a small amount of burnt sienna and Payne's grey

 **Shadow green mix:** equal parts burnt sienna, sap green, yellow ochre, Payne's grey

 **Dark wool mix:** equal parts yellow ochre, burnt sienna, Payne's grey

 **Shadow mix:** burnt sienna and Payne's grey

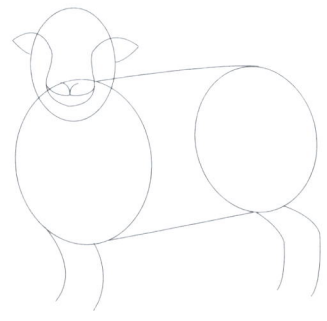
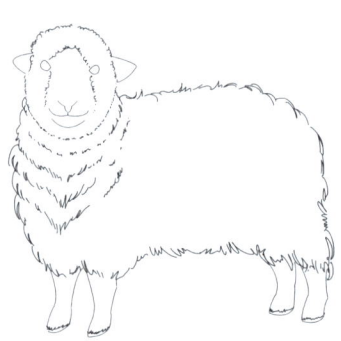

1

## 1.
Follow the drawing guides to create faint pencil body shapes for the ewe and lamb. If your pencil is heavy, lightly rub it out to leave faint lines.

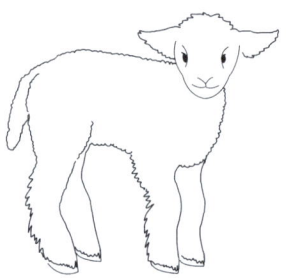

Approximate size of the ewe and lamb painting: 8 x 8cm (3 x 3in)

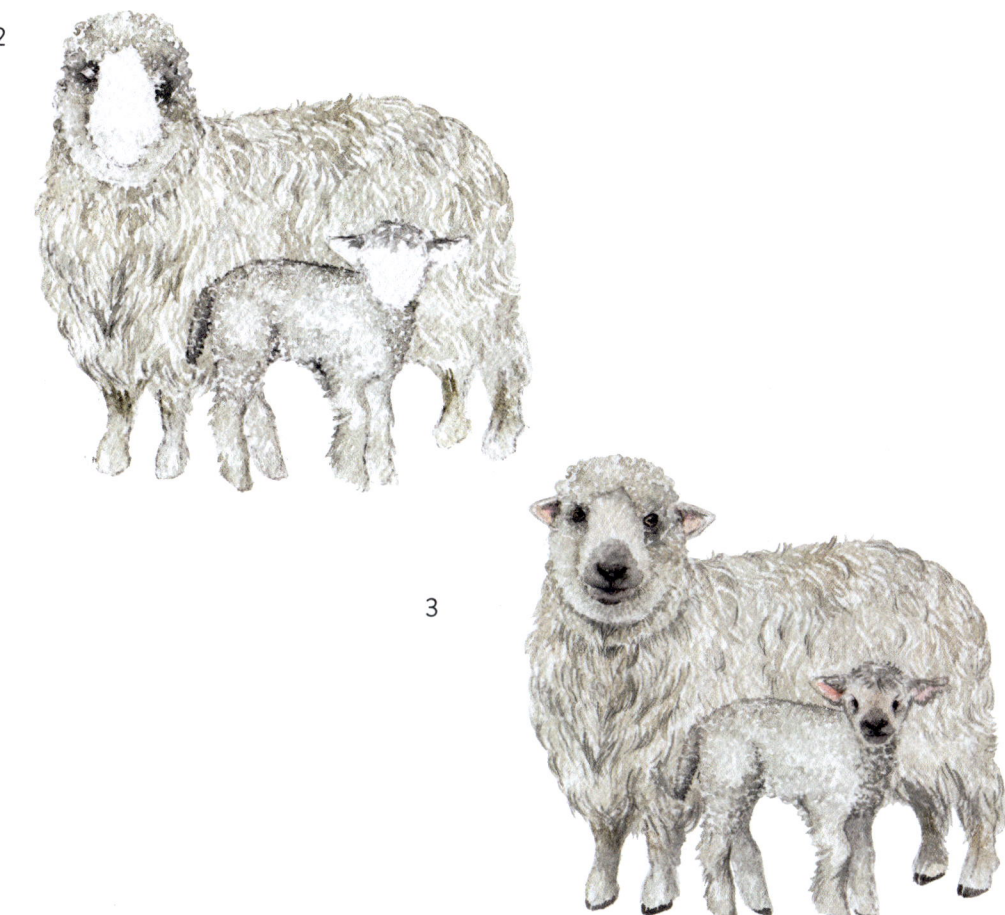

## 2.

Starting around the neck, paint the ewe's coat with C- and S-curves of light wool mix in your size 0 brush. Leave little slivers of unpainted space to create highlights. While still wet, drop in dabs of diluted dark wool mix to create darker areas down the torso and around the legs. Allow to dry, then use this stroke to create the long-haired legs, head and ears of the lamb.

Paint tight little C-curves of light wool mix for the lamb's coat with your size ⁴⁄₀ brush.

Introduce dark wool mix to the outer edges of the body and tail to create a darker edge. Paint these light wool mix tight curls around the ewe's face, adding dark wool mix into the wet paint around the eye area.

## 3.

First paint diluted burnt sienna in the eyes of both sheep and a diluted Mars black muzzle. Paint a very diluted permanent rose in the ears followed by a little shadow mix in the inner corners. Allow to dry. With your smallest brush, follow your pencil lines to paint a concentrated Mars black nose and mouth. Outline the eyes and place a little more Mars black in the eyes for pupils. Paint a Mars black sweep across the bottom of each hoof followed by little upward strokes to show the white hair coming down over the hooves.

Finally add a few extra lines of texture on the wool on the torso, around the ears and legs with dark wool mix.

4

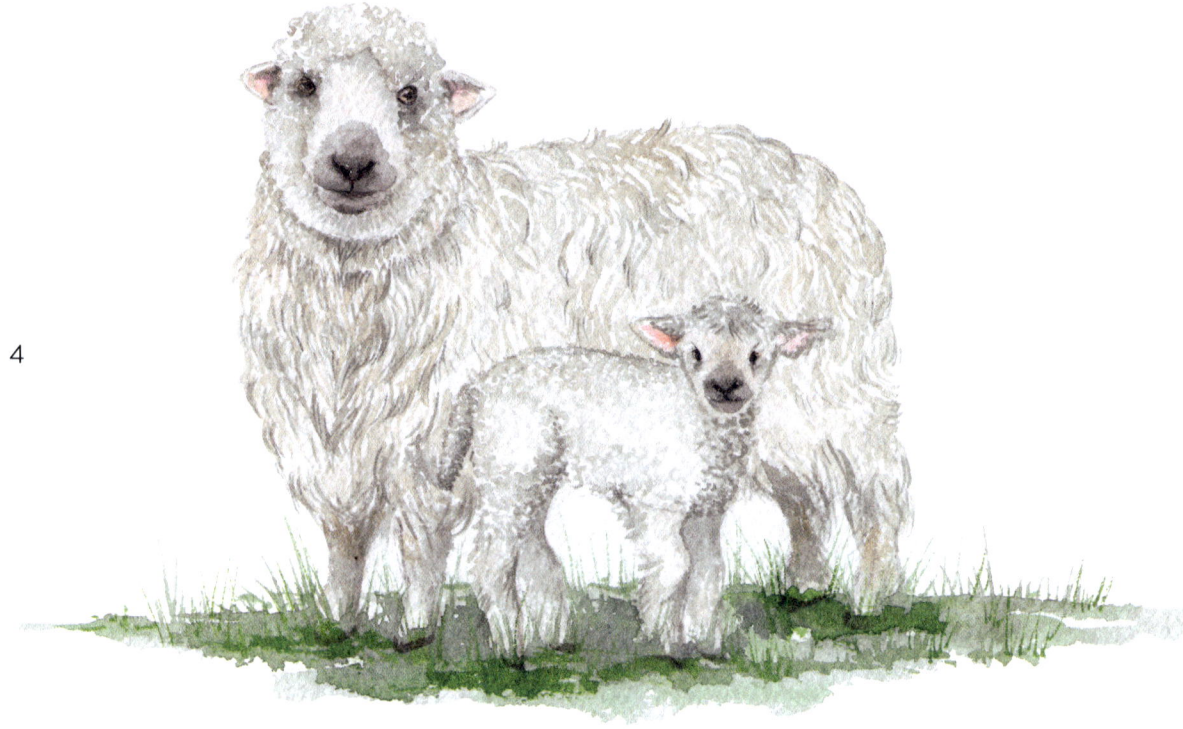

## 4.

To place the sheep in green pastures, use your size 2 brush to paint sweeps of diluted shadow green mix around their feet (so often their feet aren't visible in the long grass). While still wet, paint sap green blades of grass with your rigger brush and extra patches of sap green on the ground.

Finally, with your size 2 brush, paint diluted shadow mix down the torsos, on the back legs and on the ground beneath the two sheep. Once fully dry lightly rub an eraser over the whole piece to remove any visible pencil lines.

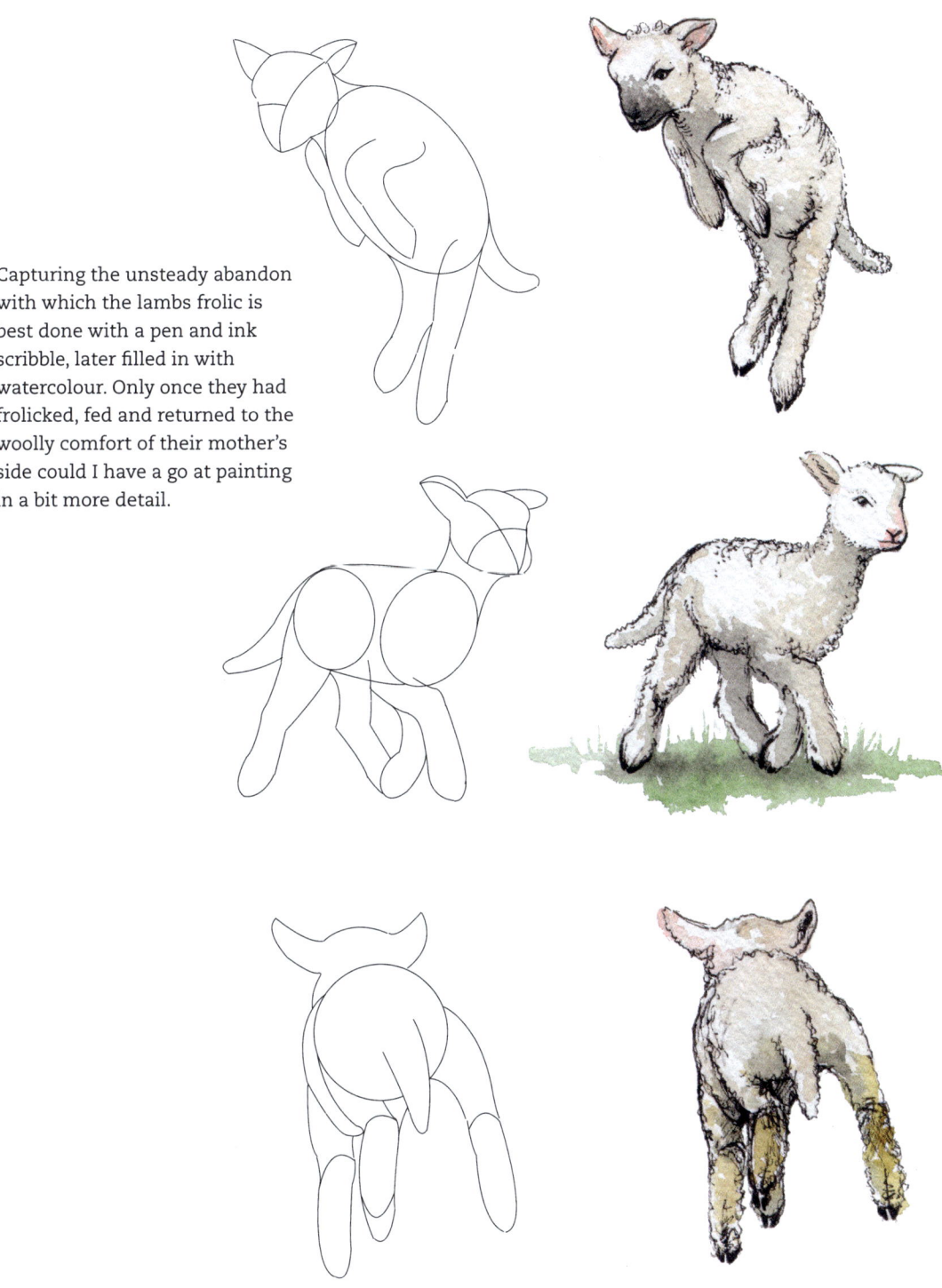

Capturing the unsteady abandon with which the lambs frolic is best done with a pen and ink scribble, later filled in with watercolour. Only once they had frolicked, fed and returned to the woolly comfort of their mother's side could I have a go at painting in a bit more detail.

# YELLOWHAMMER

There is no end to this conspicuous yellow bird's talents: inspiring poets and novelists through the ages, its musical chirp is said to have influenced the likes of Beethoven. I was just as excited to discover that its eggs, patterned with speckles and dark wobbly lines, have earned the yellowhammer the nickname 'scribble lark'.

## WHAT YOU WILL NEED

**Brushes**
Pointed round size 4, 2, 0, ⁴⁄₀

**Paper**
Cold pressed (textured)

**HB Pencil**
**Eraser**

Approximate size of the yellowhammer painting: 8 x 8cm (3 x 3in)

### Colours

yellow ochre

cadmium yellow

green gold

lemon yellow

Payne's grey

alizarin crimson

burnt sienna

Mars black

### Mix

**Red feather mix:** burnt sienna and alizarin crimson

**Shadow mix:** burnt sienna and Payne's grey

## 1.
Follow the drawing guide to create a faint pencil body shape.

## 2.
Use your size 2 brush to paint a diluted lemon yellow wash on the face and torso. While still wet, add feather strokes of cadmium yellow and green gold around the neck and face with your size 0 brush. Then add cadmium yellow and burnt sienna feather strokes on the body creating a 'bib' shape on the torso. Extend the yellow down into the tail feathers.

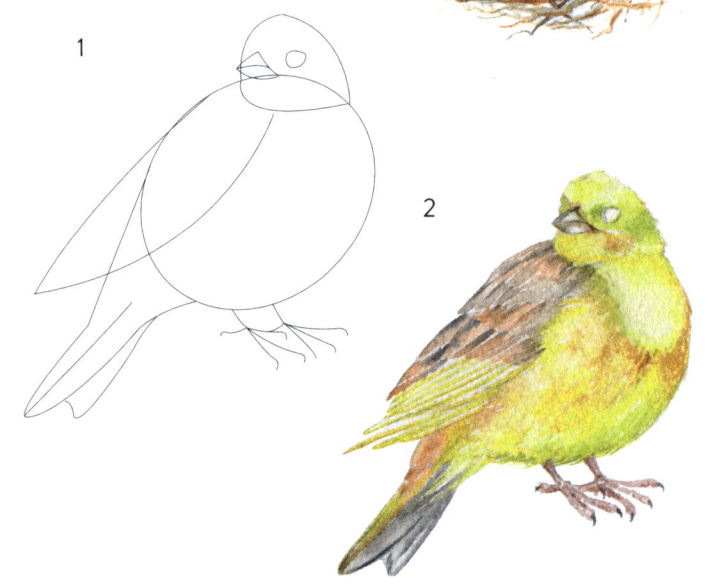

1

2

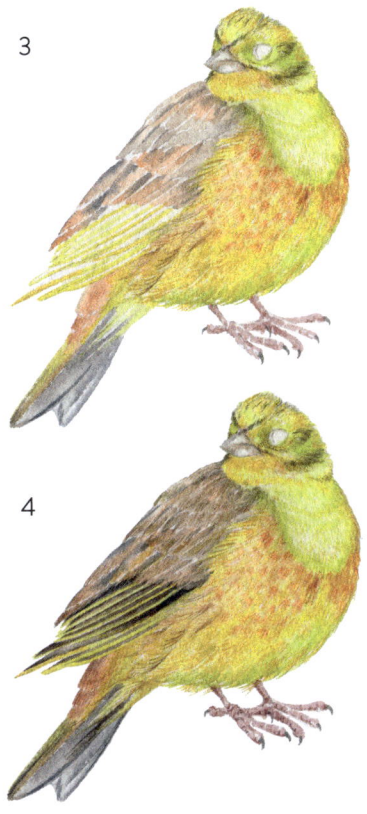

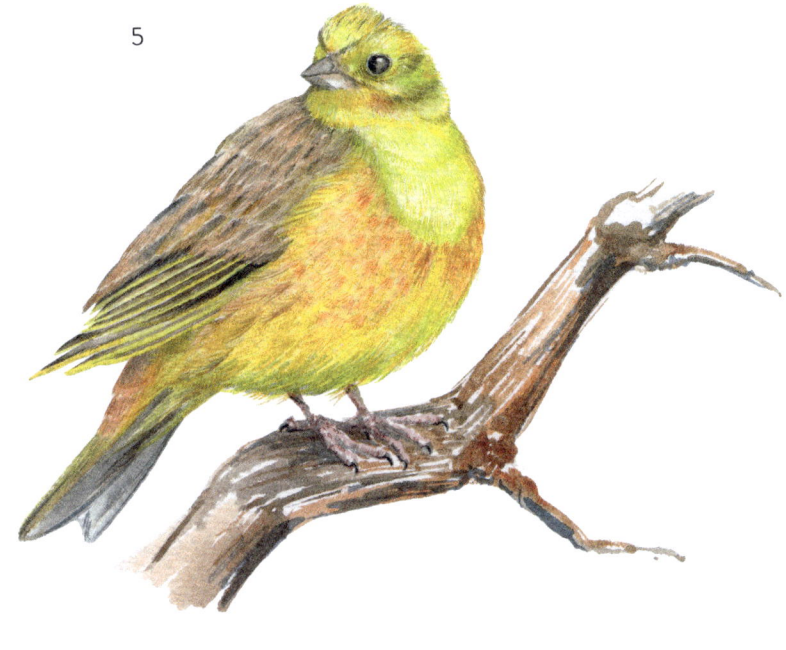

Paint in the covert wing feathers with diluted red feather mix, leaving tiny slivers of unpainted space in between, then drop in shadow mix while still wet. Paint the primaries (long slender feathers under the coverts) with long lines of cadmium yellow. Paint the underside of the tail feathers with shadow mix.

The legs and feet can be dabbed with diluted red feather mix. Add a tiny talon of shadow mix on each claw. Line the beak with shadow mix and finish with a few strokes of burnt sienna feathers around the beak. Allow to dry.

## 3.

Use your size ⅙ brush to paint in fine feather tufts across the head and torso. First paint a layer of feathers using a more concentrated version of the lemon yellow wash. Then add shadow mix lines across the face and burnt sienna tufts below the breast that blend down into yellow ochre tufts towards the legs. The feathery lines can elongate and curl as they meet the wings.

## 4.

Paint the coverts with fine feather tufts in burnt sienna. Then fill in the unpainted gaps between the yellow lines on the primaries with concentrated shadow mix and add detail to the tail feather section. Add dabs of gnarly texture to the feet with concentrated red feather mix and burnt sienna dots around the eye. Once dry, rub out any visible pencil.

## 5.

With your ⅙ brush outline the eye in Mars black. Clean your brush and use the wet bristles to draw the colour inwards leaving an unpainted 'shine'. Add some diluted shadow mix to the underside of the tail feathers, wings and torso and to the legs. To place your bird on a branch, lightly sketch a pencil branch and fill the shape with dilute strokes of yellow ochre and burnt sienna with your size 4 brush until the brush dries out giving you a dry brush texture. Add some dilute shadow mix where the birds feet sit on the branch. Once dry, add more concentrated strokes of all three colours to add further texture with your size 2 brush.

# BARE BRANCHES
# & FIRST BUDS

While we wait for flowers to bloom, there is much beauty to be found in the budding branches of early spring. Now is the perfect time to study the trees and see how the branches sprout from the trunk before they're concealed by spring leaves.

## WHAT YOU WILL NEED

**Brushes**
Pointed round size 4, 2, 0,
²⁄₀, ⁴⁄₀
Mop brush size 6

**Paper**
Cold pressed (textured)

**HB Pencil**
**Eraser**

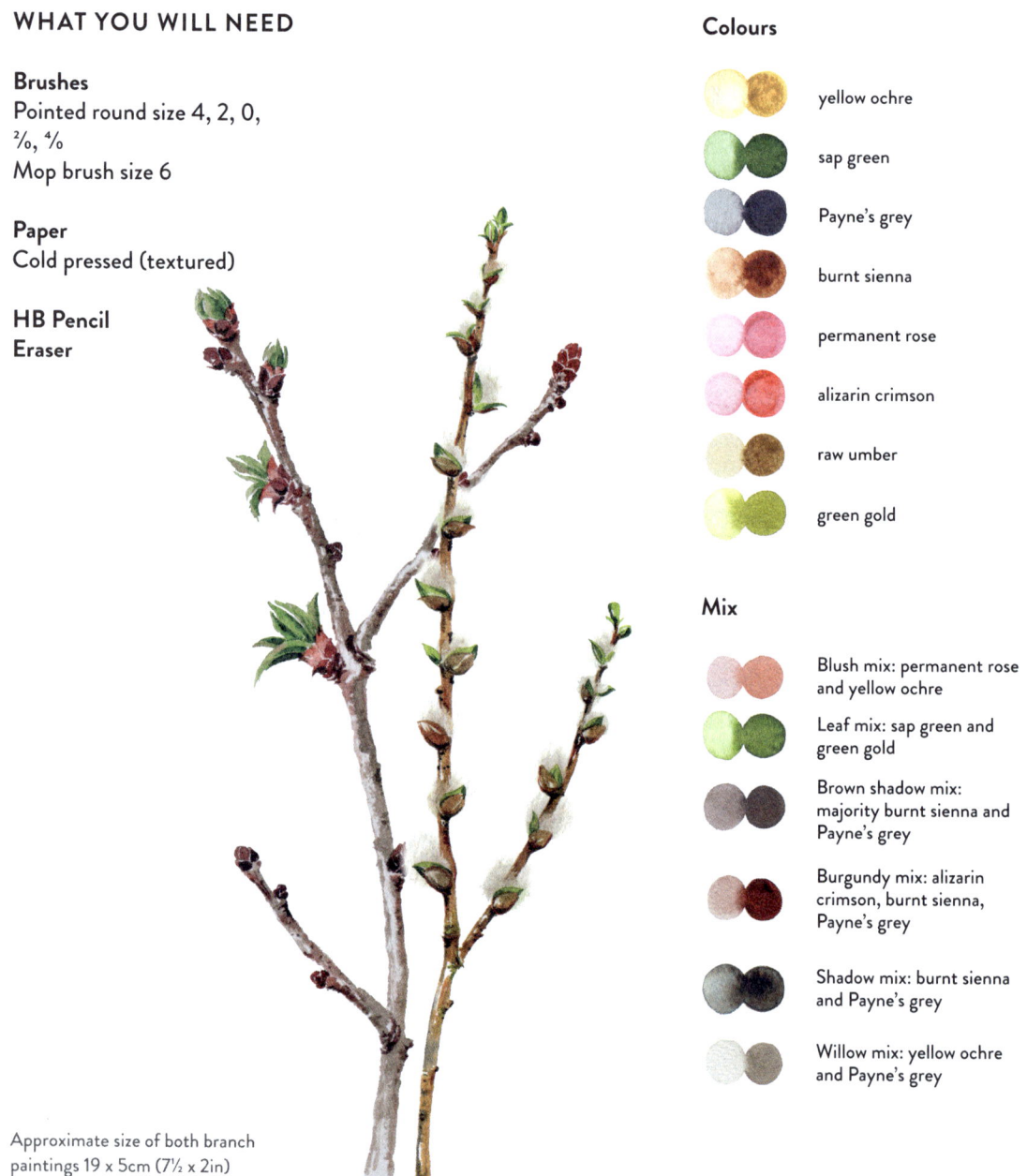

Approximate size of both branch paintings 19 x 5cm (7½ x 2in)

## Colours

yellow ochre

sap green

Payne's grey

burnt sienna

permanent rose

alizarin crimson

raw umber

green gold

## Mix

Blush mix: permanent rose and yellow ochre

Leaf mix: sap green and green gold

Brown shadow mix: majority burnt sienna and Payne's grey

Burgundy mix: alizarin crimson, burnt sienna, Payne's grey

Shadow mix: burnt sienna and Payne's grey

Willow mix: yellow ochre and Payne's grey

## WILLOW

I've always loved the fluffy buds of willows, and watercolour is the perfect medium in which to paint them.

1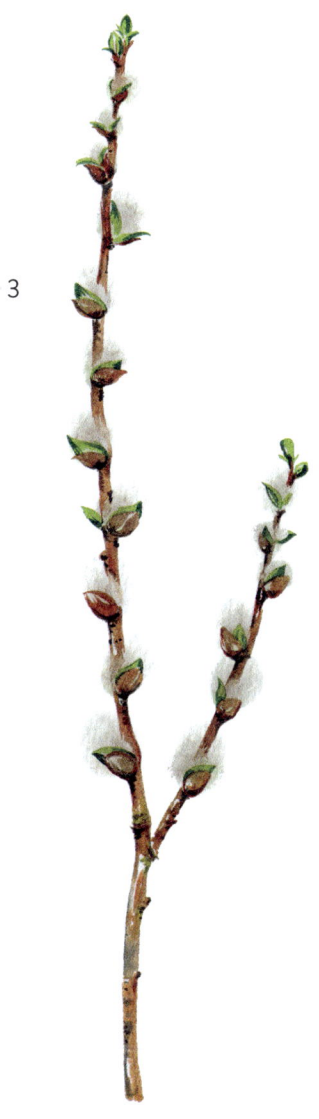

2

3

### 1.

Draw a faint pencil forked stem with a curve for the base of every bud. With your mop brush, paint a clear water wash over a section of stem (about 1cm (½in) coverage either side of the stem. While wet, dab diluted willow mix just above each curve with your size 4 brush. Pulse the brush a few times on the spot and that will help to push the paint outwards. Resist the urge to poke it and shape it. If it feels too faint, repeat the process with slightly more concentrated paint. While still wet, add a dab of leaf mix. Allow to dry fully.

### 2.

With your size 2 brush, starting at the bottom of the branch, paint a raw umber stem. Angle your brush low to create a broad line with the bristles. This will soon start to run out of paint and create a dry brushing technique that is great for branch and bark textures. Add in little knots and gnarly lumps of burnt sienna as you travel up the stem, dropping in a little green gold at the junctions and shadow mix down one side. When you reach your first bud curve, paint two mirrored C-curves to create the bud oval. Add a little burnt sienna and shadow mix to the underside. Work your way up each stem making sure to leave some space for the fluffy willow buds. Once fully dry, rub out any visible pencil.

### 3.

With your size 0 brush, paint a leaf mix sepal on each bud and sprouting shoots at the end of the branch. Once dry, add a lowlight of sap green onto each leaf with your size ⁴⁄₀ brush. Finish with a few more shadow mix marks on the branch to add more texture.

## HAWTHORN

The beady-eyed will spot how much claret colour emerges in hawthorn branches and buds long before the blossoms form.

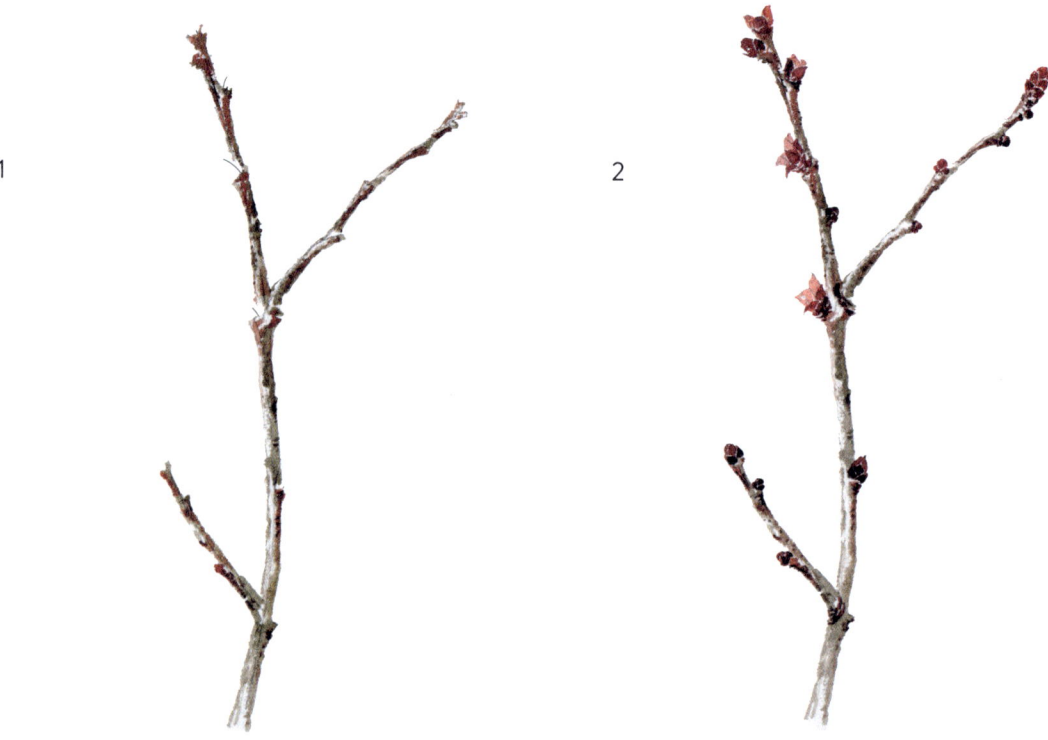

1

2

## 1.

Draw a faint pencil stem with branches. Make a note of where each bud protrudes as the stem curves out to accommodate its growth. The hawthorn is even more textured than the willow so use a size 2 brush, angled low on the page to paint a diluted brown shadow mix stem. Dry brushing will bring out the texture in the bark. The colour is more intense in the younger branches; once you have painted the branch, add lowlights of burnt sienna and burgundy mix.

## 2.

Using a ⅔ brush, paint burgundy mix C-curves for the smaller buds, interlinked and topped with a little dome. More mature buds have a second layer of C-curves and are topped with blush mix S-curves bursting outwards. Add some shadow mix to the buds' lower sections. Once dry, rub out any visible pencil.

## 3.

With your size 2 brush, paint C- and S-curves of leaf mix bursting out of the larger buds. Once dry, add lowlights of sap green and add a few more dots and strokes of texture to the branch in shadow mix.

3

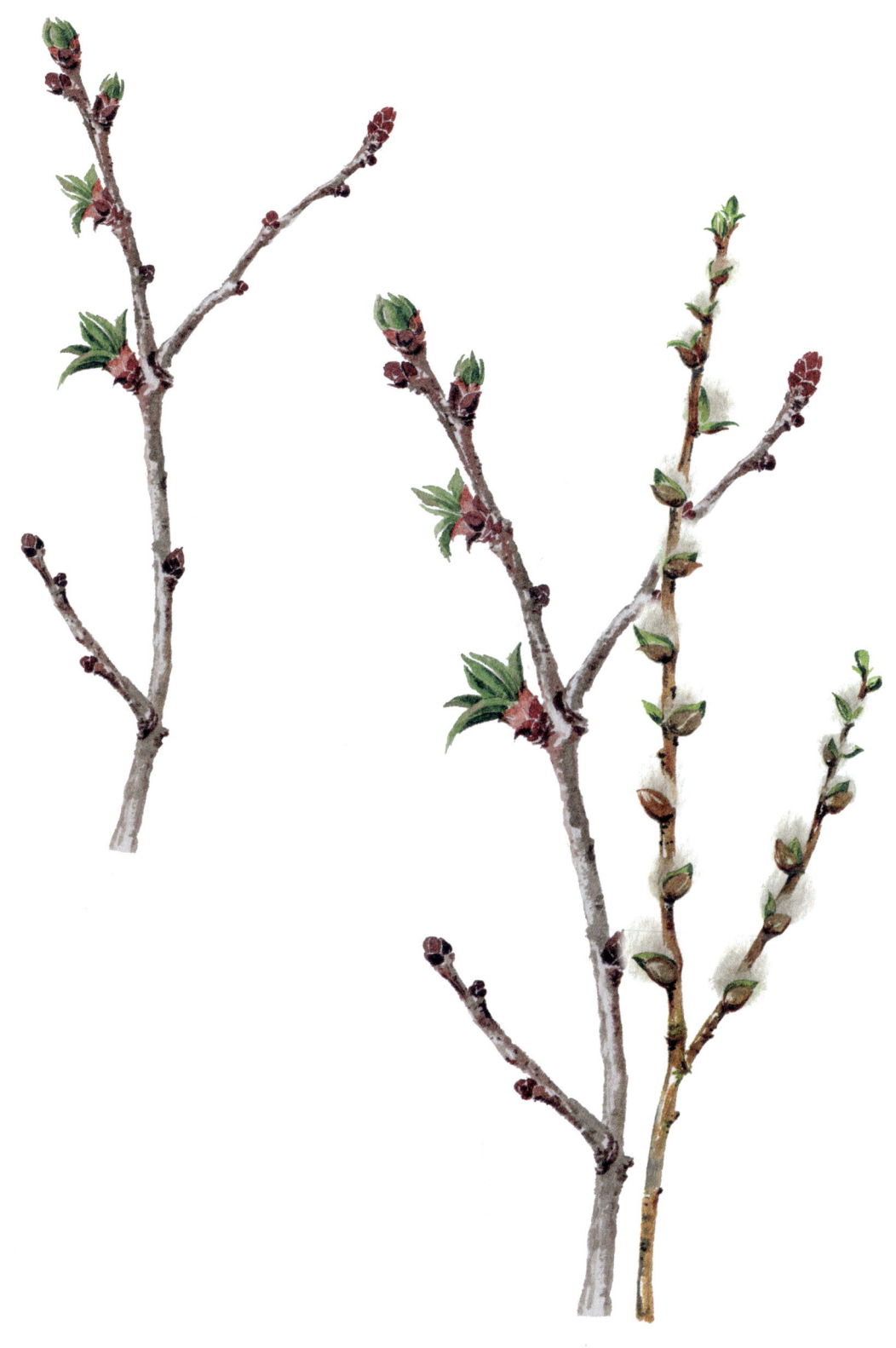

# KINGFISHER & HIS REFLECTION

The wonder of seeing a kingfisher is surely to see his reflection as he gazes into the water, looking for a fish. Here we have a tutorial that sets the scene as well as guiding you through the painting steps.

## WHAT YOU WILL NEED

**Brushes**
Pointed round size 8, 4, 2, ⁴⁄₀

**Paper**
Cold pressed (textured)

**HB Pencil**
**Eraser**

Approximate size of the kingfisher painting: 17 x 12cm (6½ x 4½in)

## Colours

yellow ochre

cadmium orange

cadmium red

sap green

green gold

Payne's grey

burnt sienna

Mars black

Winsor blue

cobalt blue

## Mix

Green water mix: green gold and Payne's grey

Feather mix: Winsor blue and Payne's grey

Shadow water mix: green gold, yellow ochre, burnt sienna, Payne's grey

Shadow mix: burnt sienna and Payne's grey

## 1.

Draw a horizontal line for your reflection line (the dotted line in the diagram) and a line for the shore in the background. Draw the kingfisher on the branch (first with an oval for the body and a smaller, squashed one for the head, before adding the beak and feathers) and then the reflected version. Use a ruler to measure up and down from the reflection line to get a rough symmetry between the two images, but remember the reflected version will be a little squashed as we are looking at it from above.

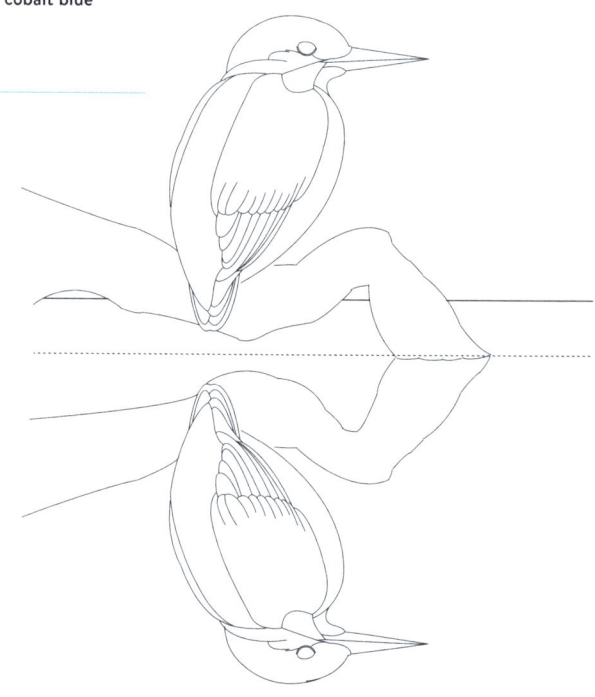

2

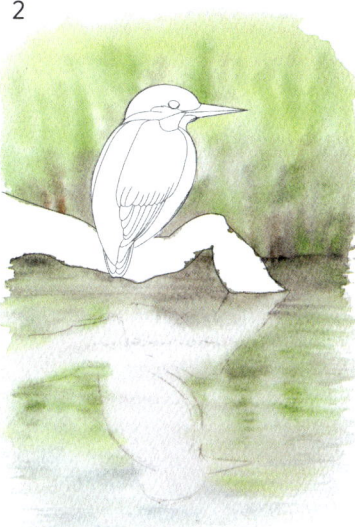

3

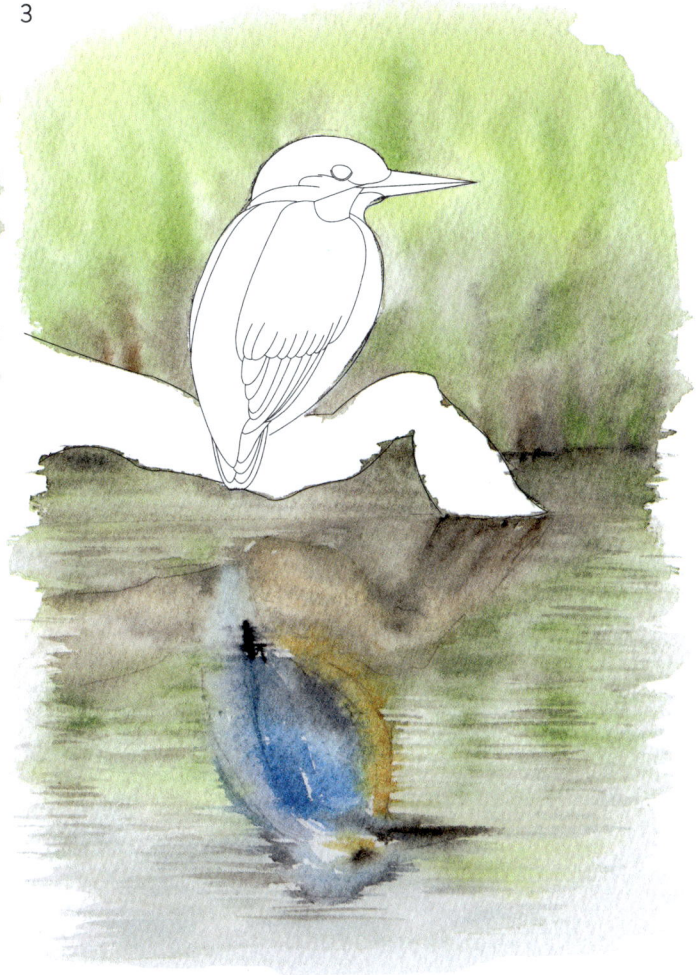

## 2.

Use your 8 brush to wet the area around the top kingfisher down to the shoreline. Paint in a wash of green gold and add flecks of sap green. Towards the bottom of the section add some shadow mix as well as flecks of sap green and burnt sienna. Now wet the whole 'water' area (including the reflected kingfisher). Paint horizontal sweeps of colour that reflect the colours you've painted above. The reflected colours should be a little more diluted and muted.

## 3.

While the water area is gradually drying, paint in a basic wash of burnt sienna on the reflected log with a little diluted shadow mix on the underside with your size 4 brush. With your size 2 brush, paint a basic wash of cadmium orange on the reflected kingfisher's chest and undereye, a cobalt blue wing and a Winsor blue head and back, down to the tail. Add Payne's grey to the wing tip, beak and eye. The aim is for the paint to softly blend on the drying page. Clean your brush and lightly sweep it back and forth horizontally across the outline of the kingfisher and it will draw the colour out in ripples into the water area. Paint ripples of diluted green water mix across the full water area.

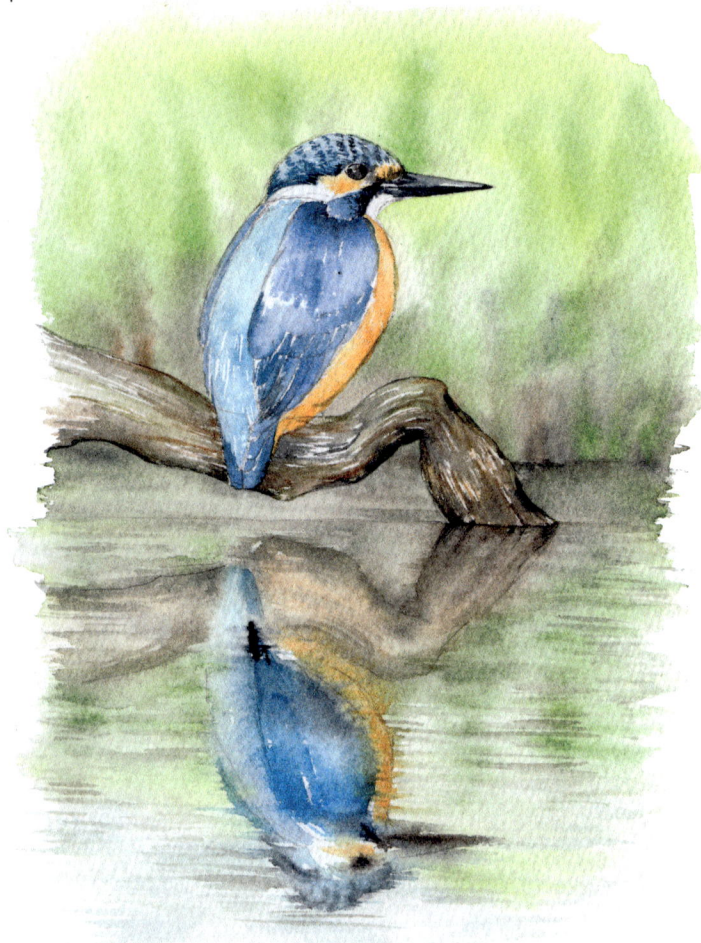

**4.**

You can now paint in the same sections on the actual kingfisher. Add a Mars black eye with a little unpainted 'shine'. Add some concentrated feather mix stripes, dabbed across the top of the head and down the neck and Payne's grey to the underside of the beak, all with your ⁴⁄₀ brush. The paper will be dry so it won't bleed. Paint the log with thin streaks of burnt sienna, yellow ochre and shadow mix to create texture. You can add some faint streaks onto the reflected log.

**5.**

With your ⁴⁄₀ brush paint fine line feather tufts across the body. Mix a little cadmium red to your cadmium orange for the orange areas. Use feather mix for the wings and tail feathers. Use Winsor blue for the back. Add a little of this detail to the reflected kingfisher. Allow to dry, then add further ripples to the water (including over the reflected kingfisher and log) using shadow water mix. Add a little shadow mix to the underside of the actual log and the area where the kingfisher is sitting.

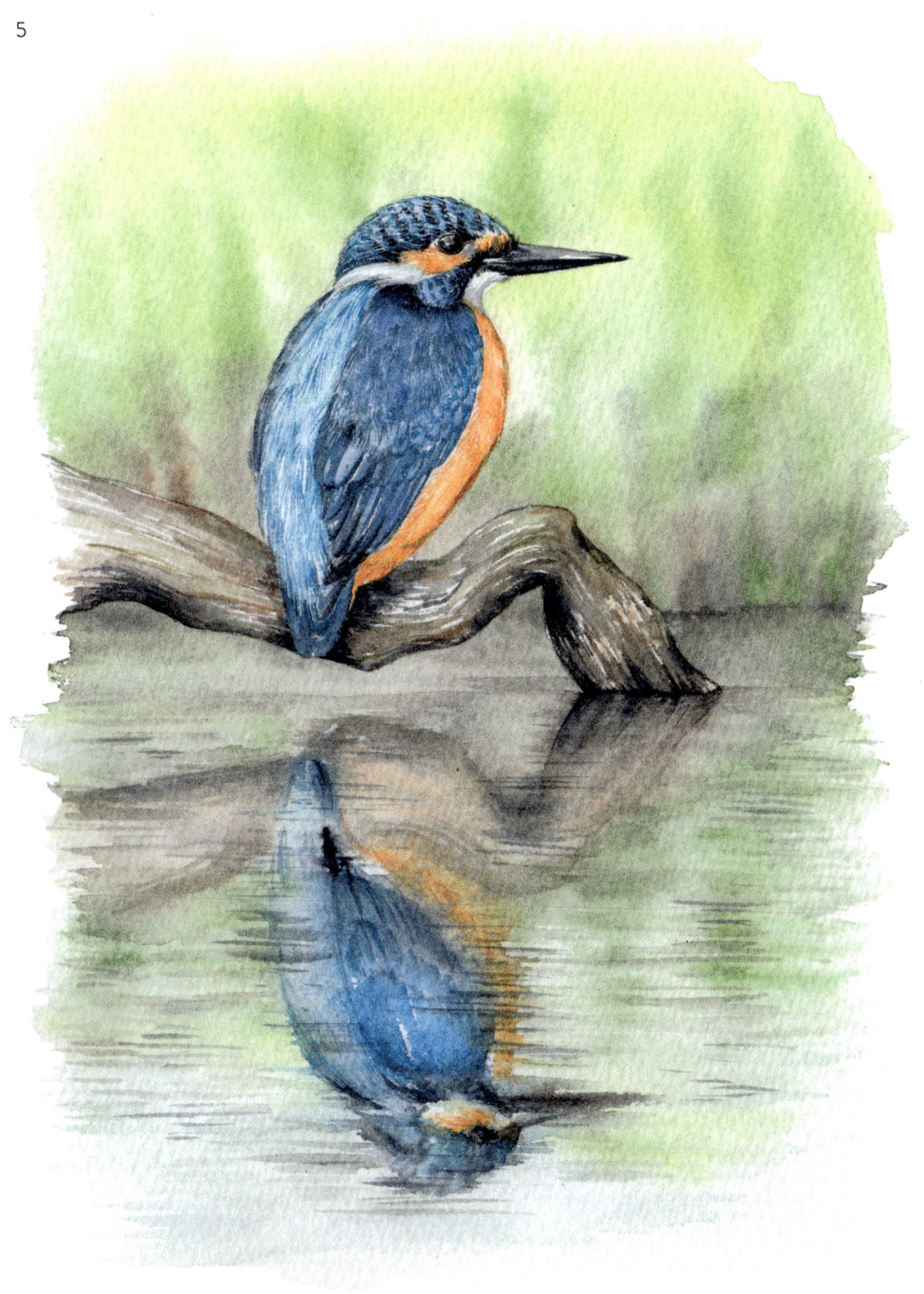

47 KINGFISHER & HIS REFLECTION

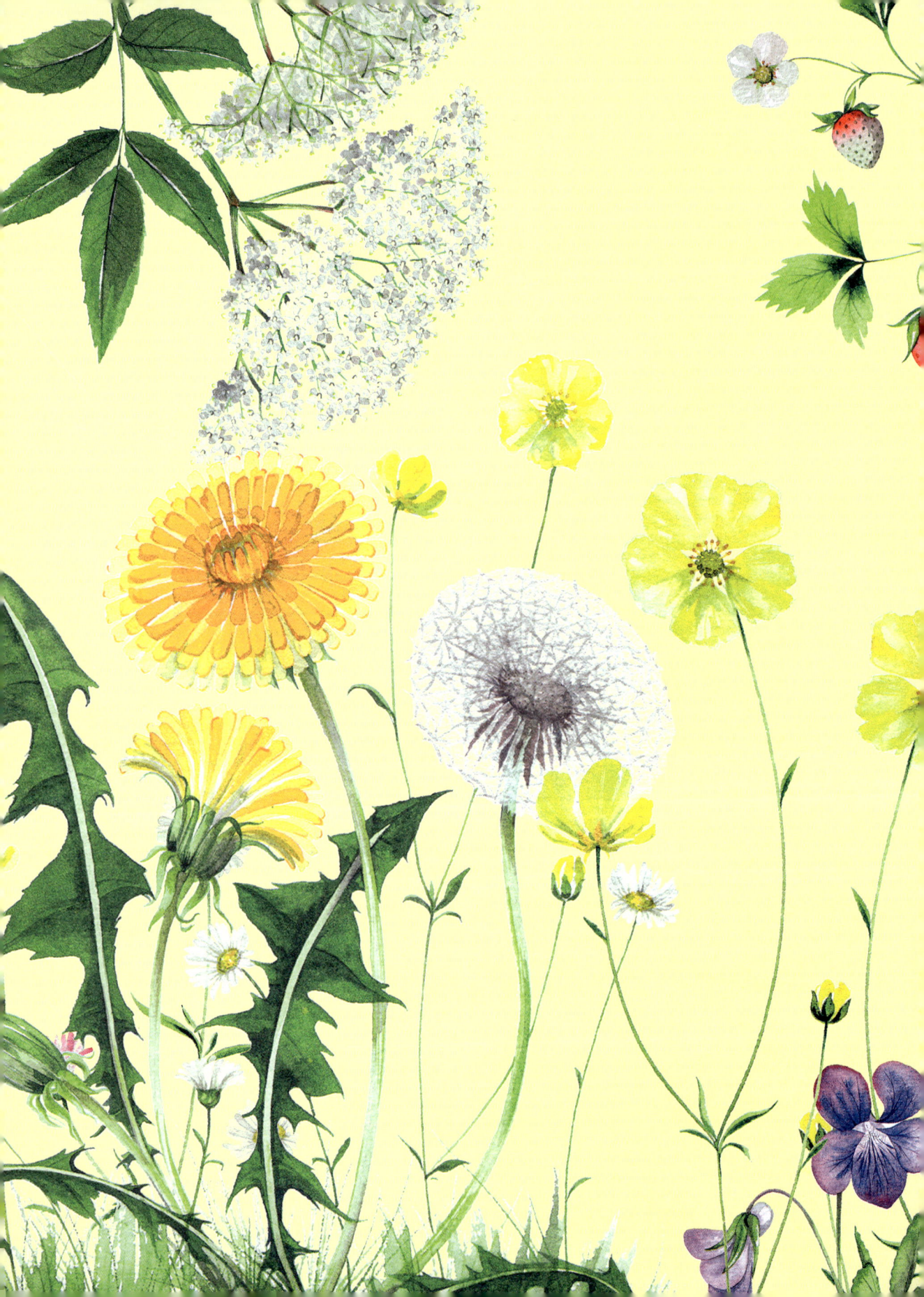

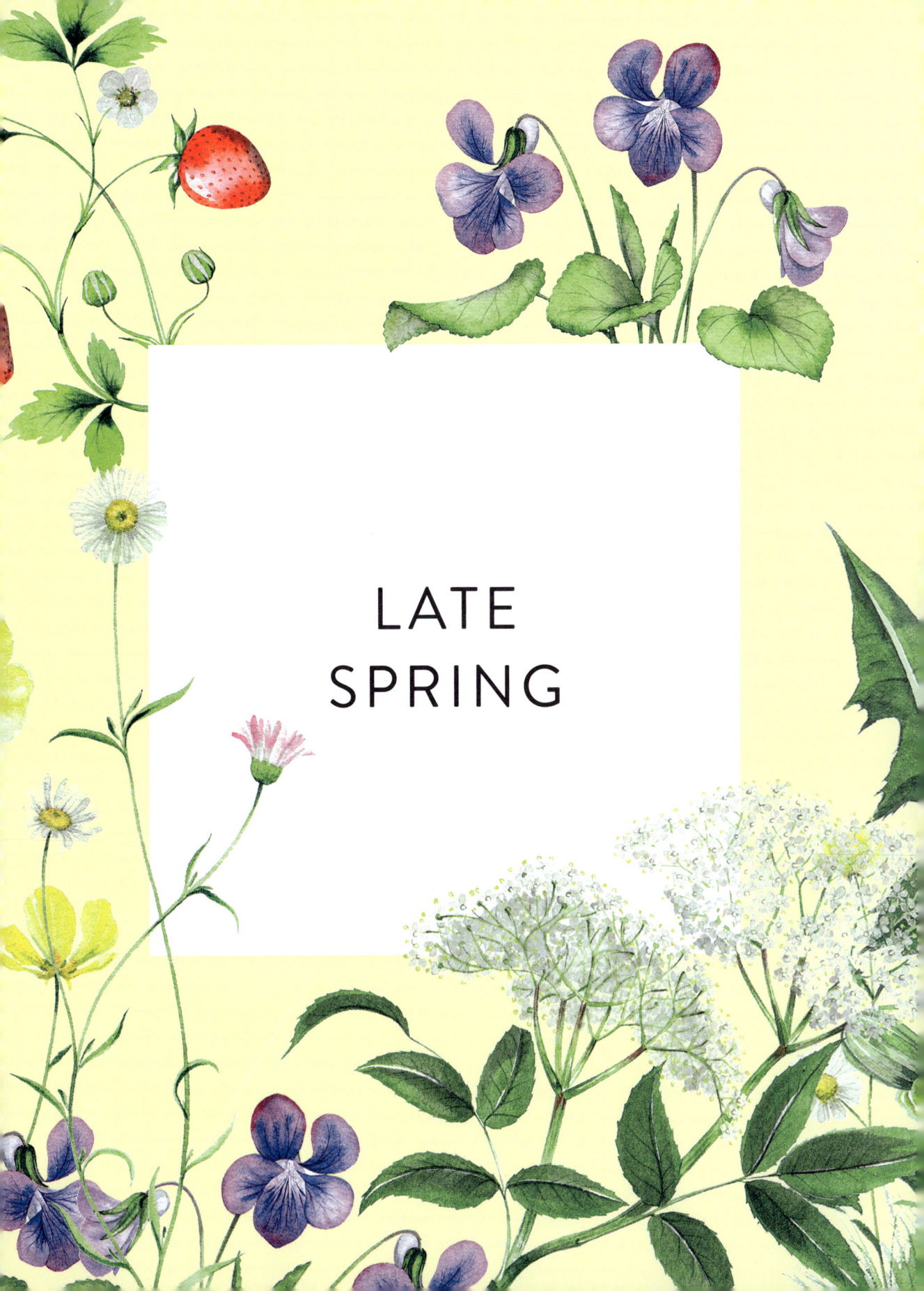

# LATE
# SPRING

# ELDERFLOWER

In late spring I noticed fluffy white clouds of elderflower growing all around us. Picking, cleaning and then turning the flowers into elderflower cordial was one of my fondest memories of that time.

This painting might seem like a tall order with all those little flowers but enjoy the process and don't rush to the end.

## WHAT YOU WILL NEED

### Brushes
Pointed round size 8, 4, 0, ⁴⁄₀
Rigger size 0

### Paper
Cold pressed (textured)

### HB Pencil
### Eraser

### Colours

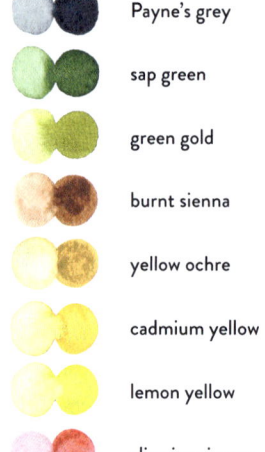

Payne's grey

sap green

green gold

burnt sienna

yellow ochre

cadmium yellow

lemon yellow

alizarin crimson

Approximate size of the elderflower painting: 19 x 17cm (7½ x 6¾in)

## Mix

 Stem mix: green gold, sap green, lemon yellow

 Shadow mix: burnt sienna and Payne's grey

 Petal mix: yellow ochre, green gold, Payne's grey

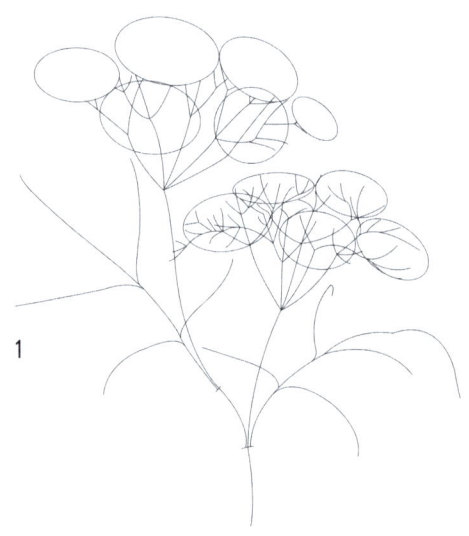

1

## 1.

Elderflower leaves most commonly grow in sets of five, so draw a curving pencil stem with extra curved branches for the leaves and a central line for each individual leaf. For each elderflower cloud, the main stem forks into five and continues to divide into smaller forked stems. For the flowers, draw a cluster of ovals in a cloud shape that encompasses the small, forked stem ends. This illustration (above right) features two clouds, one angled so we can see the stems underneath and another where the flowers conceal most of the stems.

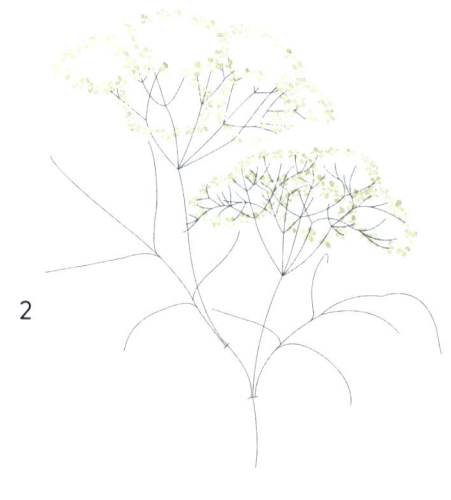

2

## 2.

Heavily dilute your petal mix and paint five-petalled flowers along the outline of each oval in your size 0 brush, spaced out so they don't touch. Allow to dry fully.

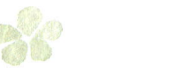

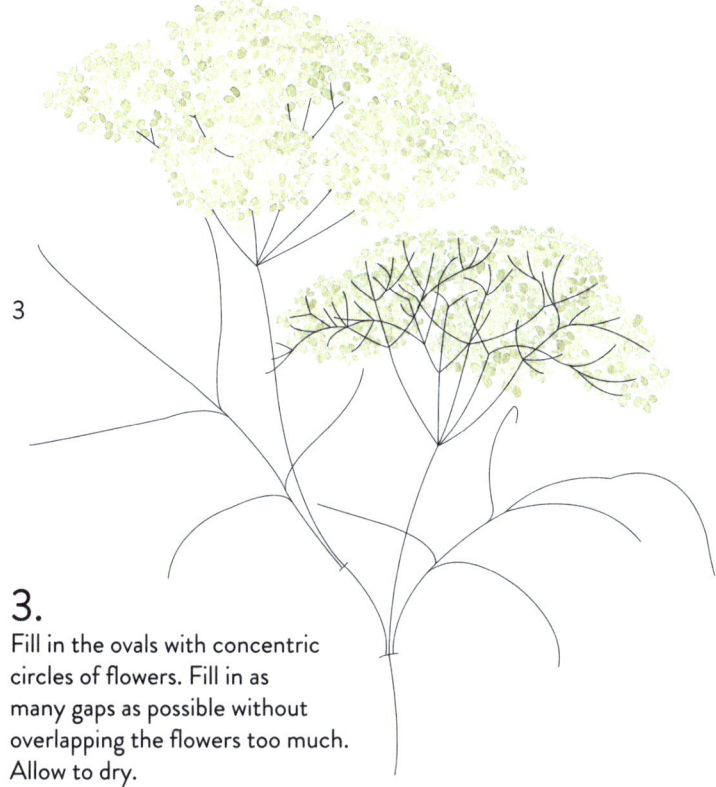

**4.**

With your size 4 brush, paint a stem mix stem that gradually thins as it reaches the five-point fork beneath the flowers. Change to a size 0 brush and paint fine lines with slivers of unpainted space to create ridged stems curving upwards into the flower cloud. As the stems fork and thin out, swap down to a ⁴⁄₀ brush. Where you can see the underside of the flowers, finish each stem with a small circular sepal. Paint the leaf branches in the same manner with your rigger brush, leaving a sliver of unpainted space.

Ensure that your size 8 brush can make a fine point by twisting the wet bristles in your palette. Fully coat it in wet stem mix and paint leaves with two mirroring C- or S-curves. While still wet, use your size 0 brush to flick little serrated edges along the edges just like the scalloped edge leaf method in the basic watercolour techniques section (see page 14).

Add streaks of alizarin crimson at each stem junction up towards the flower cloud.

The flowers need five tiny petal mix filaments and cadmium yellow anthers. Paint these in with your size ⁴⁄₀ brush and finish each one with a diluted shadow mix circle in the centre. I paint this on each flower on the edge of the cloud and then as many as I can see in the middle, but don't worry too much about painting every single one.

Once fully dry, rub out any remaining visible pencil.

**3.**

Fill in the ovals with concentric circles of flowers. Fill in as many gaps as possible without overlapping the flowers too much. Allow to dry.

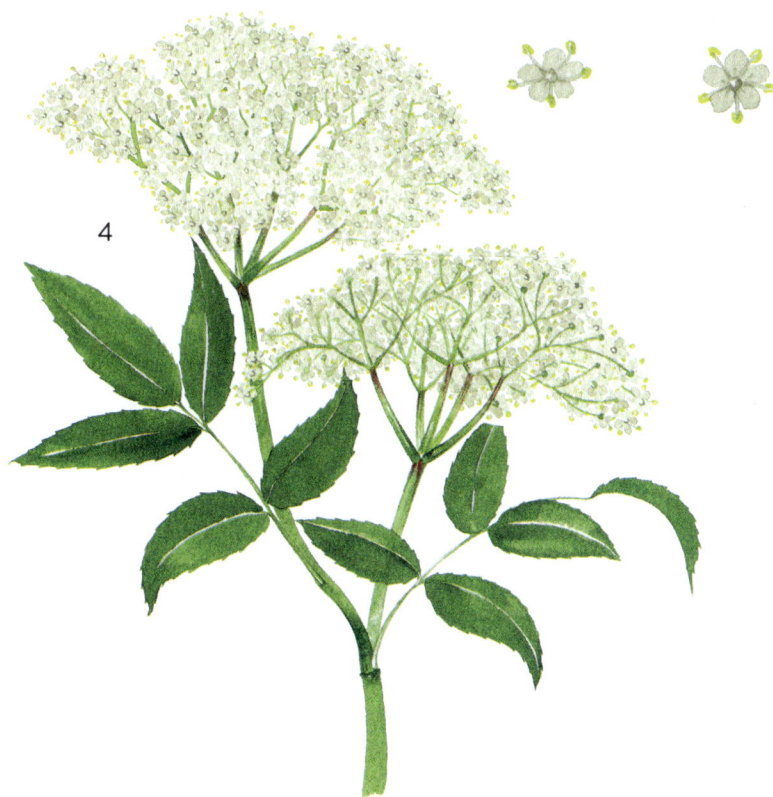

## 5.

Paint in streaks of sap green along the stems to create a ridged appearance with your size 0 brush. Dilute your shadow mix and use a size 4 brush to paint a sweep across the leaves and dab along the lower edge of the top flower cloud. Where we can see the stems underneath the other flower cloud, dab diluted shadow mix on the majority of the shape, leaving the 'top layer' of flowers untouched. Allow to dry.

Paint Payne's grey leaf lines with your rigger brush and add a few sweeps of Payne's grey along the underside of some of the thinnest stems under the flower clouds with your size ⁴⁄₀ brush.

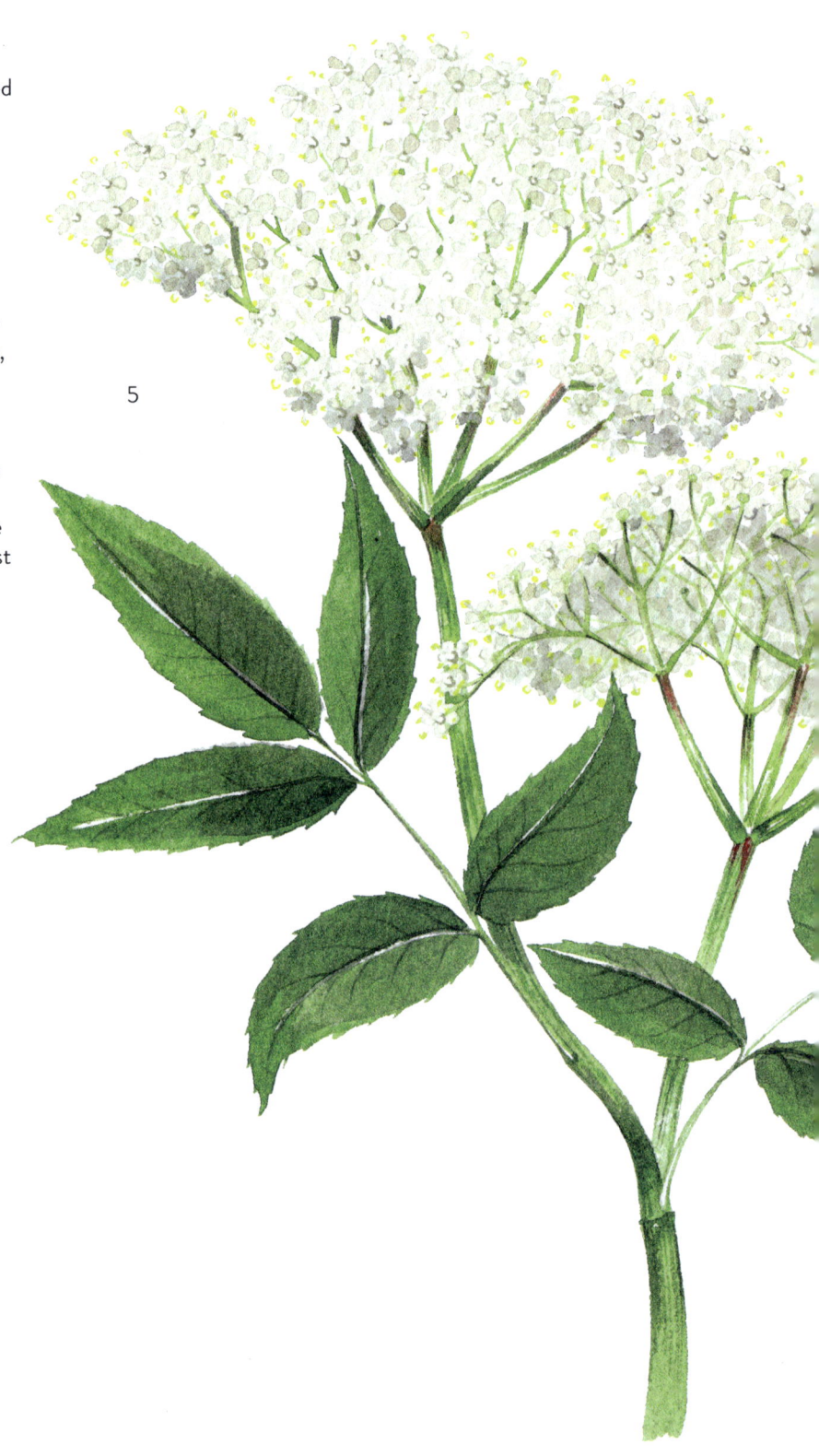

5

# ELDERFLOWER CORDIAL RECIPE

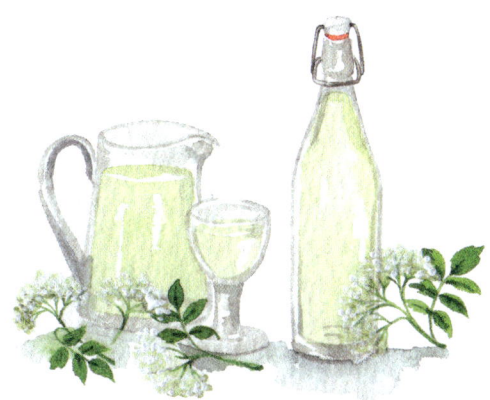

### Ingredients

15 fresh elderflower heads,
    stalks trimmed
1kg (2lb 2oz) granulated sugar
2 lemons, zested and sliced
50g (½oz) citric acid (option but
    this helps preserve the cordial)

### Method

Gently shake your flowers to loosen any dirt or bugs. Give them a gentle wash in cold water but try to avoid dislodging the pollen as that is where the flavour comes from.

In a large saucepan gently heat the sugar and 1 litres (1¾ pints) of water. You want the sugar to have dissolved but not to boil.

Stir occasionally and once the sugar has dissolved fully, turn up the heat to bring it to the boil. Once it boils turn the heat off. Add the flowers, lemon slices, zest and citric acid to the syrup and stir well. Cover the pan and leave to infuse for 24 hours.

Line a colander with a clean tea towel or kitchen paper, then sit it over a large bowl. Pour in the syrup in stages. Let the liquid drip slowly through before refilling the colander.

Funnel into sterilized bottles. The cordial is ready to drink straight away and will keep in the fridge for up to six weeks.

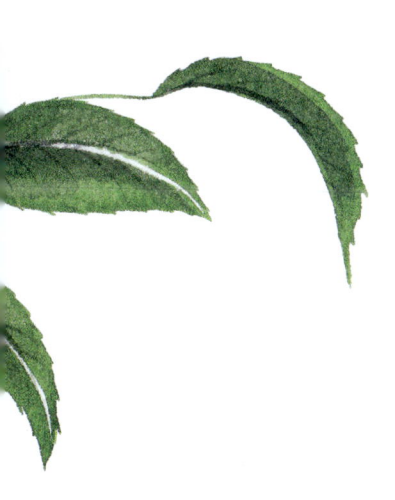

# WILD VIOLETS

This is a particularly hard-working wildflower used in scents, as an edible essence and in traditional medicine. Violets split opinion on whether they're a decorative plant or a bothersome weed, but I love to see them blooming in late spring around my birthday.

## WHAT YOU WILL NEED

**Brushes**
Pointed round size 4, 2, 0, ⁴⁄₀
Rigger size 0

**Paper**
Cold pressed (textured)

**HB Pencil**
**Eraser**

### Mix

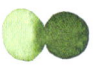 Plant mix: sap green and green gold

 Pink mix: majority permanent rose and cobalt blue deep

 Violet mix: majority cobalt blue deep and permanent rose

 Purple mix: permanent rose and French ultramarine blue

 Shadow mix: burnt sienna and Payne's grey

### Colours

 green gold

 sap green

 Payne's grey

 burnt sienna

 French ultramarine blue

 cobalt blue deep

 permanent rose

## 1.

Start by drawing pencil stems that curve and droop over at the top. Use this as the anchor point around which to draw five petals on each flower. Add heart-shaped leaves sprouting around the base of the stems.

## 2.

Each violet petal curves in a different direction. Begin with the anterior petal (central bottom) for your first wash: wet the petal shape with your size 2 brush, being careful to stay within the lines. Paint violet mix in the middle section and fill in the tip of the petal with pink mix. Leave the top unpainted and the violet mix will gradually blend upwards. While still wet, paint streaks of cobalt blue deep onto the violet mix section and an outline of permanent rose around the tip.

The aim is to paint all petals that aren't touching so they don't bleed into each other. For the curling petals there is no need to leave an unpainted area. For the partially open bud flower, wet each petal shape and paint in violet mix and allow to dry.

1

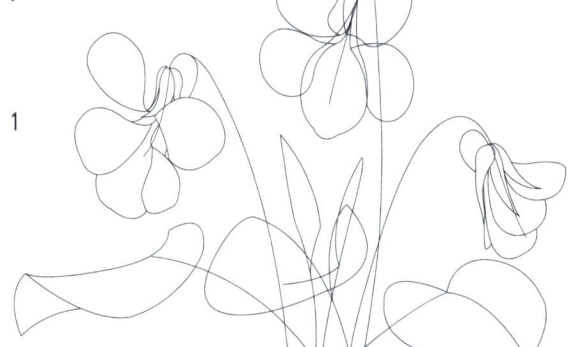

Approximate size of the wild violets painting: 15 x 14cm (6 x 5½in)

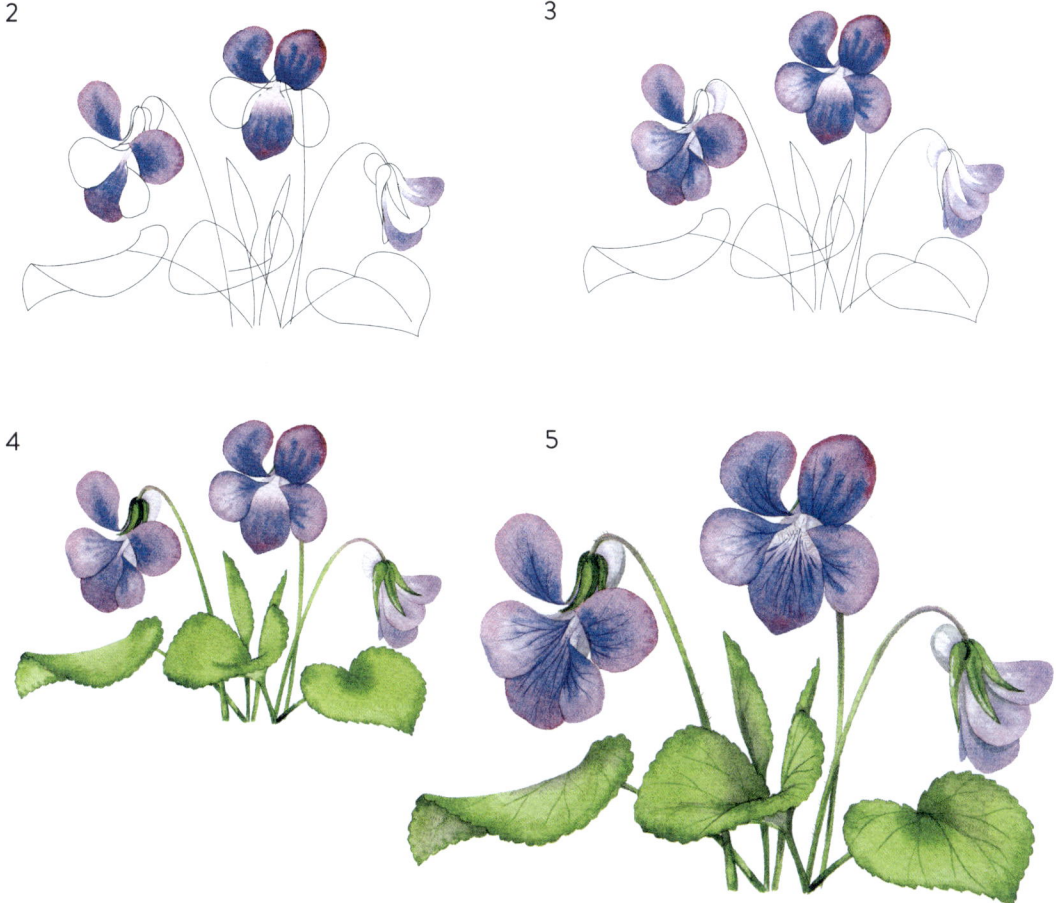

2

3

4

5

### 3.

Repeat Step 2 to paint in all the remaining petals, as well as a diluted violet mix on the bulbous spur (the pale purple lump just under the curve of the stem) and on the backs of the petals.

### 4.

With a size 4 brush, paint an unfurled leaf with wet plant mix. While still wet, dab some sap green at the point where the stem meets the leaf. Use your size 0 brush to paint a wet sap green scalloped edge around the leaf (see page 16). Work quickly and this will blend into the body of the leaf. Just like the petal painting, leave each section to dry before painting any other leaf sections that touch. Use your size 0 brush to paint plant mix stems and add some violet mix into the top, just as it curves over. Paint plant mix sepals (allowing each one to dry before painting its neighbour) and add some sap green lowlights.

### 5.

With your size ⁴⁄₀ brush paint diluted shadow mix lateral hairs (they look like tiny pointed teeth) on the two lateral (lower side) petals. Add some fine line shadow mix hairs to the stems too. Add sap green leaf veins with your rigger brush. Then use the rigger brush or your ⁴⁄₀ brush, depending on which gives you better control, to paint the concentrated purple mix veins on the inside of the petals.

Once everything is dry, lightly rub out any visible pencil. Then with your size 2 brush, paint diluted shadow mix on the underside of the petals, sepals and leaves.

# DANDELIONS & OTHER WONDERFUL WEEDS

I need look no further than our own imperfect lawn in the late spring and early summer months for a riot of colour. Dandelions, daisies and buttercups are some of the first flowers we take notice of as children – growing where they shouldn't – and their charm endures all these years later.

## WHAT YOU WILL NEED

**Brushes**
Pointed round size 6, 4, 2, 0, ⅔, ¾
Rigger size 0

**Paper**
Cold pressed (textured)

**HB Pencil**
**Eraser**

**Colours**

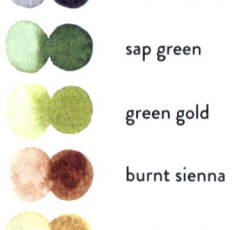 Payne's grey

sap green

green gold

burnt sienna

yellow ochre

cadmium yellow

lemon yellow

cobalt turquoise

cadmium orange

permanent rose

Approximate size of the dandelions painting: 15 x 13cm (6 x 5in)

## Mix

 Stem mix: green gold, sap green, cobalt turquoise

 Shadow mix: burnt sienna and Payne's grey

 Brown shadow mix: majority burnt sienna and Payne's grey

 Petal mix: lemon yellow and cadmium yellow

## DRAWING DANDELIONS

Draw a series of curved pencil stems for the flowers and leaves. For the open-face flower and clock, draw a small oval at the top of the stem, and a much larger one to form the outer edge of the flower. For the side-on flower and bud draw a curve that dissects the end of the stem 1cm (½in) down. Paint in all stems with your size 2 brush in diluted stem mix. Follow the steps that follow for each element of the plant.

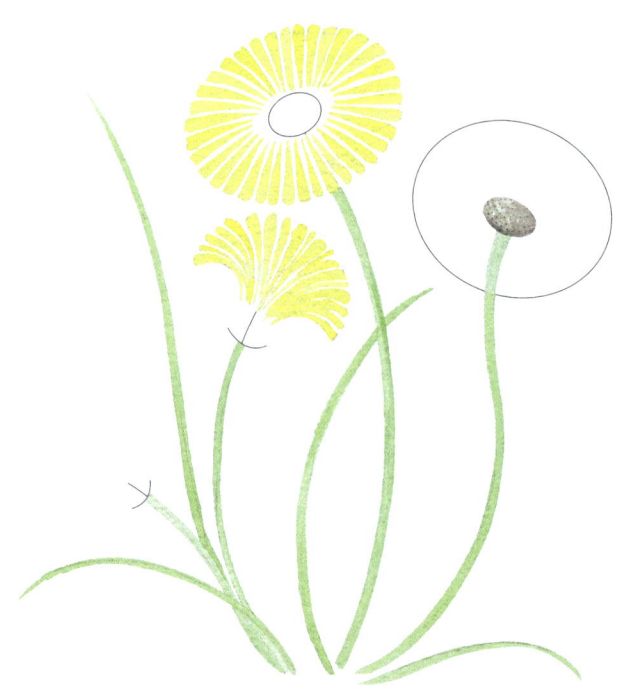

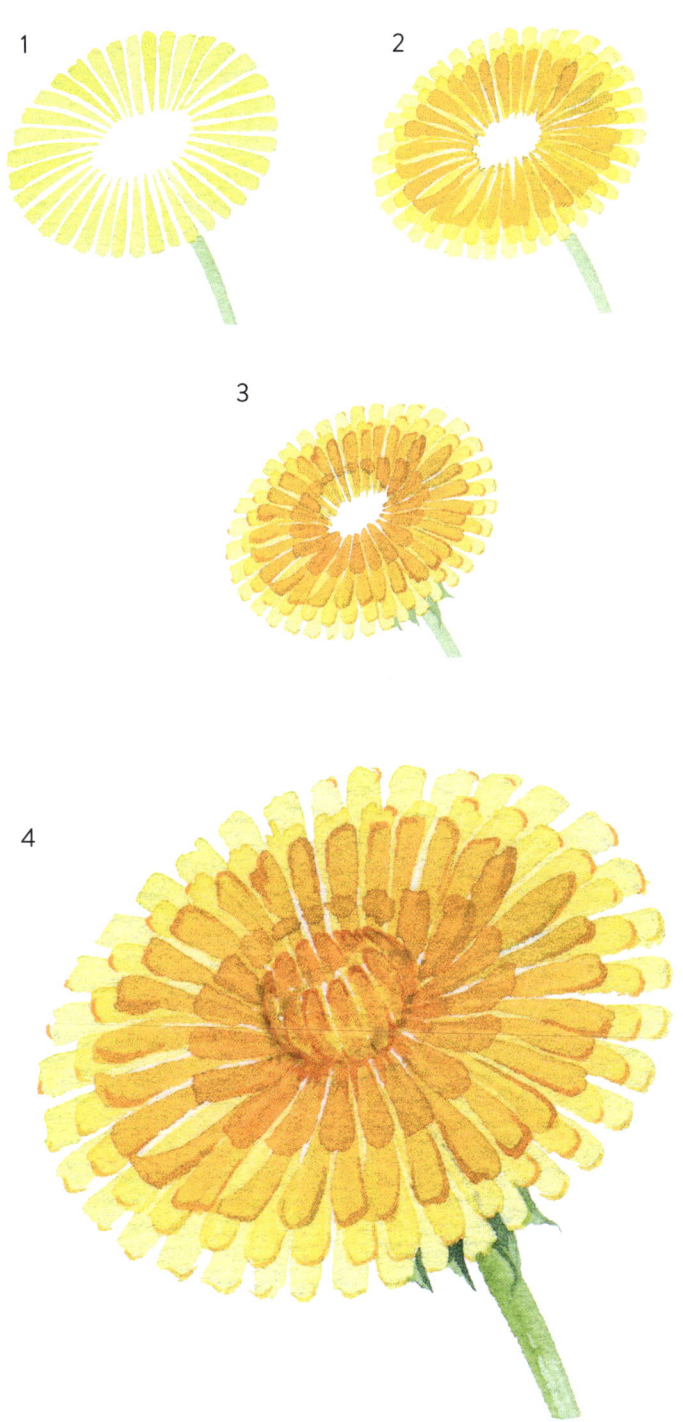

## OPEN-FACE FLOWER

### 1.

With your size 0 brush, paint tapering lines of diluted petal mix (it's really important to start diluted, so you can layer up on top) using the outer and inner pencil ovals as your guide. Allow to dry.

### 2.

Paint another layer with shrinking petals in a more concentrated petal mix. Then add a little cadmium orange to the mix and paint another layer of even shorter petals on top.

### 3.

Add a little more orange and paint another more concentrated layer. Shorten the petals around the back to accommodate a circular space for the flower centre. Use your size ⁴/₀ brush to edge some of the fainter petals with a little of this orange petal mix. Add some stem mix sepals.

### 4.

Dry brush some green gold streaks down the stem in your size 0 brush. Add a little cadmium orange to the petal mix and paint upturned petals in a cup formation in the centre of the flower. Once dry, use concentrated cadmium orange to outline the tops and bottoms of these petals with your size ⁴/₀ brush. Add some sap green lowlights to the sepals.

With your size 0 brush, paint some diluted shadow in the centre of the flower, around the central cup and on the stem.

## SIDE-ON FLOWER

### 1.

With your size 0 brush, paint a fan of tapering lines of diluted petal mix (it's really important to start diluted so you can layer up on top). Allow to dry.

### 2.

Paint a layer of petals in a more concentrated petal mix. Then add a little cadmium orange to the mix and paint another layer with fewer petals.

### 3.

For the upturned sepals, paint C- and S-curves with stem mix in your size 0 brush to house the petals. Allow to dry and then paint more unfurling downwards. Add a little more cadmium orange to the petal mix and use your size ⁴⁄₀ brush to edge some of the fainter petals with a little of this orange petal mix.

### 4.

Dry brush some green gold streaks down the stem and on the downturned sepals with your size 0 brush. Add some sap green lowlights to the upturned sepals with your size ⁴⁄₀ brush.

### 5.

Paint some diluted shadow mix on the petals that surround the central cup and on the stem with your size 0 brush.

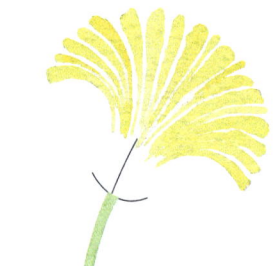

1

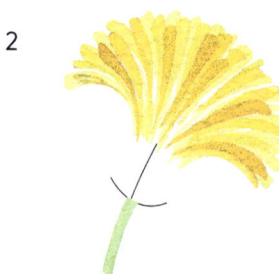

2

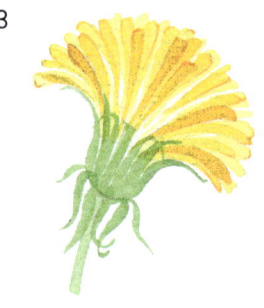

3

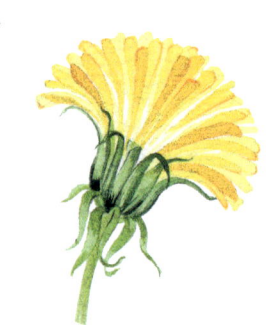

4

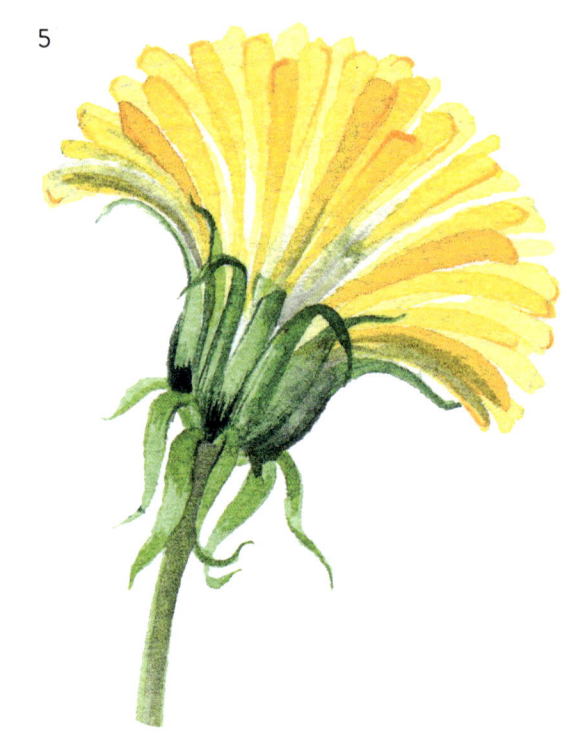

5

# DANDELION CLOCK

## 1.

With your size 0 brush, dilute some of your brown shadow mix to almost clear water. Paint the smaller central oval at the top the stem. Add a little shadow mix to the bottom half. Allow to partially dry and dot with concentrated brown shadow mix. Allow to dry.

## 2.

Each dandelion clock has approximately one hundred feathery bristles known as a pappus. With your size 0 brush, paint brown shadow mix dried sepals beneath the oval, and add a little shadow while still wet. Add some yellow ochre to your diluted brown shadow mix. With your size ⅙ brush paint diluted fine lines from the outer edge into the centre, just stopping short. On the outer end of that line, paint a series of small C-curves to create an inside-out-umbrella-star shape. Paint these little shapes around the edge of the whole oval.

## 3.

Paint concentric circles of these feathery bristles until you have covered the entire area. Allow to dry.

## 4.

Wet your size 6 brush and paint a wash over the whole oval. The aim is to gently blend the pappus so you can still see some detail, but it feels more cohesive. Dry brush some green gold streaks down the stem with your size 0 brush.

## 5.

Paint some diluted shadow mix on the stem.

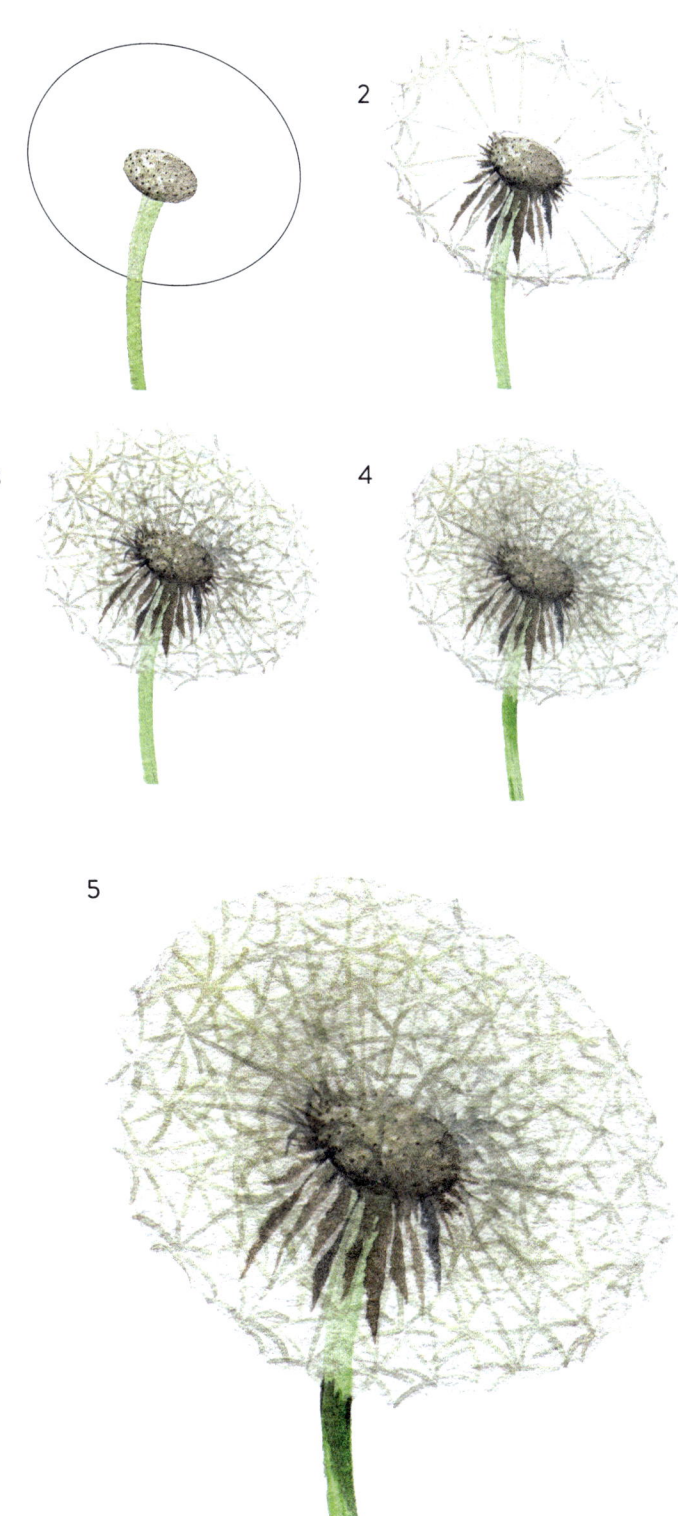

## LEAVES AND BUD

### 1.

With your size 4 brush, start at the top of the leaf with a fine point and paint wet sap green triangular leaf shapes down one side and then the other, leaving the faint stem mix of the leaf vein visible. Work fast to ensure the colour blends smoothly.

### 2.

For the bud, paint stem mix C-curves with small slivers of unpainted space in between. Then paint downturned sepals. For the leaf, dilute some Payne's grey into your sap green and with your size 2 brush, paint a line down one side of the central vein. Then with a wet brush, draw the colour outwards to create shadow leaf veins. Also paint some of this colour into the underside of each curve of the leaf and blend.

### 3.

Dry brush some green gold onto the bud stem and downturned sepals. Add some sap green lowlights to the bud with your size ⁴⁄₀ brush. Paint Payne's grey leaf lines onto the leaf with your rigger brush.

### DANDELION LAST STEP

With all your elements painted in, add diluted shadow mix wherever a leaf overshadows a stem or the open-face flowers shelter buds and stems beneath them.

Why not add in a handful of buttercups and daisies to complete the piece?

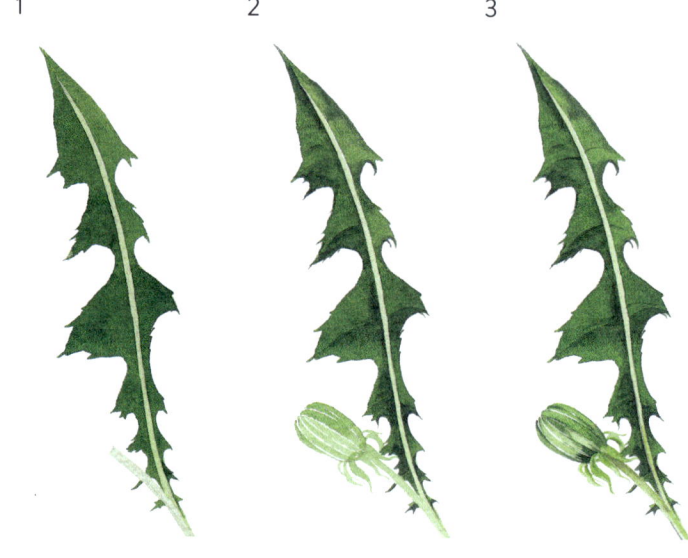

1     2     3

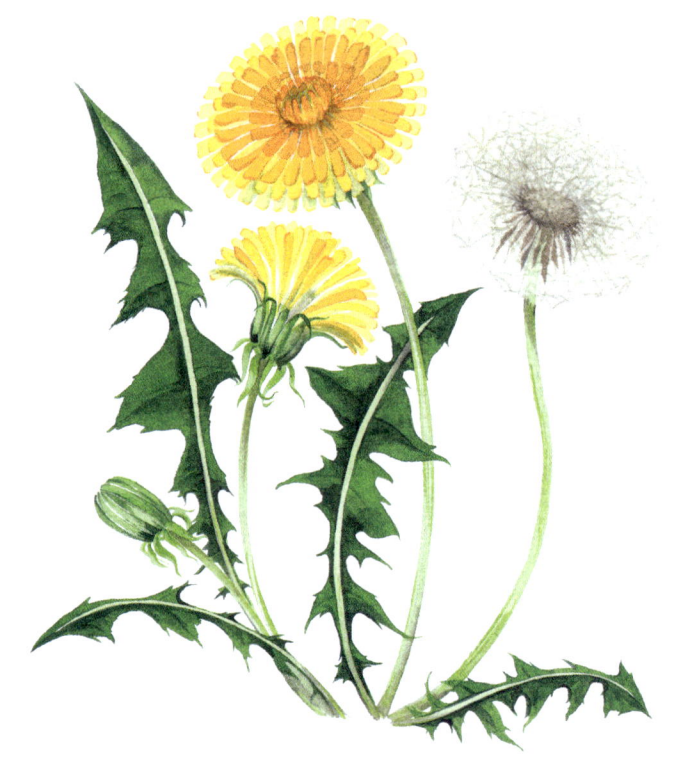

## BUTTERCUP

### 1.

Draw a slender forked stem in faint pencil. Paint this in stem mix with your rigger brush and add a few small C- and S-curve leaves with your size 0 brush. For an open flower paint a wet blob of lemon yellow. Wet your size 0 brush and draw out a fine line of paint from the blob, then fan your brush out to create a broad wet petal. Paint five of these around the blob. For a side-on flower paint curved C-curves from a central point with your size 2 brush, starting with a fine point and fanning out the brush. For an opening bud paint a couple of petal mix dabs, allow to dry and then paint 3 C-curve sepals in stem mix.

### 2.

Paint streaks of concentrated petal mix onto the petals to create a bit more shine and texture. Add sap green lowlights to the leaves and bud sepals with your ⁴⁄₀ brush. Paint green gold dabs in the centre of the open face flower and fine line cadmium yellow filaments around the edge. Dot each one with cadmium orange. For the side-on flower, paint cadmium yellow sepals at the base of the flower and a tiny bit of green gold in between each petal. Once dry, add some very diluted shadow to the bottom half of the open flower petals and under the side-on flower.

## DAISY

### 1.

Draw a slender, curling forked stem in faint pencil with a small circle for the open-faced flower and an oval for the angled flower. Paint the stem in stem mix with your rigger brush, add a few small leaves with your size 0 brush and a filled-in 'U' shape for the side-on flower. Paint the same diluted mix used for the dandelion clock pappus to paint spaced-out petals around the circle and oval with your size ⅔ brush. Paint a fan of petals on the side-on flower. Feel free to drop in diluted permanent rose to the petals.

### 2.

Once dry, add a second layer of diluted petals in the gaps on each flower. Add sap green lowlights to the leaves and bud sepals with your ⁴⁄₀ brush. Once the petals are dry, dab cadmium yellow into the central shape with a little dab of green gold and burnt sienna in the centre while still wet. Once dry, add some very diluted shadow to the bottom half of the open flower petals.

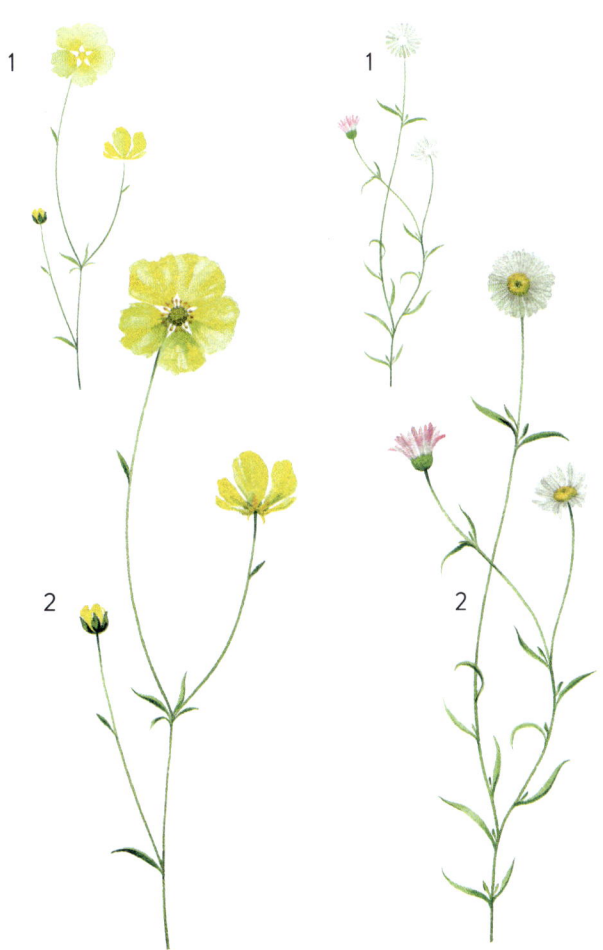

# STRAWBERRIES & STRAWBERRY THIEVES

I've barely ever tasted one of our home-grown strawberries; I'm far behind our garden's bird population in the pick-your-own queue. We've never acted on this 'problem' and I think my husband Ant's joy at enticing so many birds into the garden – even if they are plundering our produce – is, for him, a highlight of growing your own.

We're not experienced gardeners, preferring to feel our way through trial and error, but an accidental run over with the mower brought a triumphant strawberry crop the following year. The blackbirds were thrilled.

## WHAT YOU WILL NEED

**Brushes**
Pointed round size 4, 2, 0, ⁰⁄₀
Rigger size 0

**Paper**
Cold pressed (textured)

**HB Pencil**
**Eraser**

Approximate size of the strawberries painting: 14 x 16cm (5½ x 6¼in)

## Colours

- yellow ochre
- sap green
- Payne's grey
- burnt sienna
- cadmium yellow
- cadmium orange
- cadmium red
- alizarin crimson
- permanent rose

## Mix

- Plant mix: sap green and cadmium yellow
- Berry mix: cadmium red and permanent rose
- Blossom mix: yellow ochre, burnt sienna, Payne's grey, cadmium yellow
- Seed mix: alizarin crimson and yellow ochre
- Shadow mix: burnt sienna and Payne's grey

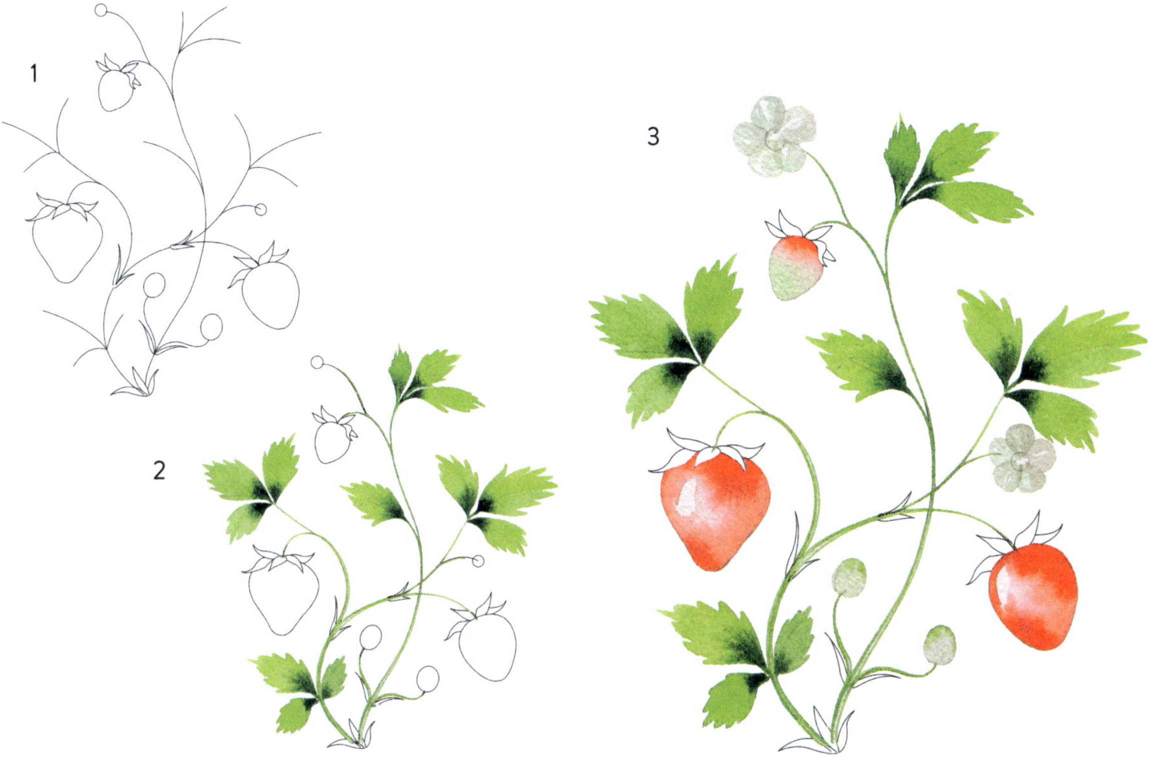

**1.**

Follow the drawing guide to create a faint pencil outline of a strawberry plant.

**2.**

Strawberry leaves tend to grow in threes. For each leaf, use your size 4 brush to paint plant mix serrated edge leaves, following the serrated edge leaf demo in the watercolour techniques section (see page 14). While still wet, dab some sap green into the base of the leaf and it will slowly bleed up. Paint in the plant mix stems with a rigger brush, thickening the stem at the base of the plant.

**3.**

Dilute the blossom mix almost to the point of invisibility; when it dries on the paper it will form a beautiful, crisp edge. The strawberry blossom has five petals; paint two rounded petals with your size 0 brush anchored in the middle of the central pencil circle and allow to dry. Then paint in the remaining three. Use the blossom mix to paint in the little unripe strawberries, adding a dab of plant mix at the end of each berry. For the ripening strawberry, paint the lower half of the berry in blossom mix. While still wet, paint some diluted berry mix at its top, clean your brush and use the wet bristles to draw the two colours together. Once they touch and start to blend, leave them alone.

For the ripe strawberries, with your size 2 brush paint in a very diluted berry mix leaving a small area of unpainted space. While still wet, introduce more concentrated berry mix to the outer edges and pulse the brush to push the paint into the berry centre. You can always add more concentrated cadmium red or alizarin crimson to areas for a more intense colour.

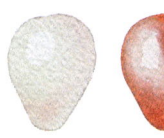 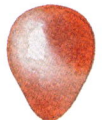 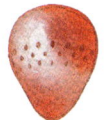

## 4.

Paint plant mix sepals on the berries, stem and blossom with lowlight accents of sap green while still wet. Use the rigger brush to paint sap green leaf veins: a central long line along each leaf and then smaller, branching lines angled towards the end of the leaf.

## 5.

With your size ⁴⁄₀ brush, paint a curved row of seeds (two tiny mirrored C-curves) across the broadest part of the ripe strawberry with seed mix. From there, paint further curved rows of seeds, with each new one in a gap from the previous line. The seeds shrink in size towards the bottom of the berry. For the ripening strawberry, paint these seeds in sap green.

Fill in the pencil circle on the blossoms with dabs of concentrated cadmium yellow. Circle that with a few larger dabs of cadmium orange. Add a few dabs of shadow mix on the underside of the yellow circle to create a rounded shape.

Add some burnt sienna C- and S-curves at the base of the plant and paint a sweep of diluted shadow mix down the side of the strawberries.

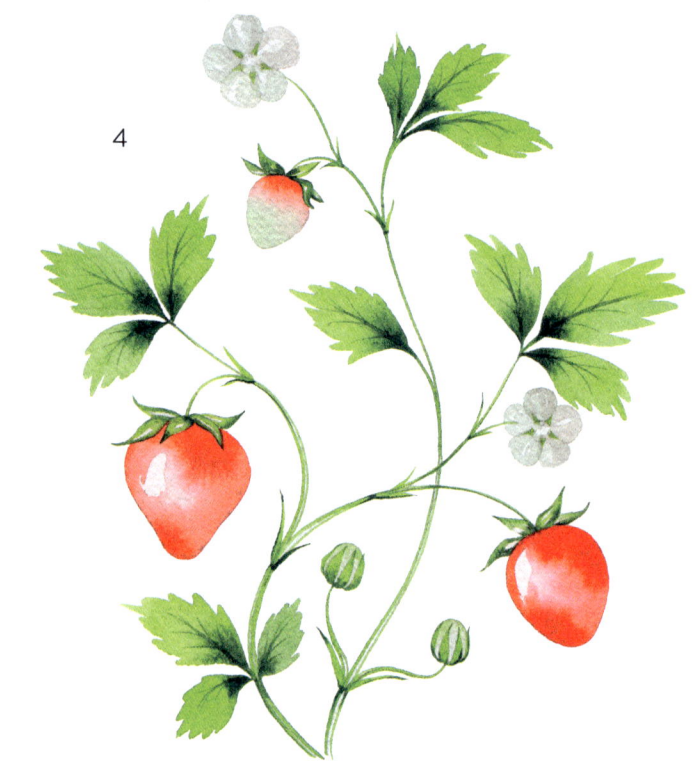

4

If you're lucky enough to be ready with art supplies when the culprits strike, these blackbirds are best captured by a pen and ink scribble in the moment. These sketches are a useful way to capture their speedy movements, and can then be used as reference to put into a full watercolour piece later on.

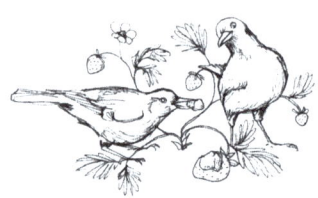

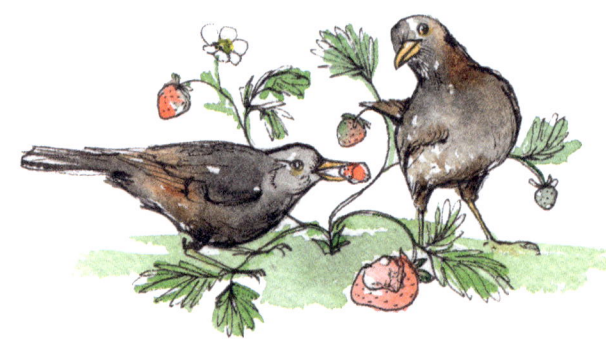

5

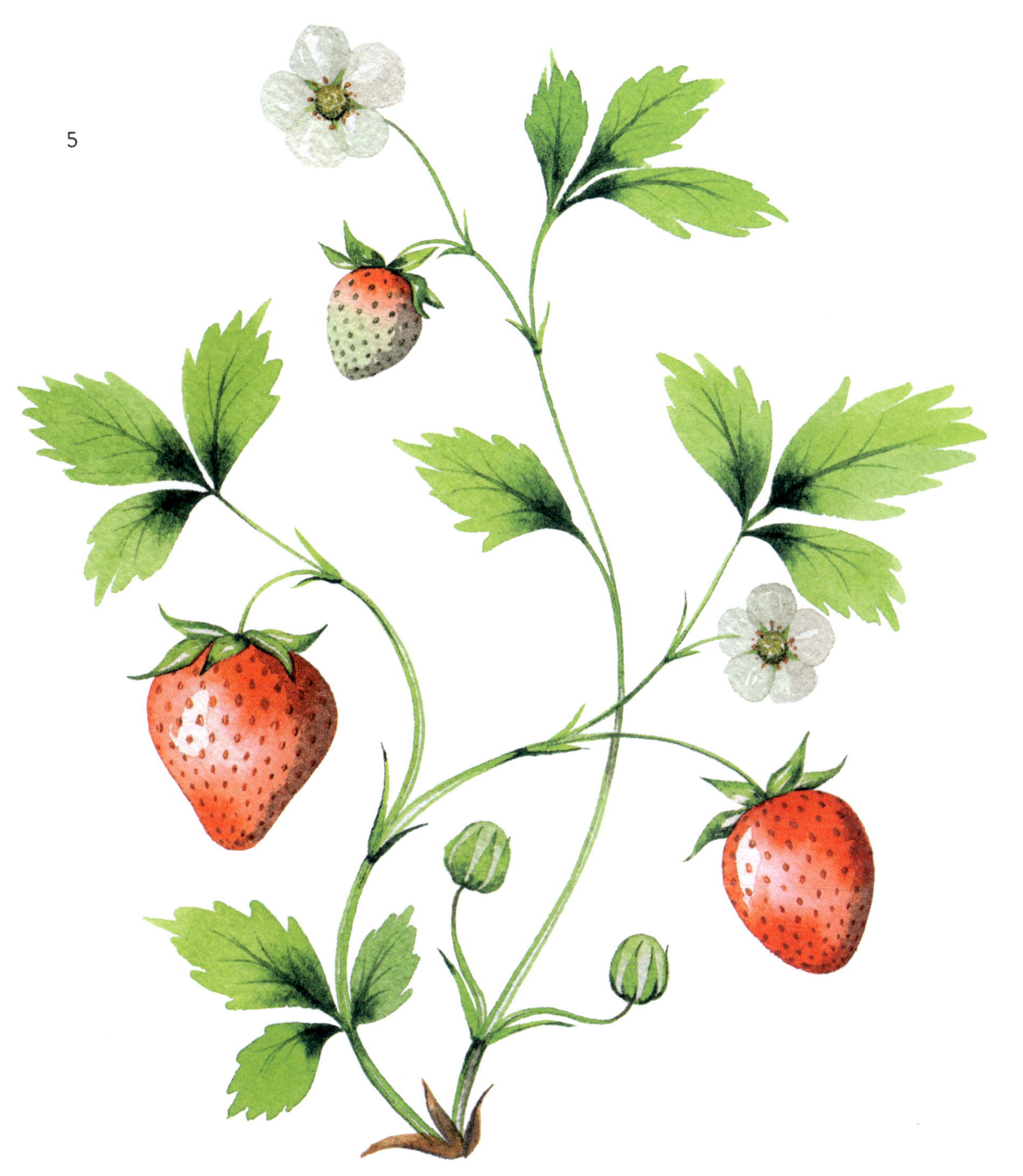

# THE WOODPECKER
# AT THE BIRD FEEDER

There is no greater example of hierarchy and mob rule than at
our garden bird feeder. The house sparrows arrive in packs and
bully away the various finches and blue tits, but all birds hurriedly
disperse with the arrival of the great spotted woodpecker. Swinging
the peanut feeder with the force of his arrival, he aggressively pecks
away while the other birds patiently wait at a respectful distance.

I tried to observe the daily bird feeder politics while sat in the
garden, but every time I picked up a pencil to sketch, they flew away.
The distance of the view through the kitchen window meant only
capturing the simpler block colours of each bird, which led to an
enjoyable series of simplified, miniature paintings. These are so much
quicker than a detailed piece and you might even manage to finish a
simple study (see page 69) before they've flown away.

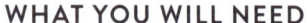

## WHAT YOU WILL NEED

**Brushes**
Pointed round size 0, ⅘

**Paper**
Cold pressed (textured)

**HB Pencil**
Eraser

**Colours**

    Payne's grey

    burnt sienna

    Mars black

    cadmium red

    yellow ochre

**Mix**

    Shadow mix: burnt sienna
and Payne's grey

    Brown shadow mix:
majority burnt sienna and
Payne's grey

    Black feather mix: Mars
black and Payne's grey

    Feather mix: burnt sienna,
Payne's grey, yellow ochre

Approximate size of the detailed
woodpecker painting: 13 x 8cm (5 x 3in)

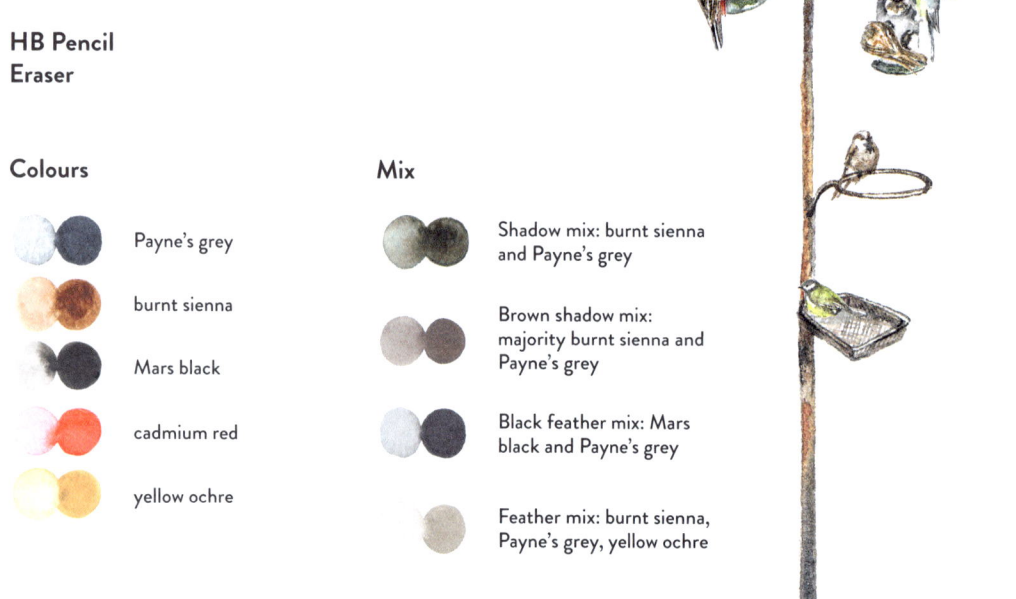

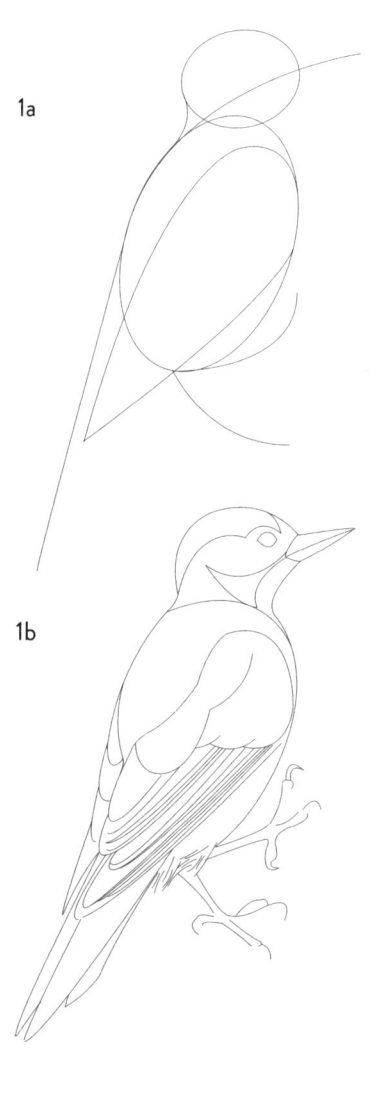

1a

1b

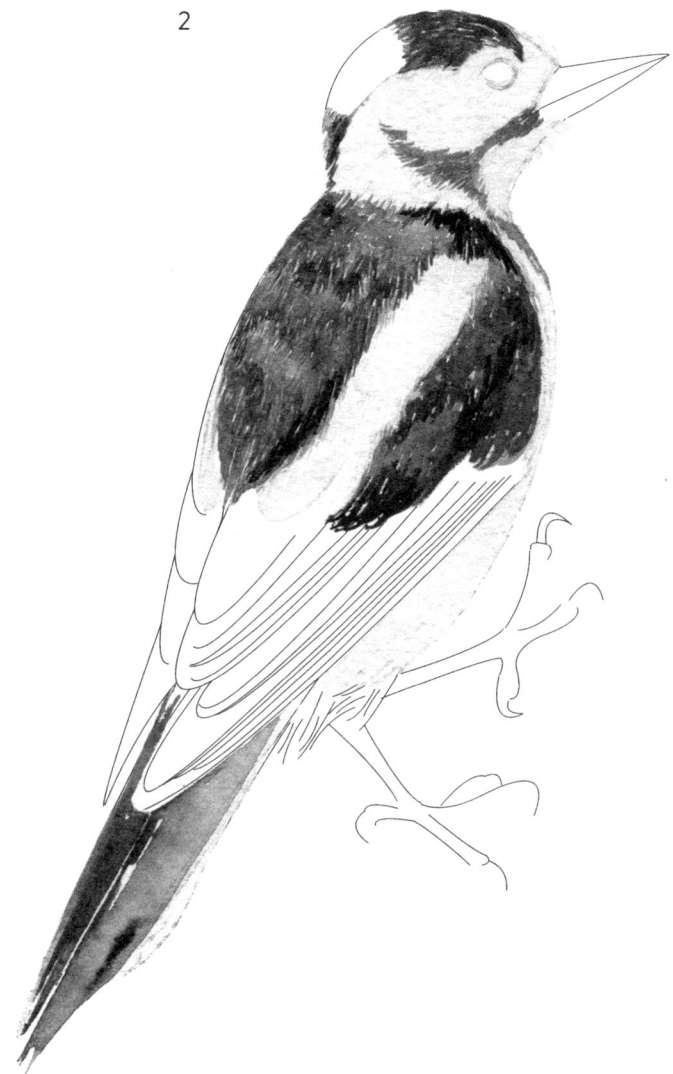

2

## 1.
Follow the drawing guide to create a faint pencil body shape.

## 2.
Use your size 0 brush to paint strokes of diluted feather mix over the face, neck, torso, lesser coverts and undertail coverts. Allow to dry. Paint feathery strokes of black feather mix over the head, neck, back, wings and tail feathers.

## 3.

The long thin feathers on the wings are called the primaries and secondaries and these are the feathers with the distinctive white spots. Paint each feather in brown shadow mix with your size 0 brush, leaving unpainted white spots down each one and a fine sliver of unpainted space between. Add extra lowlights of the black feather mix.

## 4.

Dilute your black feather mix to a translucent grey and using a size 0 brush, dab textured marks on the legs and feet with a tiny talon on each claw. Paint the beak and add a more concentrated dab at the tip and nostril.

Clean off your size 0 brush and paint cadmium red feathery streaks on the back of the head and longer strands on the abdomen behind the legs. Mix a little shadow mix into your red and add a few streaks to both sections. Once dry, rub out any visible pencil.

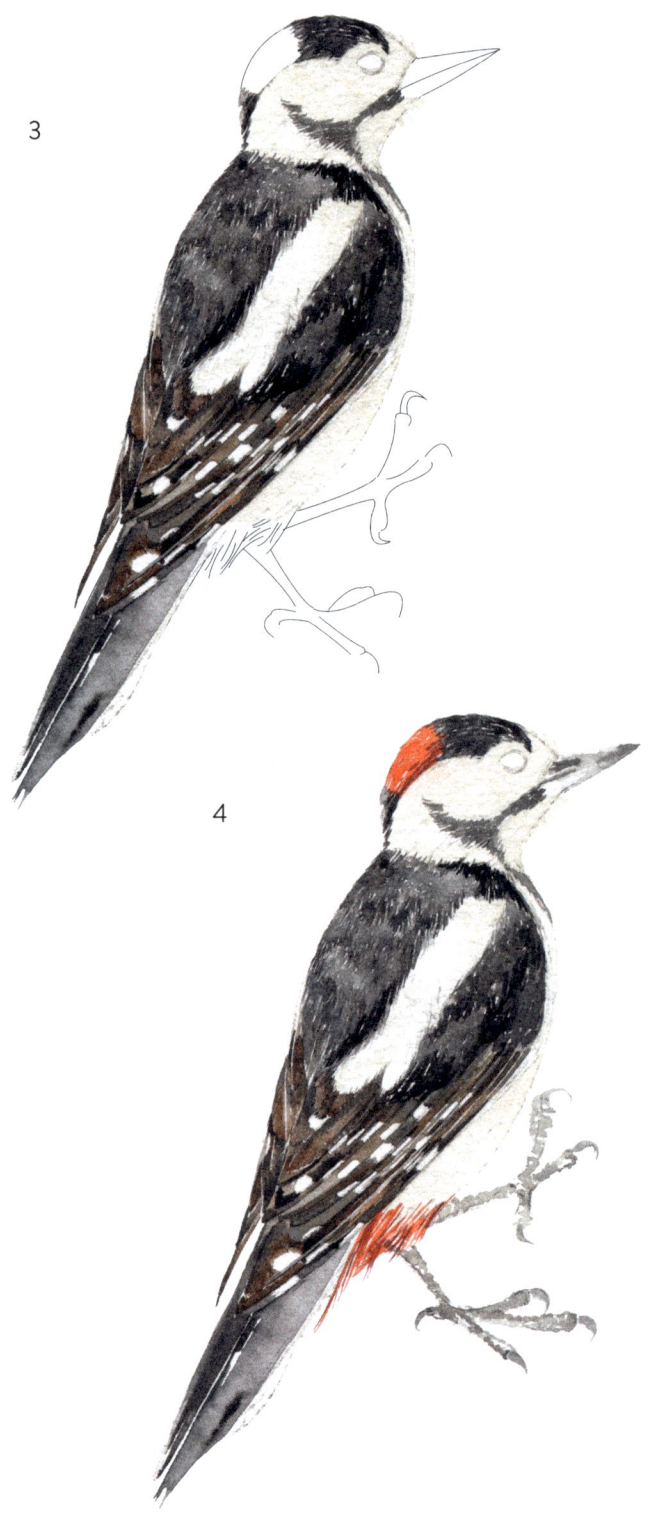

3

4

5

Draw the simplified pencil line drawing and add basic colour blocks with a size 0 brush in the same arrangement as the detailed painting. Once dry, paint in a few lowlights with a size 4/0 brush.

Approximate size of the miniature woodpecker painting: 2.5 x 1cm (1 x ½in)

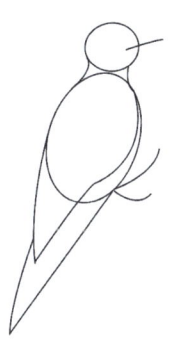

### 5.

Wet the area around the eye and paint a diluted sweep of burnt sienna, allow to dry. Use your size 4/0 brush to paint in fine feather tufts across the head and torso using a more concentrated version of each colour. Then add shadow mix lines across the face. Repeat this technique down the body. Add concentrated shadow mix lowlights to the legs, feet and bill.

Outline the eye in Mars black. Clean your brush and use the wet bristles to draw the colour inwards, leaving an unpainted 'shine'. Add some diluted shadow to the underside of the tail feathers, wings and torso and to the legs.

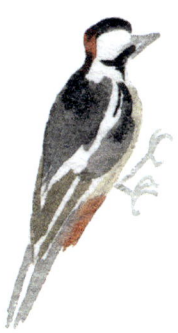

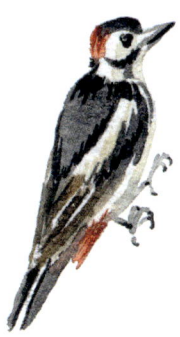

# CHERRY BLOSSOM TREE

Crumble and I found walking routes close to home in spring 2020, which led us to a path lined with cherry blossom trees. Our repeated daily trek down this same path allowed me to track the subtle stages of growth in the early cold weeks and then the burst of blooms as spring warmed up.

A blossom tree's growth through spring is the most rewarding subject to journal: beginning with the wintery bare branches that show just how the tree is structured; then come the buds that eventually burst into blooms. As fast as these changes occur, the subject will remain perfectly posed for you all year.

## WHAT YOU WILL NEED

### Brushes
Pointed round size 2, 0, ⁴/₀
Rigger size 0

### Paper
Cold pressed (textured)

### HB Pencil
### Eraser

Approximate size of each cherry blossom tree painting: 13 x 8cm (5 x 3in)

### Colours

 permanent rose

 alizarin crimson

 yellow ochre

 green gold

 sap green

 Payne's grey

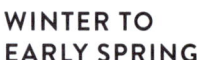 burnt sienna

### Mix

 Tree mix: majority burnt sienna and Payne's grey

 Shadow mix: burnt sienna and Payne's grey

 Blossom mix: permanent rose and yellow ochre

## WINTER TO EARLY SPRING

### 1.
Draw the trunk in faint pencil and from there, see how the trunk separates to form a few thick branches before fanning out into the full fan of the tree. It can be helpful to sketch a faint halo around the tree – a boundary for your branches to reach. Fill the space with thinning branches, growing in parallel pairs.

1

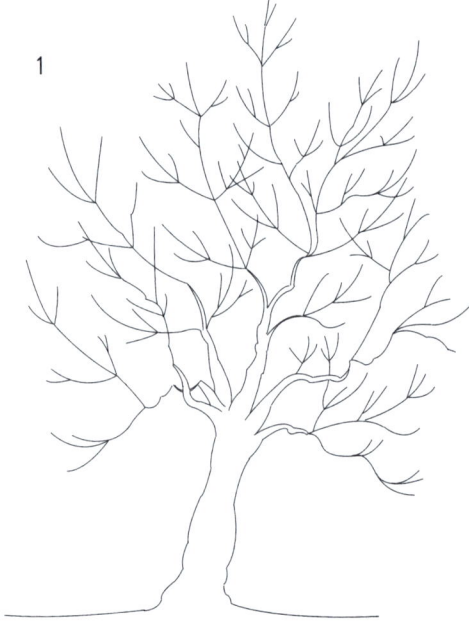

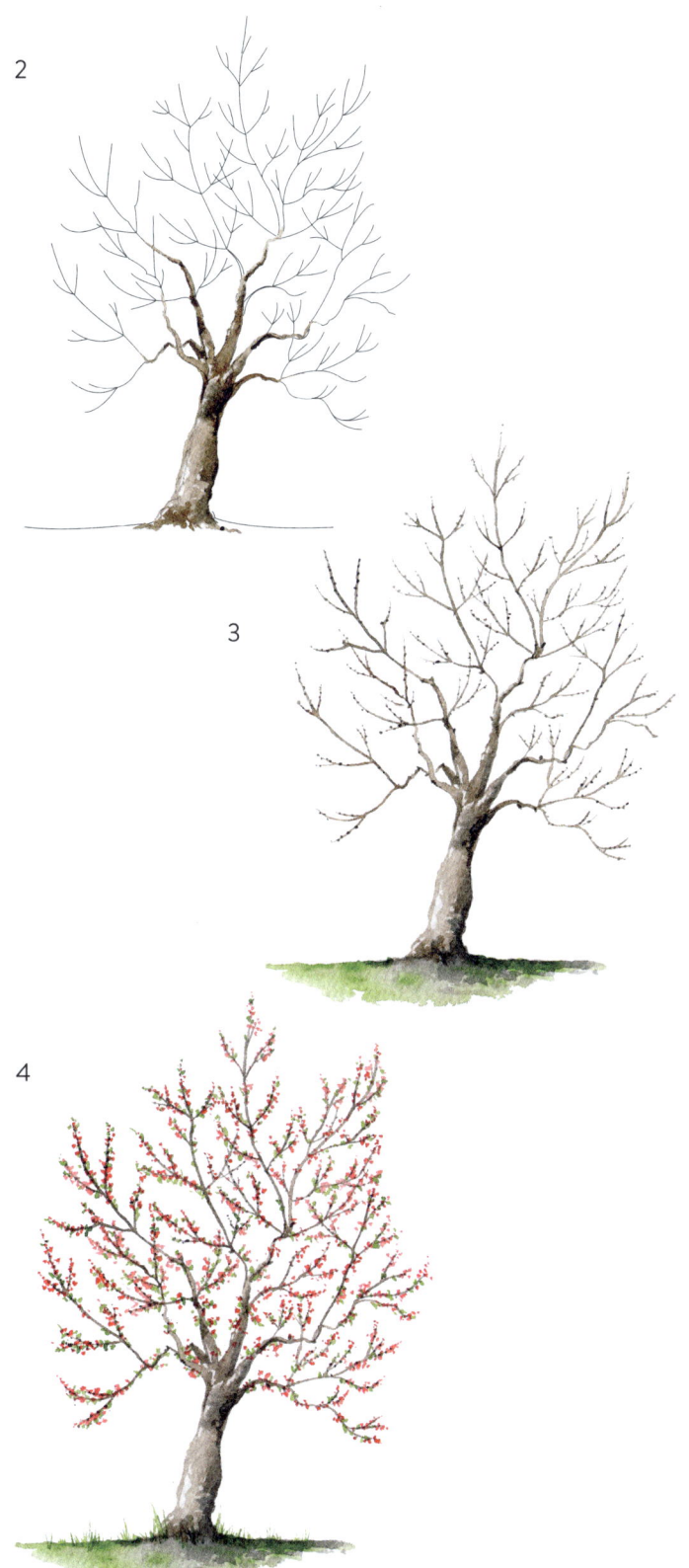

## 2.

With your size 0 brush, paint a diluted tree mix wash on the trunk. While still wet, add dabs of more concentrated shadow mix to create dark areas on the bark, as well as leaving small highlights of unpainted space on the other side of the trunk. Paint up into the thicker branches using the same method.

## 3.

Paint the rest of your branches with the rigger brush using tree mix and occasional dashes of shadow mix. The long bristles of the rigger brush allow for fluid lines and great control. Allow to dry, then with your size ⁴⁄₀ brush, paint small, concentrated shadow mix dots along the outer branches to show the early buds. Add a diluted green gold sweep of grass along the bottom of the tree trunk with your size 2 brush. Add dabs of sap green while still wet and a little more regular shadow mix.

You've now painted the tree in its winter stage.

## 4.

To bring the tree into early spring, add clusters of alizarin crimson dots around the branches with your size ⁴⁄₀ brush. Once dry, add green gold leaves among the pink buds. Paint a few sap green shoots of grass sprouting on the ground below.

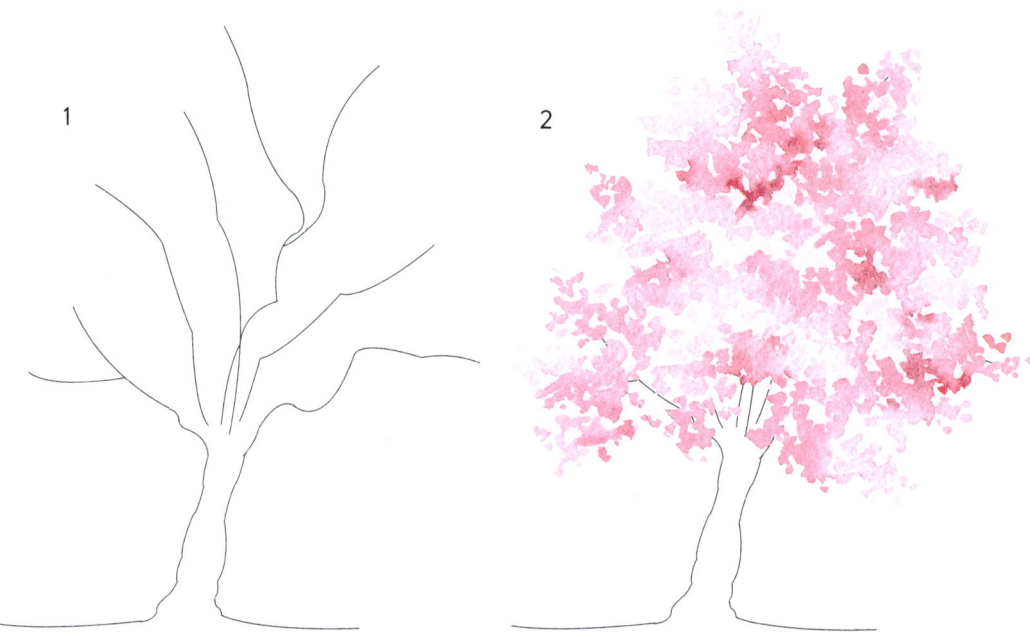

## 1.

A tree in full blossom doesn't require a fully drawn set of branches. Instead, draw the trunk and a few key branches. Lightly rub out the pencil so it is faintly visible.

## 2.

Paint clusters of diluted blossom mix dots along each branch with your size 2 brush. Leave little areas of unpainted space and dab permanent rose onto the wet blossom clouds every now and then. Allow to dry fully.

## 3.

With your size 0 brush, paint clusters of alizarin crimson dots along the underside of each bough to create a rounded texture to the blossom. Once dry, follow steps 2 and 3 on page 71 to paint the tree trunk. Use your ⅛ or rigger brush and a concentrated tree mix to track the branches up through the blossom by painting tiny branch lines in each unpainted section. You may want to paint a few branches reaching out beyond the blossom and add a final few dots of alizarin crimson to the branch ends.

## 4.

Finish the piece with a sweep of diluted green gold along the ground. Add some blades of sap green grass while still wet. Once dry, add a few dabs of diluted shadow mix on the lower blossom boughs, down the tree trunk and onto the grass.

You can also substitute blossom mix for leaf colours and use this tutorial to paint leaves in full foliage.

3

4

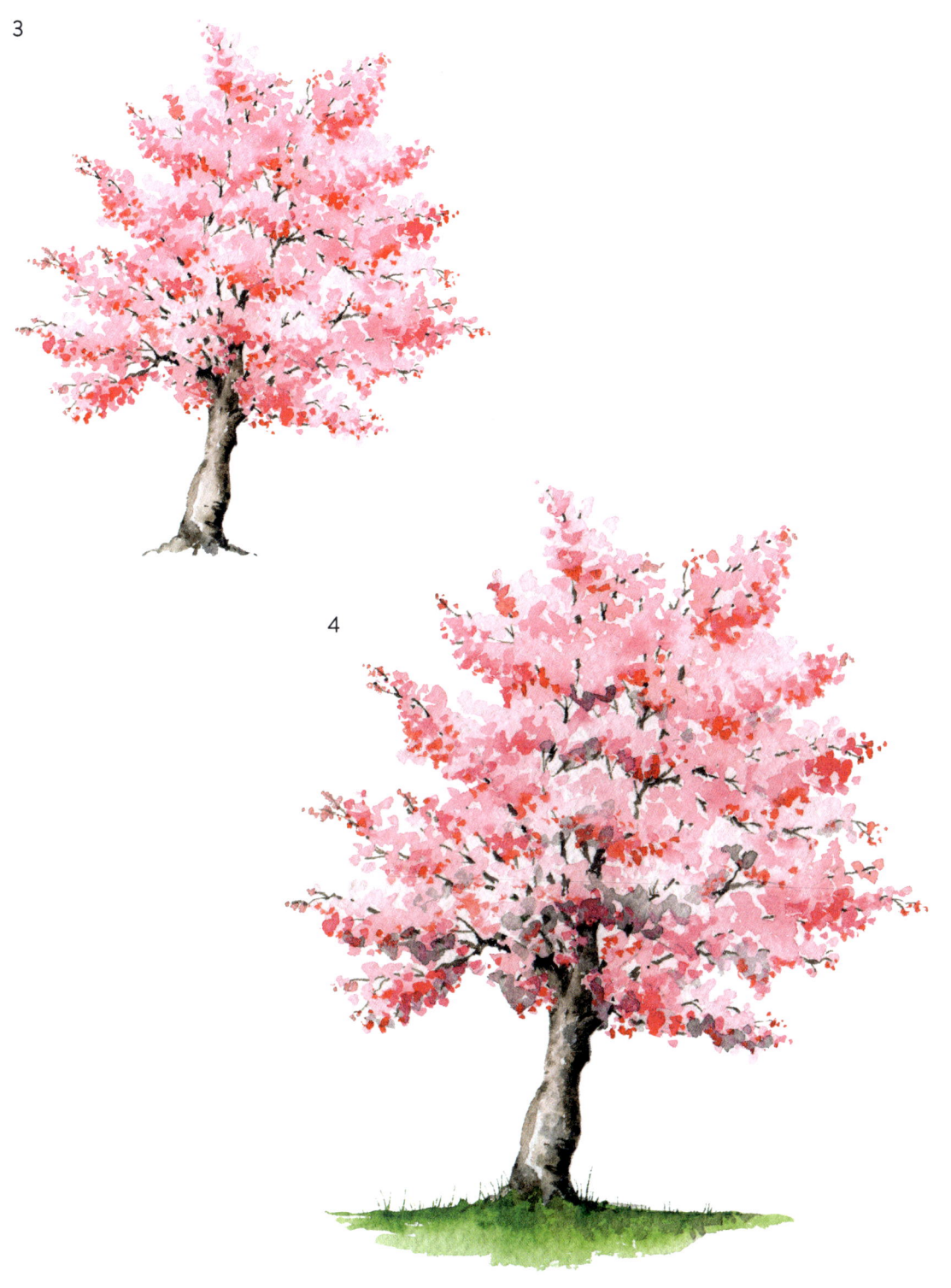

73 CHERRY BLOSSOM TREE

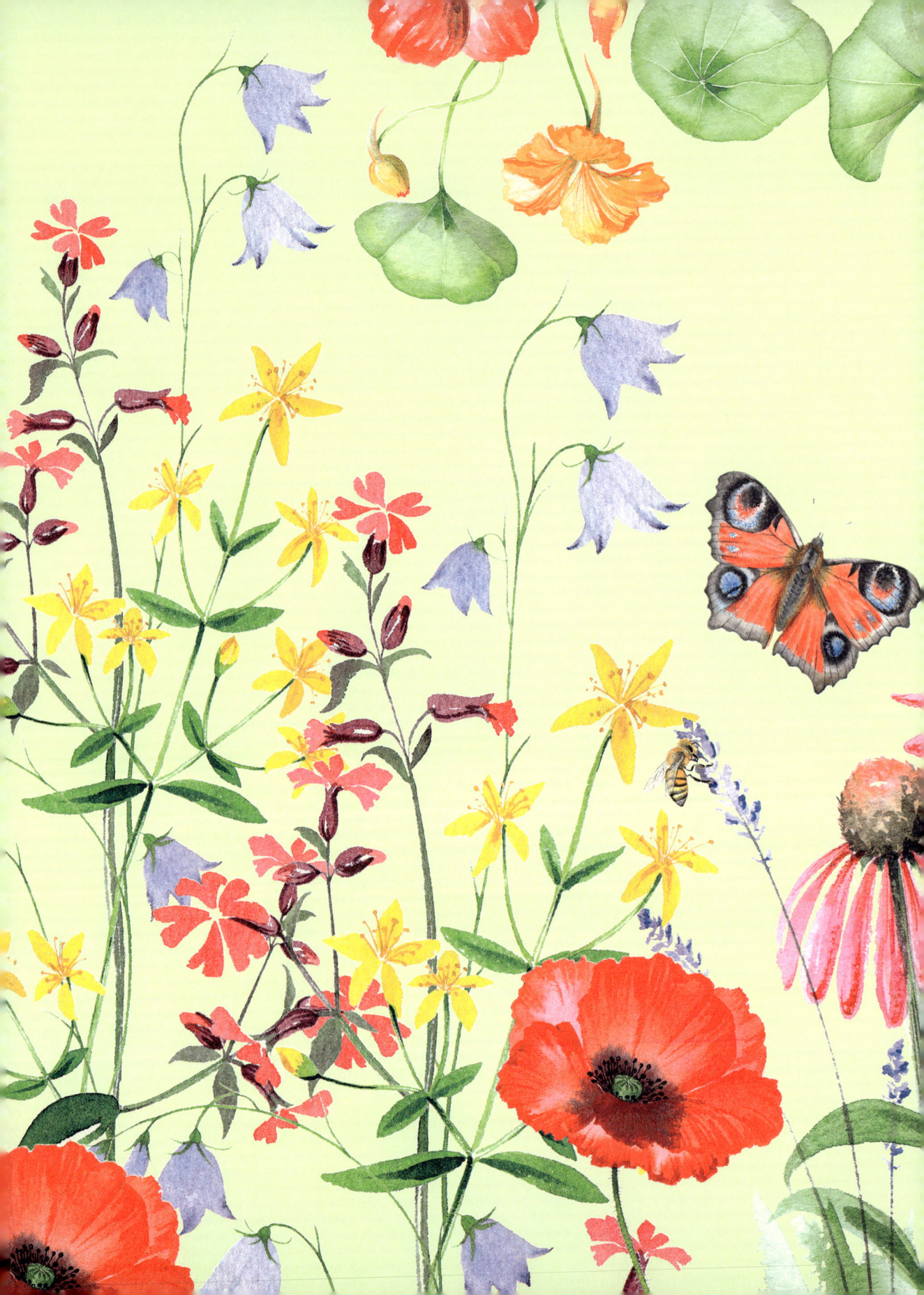

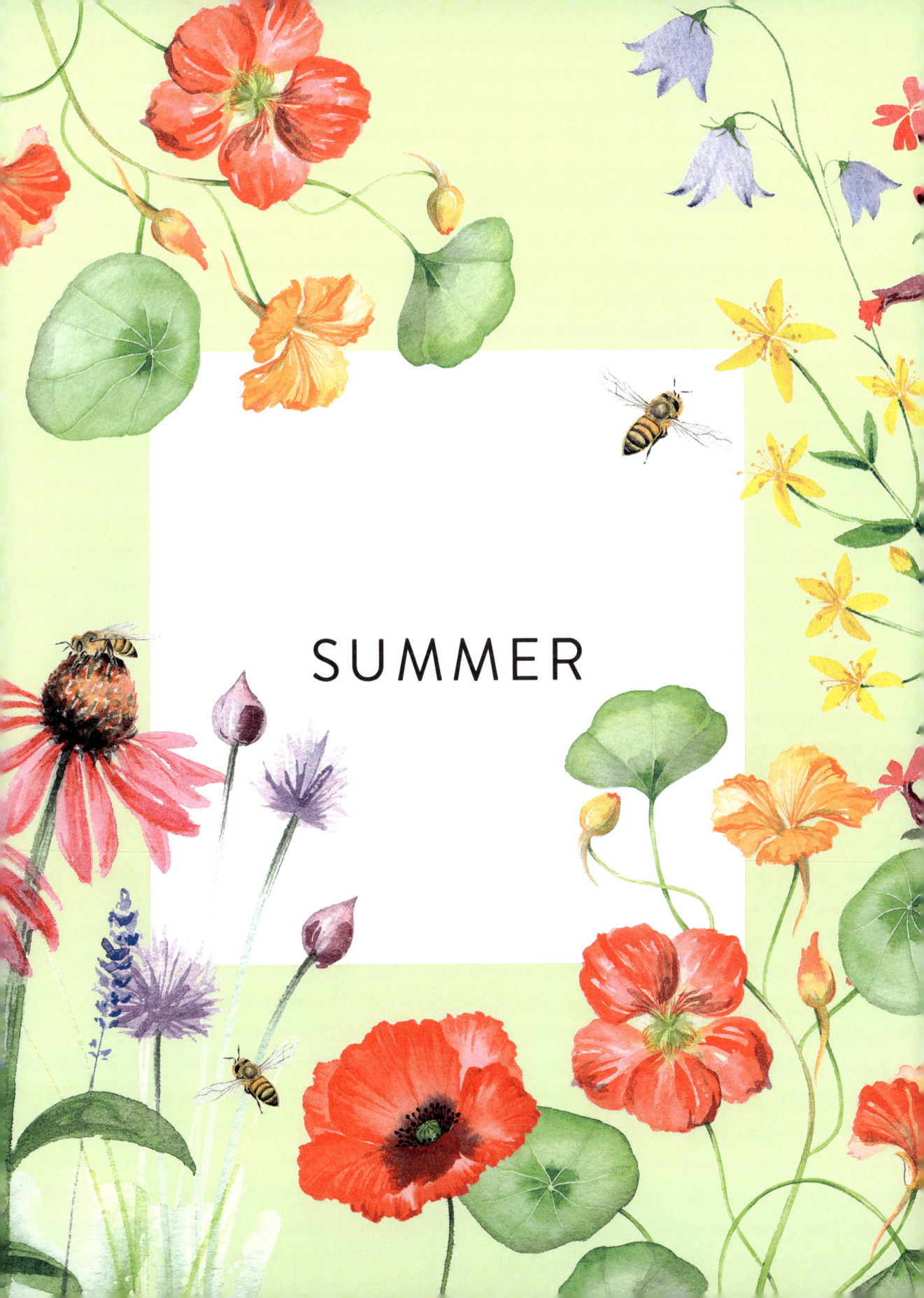

SUMMER

# HONEYBEES & SOME OF THEIR FAVOURITE FLOWERS

Our wildflower meadow bursts forth in summer and spotting a tiny bee flying among the flowers can be tricky. I found contrasting a detailed bee painting with looser watercolour flowers captured this moment perfectly. There are many detailed plant paintings in this book, but sometimes it's good to loosen up with the brush and try to capture a subject in as few brush strokes as possible.

## WHAT YOU WILL NEED

**Brushes**
Pointed round size 4, 2, 0, ²⁄₀ ⁴⁄₀

**Paper**
Cold pressed (textured)

**HB Pencil**
**Eraser**

**Colours:** Bees

Payne's grey

burnt sienna

yellow ochre

cadmium yellow

Mars black

**Mix:** Bees

Gold mix: cadmium yellow and yellow ochre

Brown shadow mix: majority burnt sienna and Payne's grey

**Colours:** Flowers

sap green

permanent rose

cobalt blue deep

alizarin crimson

cadmium orange

cadmium red

burnt sienna

Payne's grey

**Mix:** Flowers

Chive mix: majority permanent rose and cobalt blue deep

Lavender mix: majority cobalt blue deep and permanent rose

Shadow mix: burnt sienna and Payne's grey

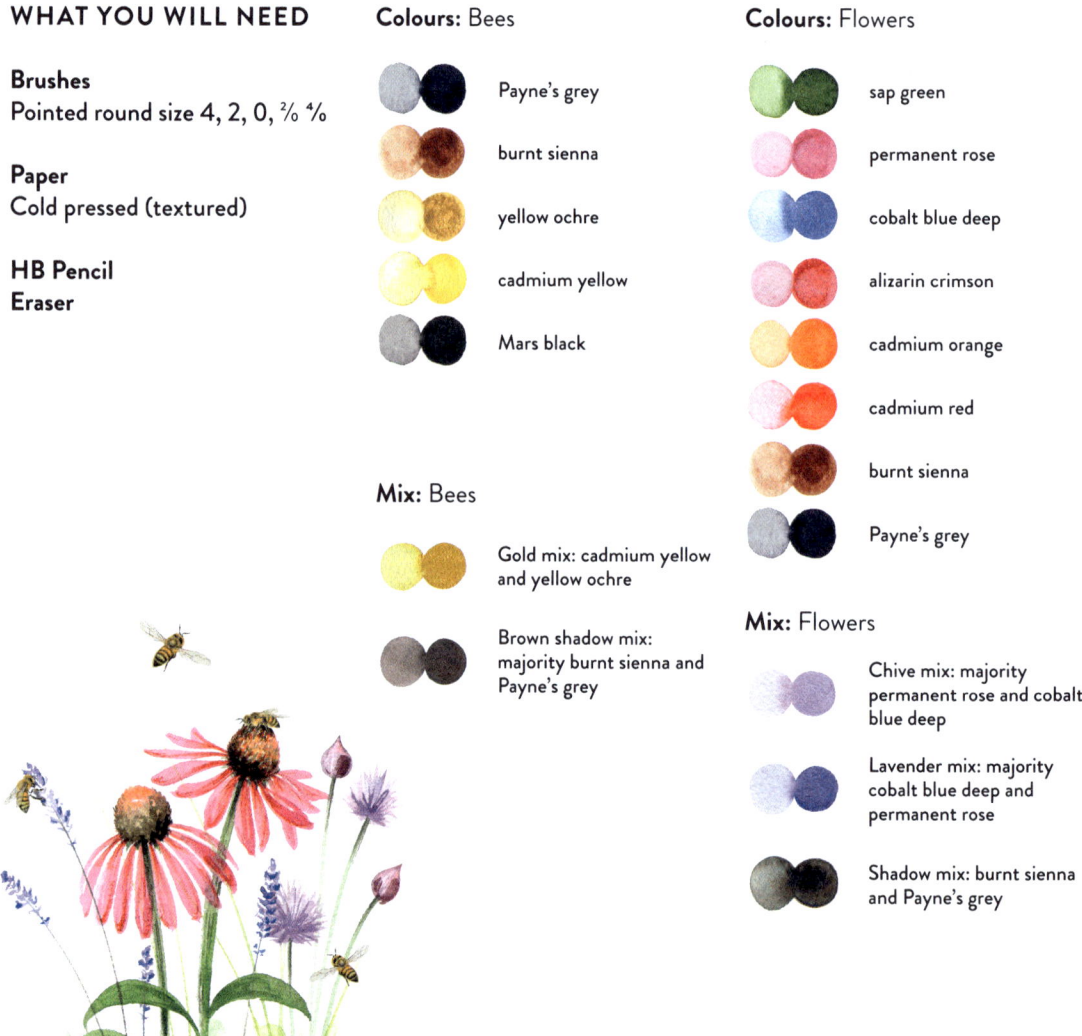

Approximate size of the wildflowers and honeybees painting: 11 x 14cm (4¼ x 5½in)

## HONEYBEE

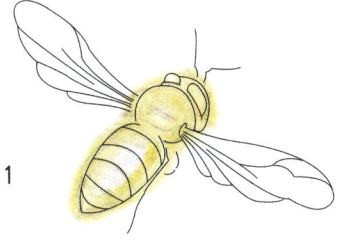

1

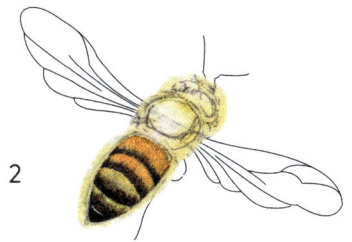

2

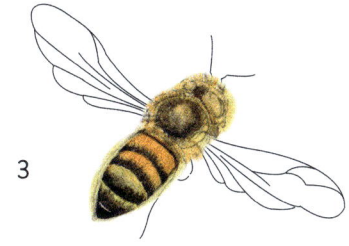

3

### 1.

Draw a curved line to dictate the curvature of the bee's body, then add a round thorax with a pointed abdomen below it. Add a curve for the head with bulbous eyes. Where visible, add legs, antennae and wings. Lightly rub out your pencil to leave a faint outline.

With your size 2 brush, paint a clear water wash over the body of the bee and in the surrounding area. Don't flood the page, it just needs to be slightly damp. Then paint a gold mix outline over the body and allow it to bleed over the pencil outline. This golden fuzz helps depict the many tiny hairs on the bee's body. Allow to dry.

### 2.

Paint the top section of the abdomen in gold mix with your size 0 brush, while still damp, paint a line of concentrated brown shadow mix along the bottom of the section with your size ⁴⁄₀ brush. If the wing overlaps this section, paint a more diluted version as if the colour is clouded behind the wing. Allow to dry, repeat the step for the next section down. For the next two sections, paint cadmium yellow instead of gold mix. For the final pointed section, paint in brown shadow mix.

### 3.

Using your 0 brush, paint the thorax and head in diluted yellow ochre (making sure to leave the wings unpainted), then with your ⁴⁄₀ brush push the paint outwards in fine hair-like lines. While still wet, drop a dab of brown shadow mix into the middle of the thorax and between the eyes.

5

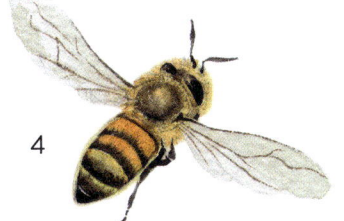

### 4.

Dilute the brown shadow mix to almost clear water and paint a few strokes on the wings. Outline the legs in Mars black with your size ⁴⁄₀ brush. Then clean your brush and use the wet bristles to draw the colour inwards creating a little 'shine'. Repeat this process with the eyes and antennae. When the wings have dried, paint brown shadow mix wing veins with your size ⁴⁄₀ brush. Once fully dry, rub out any visible pencil.

### 5.

Paint fine yellow ochre hairs around the outline of the body, on the thorax, head and legs.

4

## SIMPLE SUMMER WILDFLOWERS

### Chive Flower

### 1.

Paint a sap green stem with your size 2 brush and then scribble a burst of C- and S-curves in chive mix from the central point. Add a stroke of permanent rose curling down beneath the plant for the unfurled bud case.

### 2.

Increase the concentration of your chive mix and scribble a slightly smaller star of petals over the top. Allow to dry and repeat once more. Add some shadow mix to your sap green and add streaks to the top of the stem.

### Echinacea Flower

### 1.

Although it's a loose painting, it's still advisable to sketch a stem with a cone flower centre. Paint permanent rose petals from the centre, curling down, starting with the tip of your size 4 brush and adding pressure to thicken the stroke at the end of the petal. Add a streak of alizarin crimson to the fine end while still wet.

### 2.

Paint the cone flower with diluted cadmium orange; while still wet, use your ⅔ brush to add cadmium red serrated sides and shadow mix along the bottom edge.

### 3.

Scribble alizarin crimson along the petals, don't worry about perfect blends, the dry brushing adds wonderful texture to this loose painting. Dab cadmium red and orange onto the cone flower with your size 0 brush. Add in shadow mix halfway down and don't be afraid to be expressive with the brush. Finish with a sap green stem and sepals. Add a few streaks of shadow mix down the stem once dry.

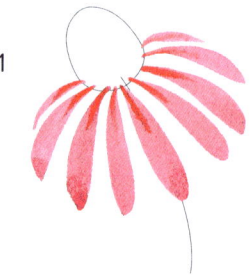

1

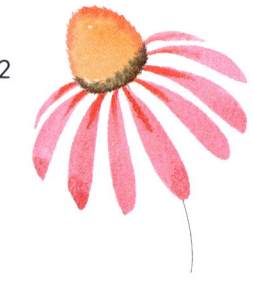

2

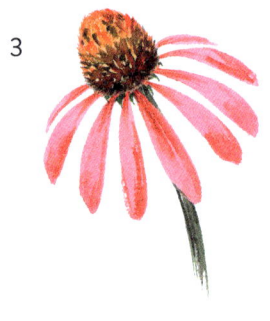

3

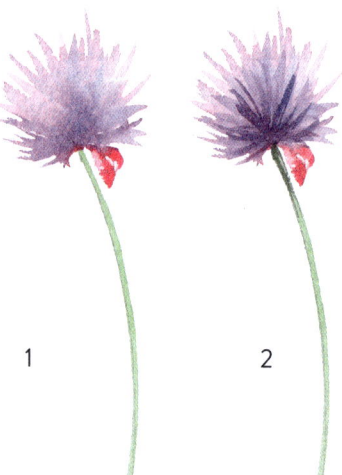

1

2

**Flowering Lavender**

## 1.

Draw a faint pencil curve. With a size 0 brush paint lavender mix assorted C-curves protruding upwards from the stem, starting at the top. Work your way down and then paint a sap green stem downwards for the remainder of the pencil curve. Drop a little lavender mix into the top of the green stem and allow it to blend.

## 2.

Dilute your lavender mix and paint frilly and loose flowers growing out of the buds with your size 0 brush. Keep your brush free and easy and don't focus on perfection. Allow to dry. Paint concentrated lavender mix scribbles on the buds and down the stem to add a little texture.

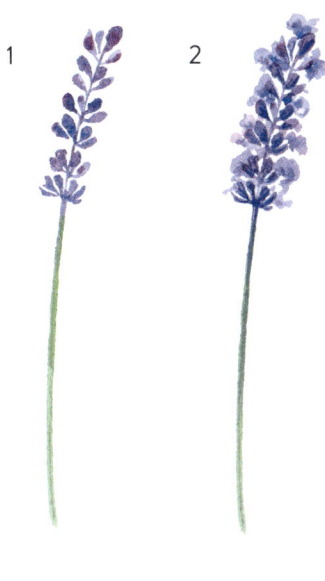

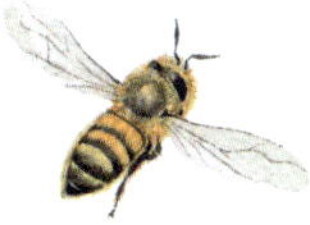

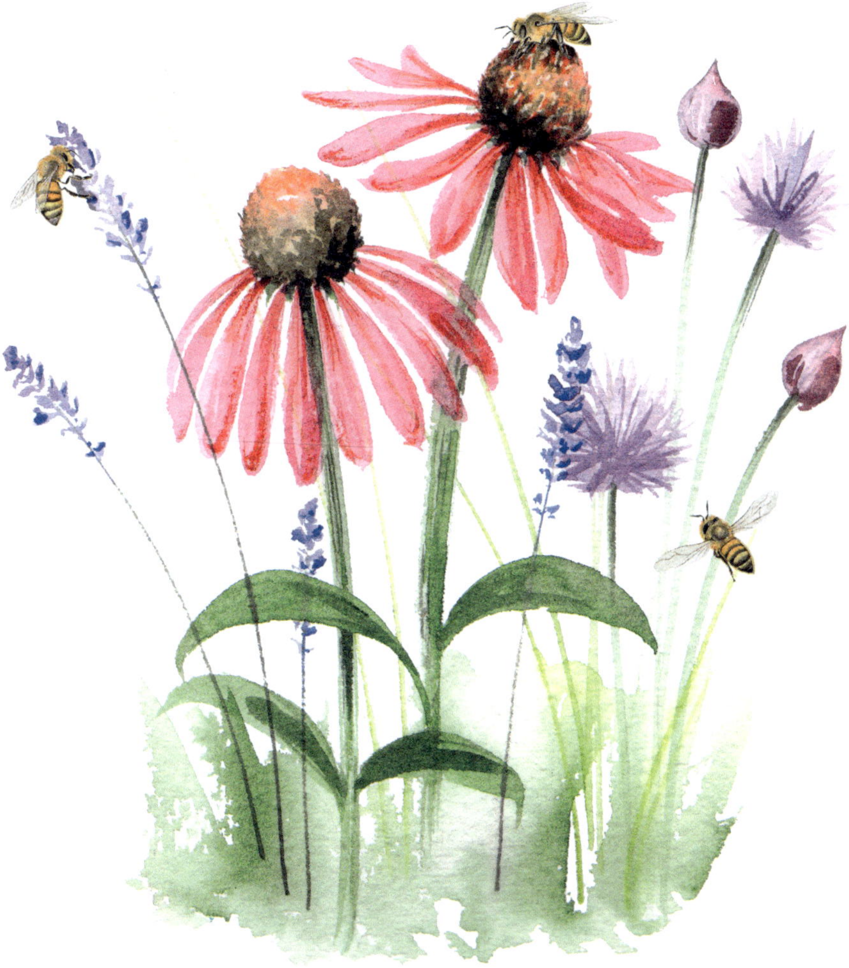

# NASTURTIUMS

Our gardening efforts have always focused on fruit and vegetables so imagine my joy when my husband Ant grew bright and beautiful nasturtiums – on the proviso that they will be eaten once I've had my fill of painting them!

These have been great to observe since planting in spring. The tangle of stems undulates across the ground and the flowers are unlike any I've painted before: after numerous experiments I found the best way to capture the bright, crumpled petals is to scribble the paint onto the page. This is a technique I'm sure I wouldn't have found, had I not been able to sit and study the real thing.

## WHAT YOU WILL NEED

**Brushes**
Pointed round size 4, 2, 0, ⁰⁄₀
Rigger size 0

**Paper**
Cold pressed (textured)

**HB Pencil**
**Eraser**

### Colours

cadmium yellow

cadmium orange

cadmium red

sap green

green gold

alizarin crimson

Payne's grey

burnt sienna

### Mixes

**Plant mix:** sap green and green gold

**Shadow mix:** burnt sienna and Payne's grey

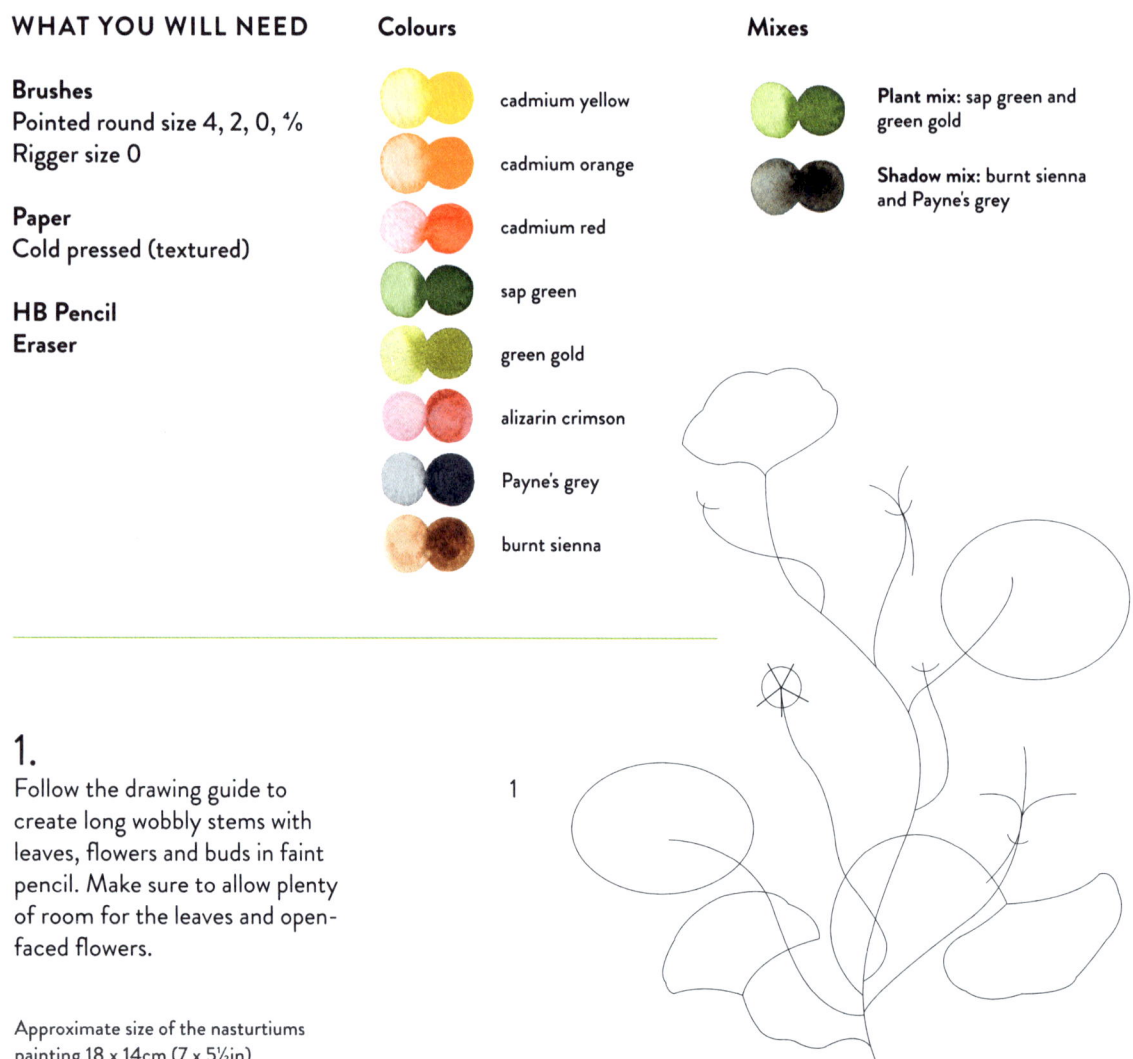

## 1.

Follow the drawing guide to create long wobbly stems with leaves, flowers and buds in faint pencil. Make sure to allow plenty of room for the leaves and open-faced flowers.

1

Approximate size of the nasturtiums painting 18 x 14cm (7 x 5½in)

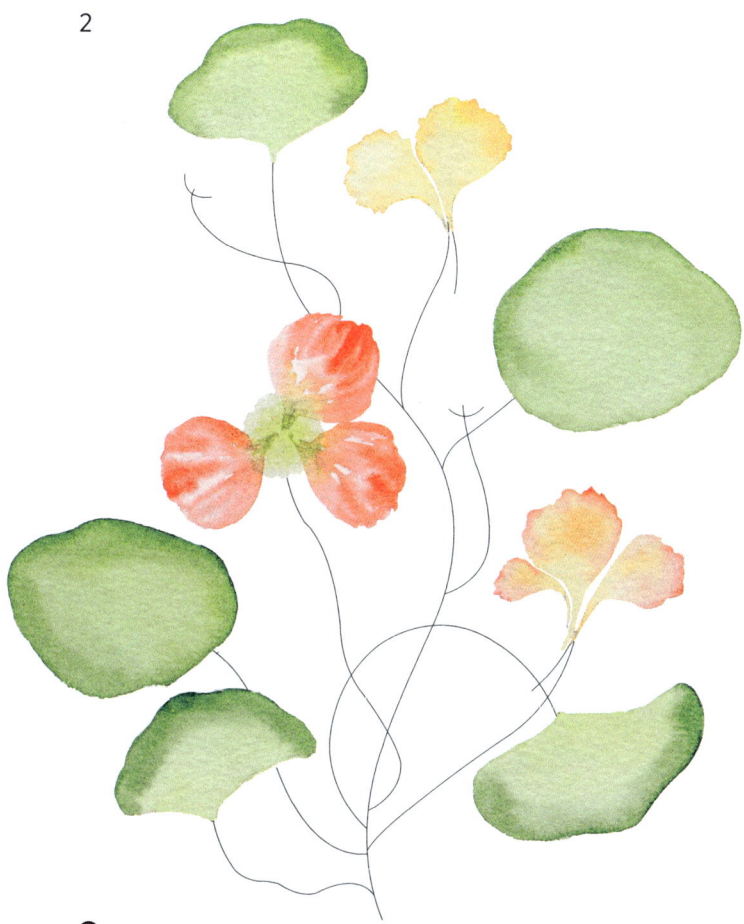

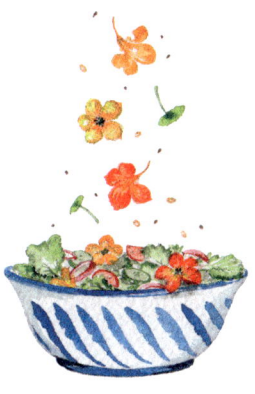

**What's edible?**
You can eat the leaves, the flowers, seeds and stems of a nasturtium. All components have a peppery taste, not unlike a radish. The flowers are a brilliant splash of colour on the plate. I love to freeze them into ice cubes to brighten up my endless glasses of orange squash in summer.

## 2.

With a size 2 brush, paint a circle of diluted green gold over the centre of the open-face flower pencil circle. Dab a little cadmium yellow while still wet. While that dries, move onto the leaves: with your size 4 brush, paint a diluted green gold leaf shape and quickly edge it with wet sap green.

For the side-on flowers, start with a diluted colour (I painted one in cadmium orange and one in cadmium yellow). With the tip of your size 4 brush, gradually paint up and out from the base of the petal, pressing down and fanning out the bristles. A few brush strokes like this will create a petal. Don't tidy up the rough edges but add cadmium red or orange into the edge of the petals and allow to bleed down.

Now the open-face flower circle is dry, paint three spaced out petals in diluted cadmium red with your size 4 brush. While still wet, add a little green gold into the fine tips at the centre of the flower and some streaks of more concentrated cadmium red on the petals.

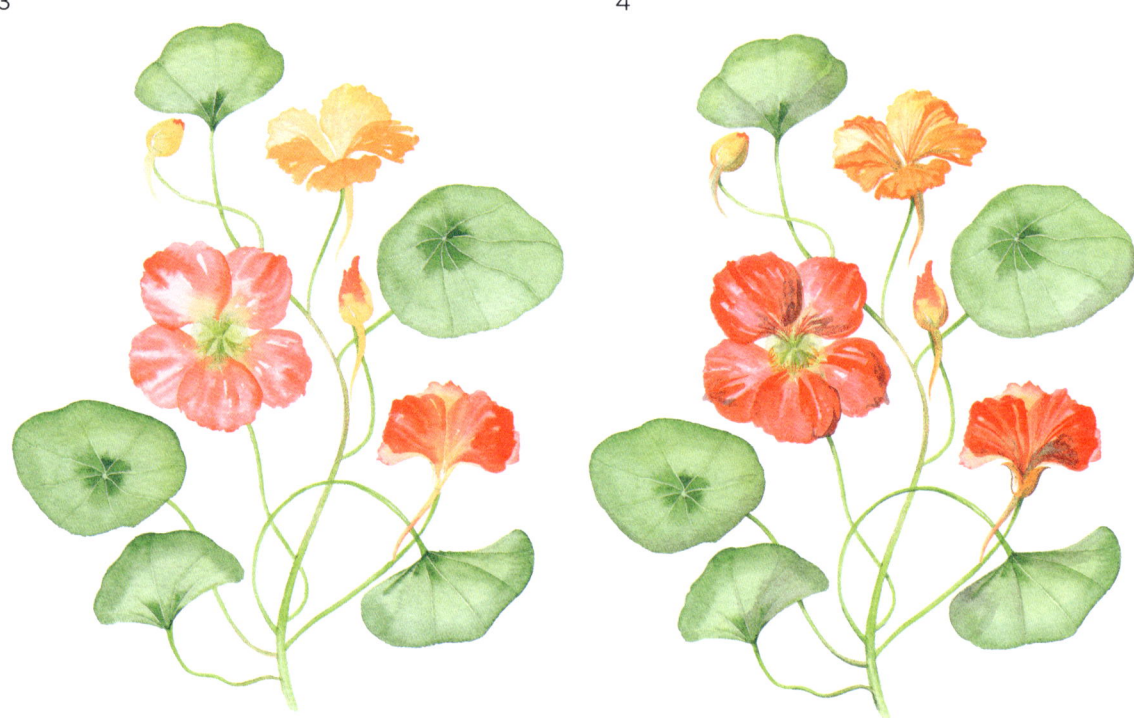

## 3.

Paint in a layer of more concentrated petals over the side-on flowers and the remaining petals on the open-face flower with your size 2 brush.

On the back of each flower is a 'calyx', which forms the sepals and a tail. With your size 2 brush, paint in the closed calyx and tails in a mix of cadmium yellow and cadmium orange, with a tuft of cadmium red petals starting to show. Paint in the visible tails on the other flowers. Starting at the top of the plant, paint diluted plant mix stems with your rigger brush. Use a size 0 brush to make the main stem a little thicker as you work your way down and add a tiny bit of cadmium yellow to the plant mix.

To create the leaf detail, paint diluted plant mix triangles from the centre to the edge with your size 2 brush. While still wet, dab some sap green in the central part of the triangle. Leave a tiny sliver of unpainted space between triangles.

## 4.

To add the crumpled petal texture, scribble lines of a more concentrated version of each petal colour from the petal edge down into the tapered base with a size 0 brush.

The lower three petals of the open-face flower have a fringe of lateral hairs. With a size ⁴⁄₀ brush, paint these in cadmium yellow and then edge with cadmium red

when dry. For the top two petals, add thin alizarin crimson stripes that fan out from the fine green tips into the main red body of the petal.

Add a sweep of diluted shadow mix to the edges and undersides of the leaves with a size 4 brush. Add sap green to areas of stem you want to accentuate, and paint lines of diluted shadow mix up the closed buds' calyx and side-on flower petals to help create roundness. Add a little alizarin crimson to your shadow mix and scribble a bit more texture onto the red, open-faced flower with a size 0 brush.

1

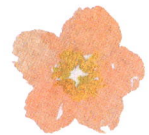

2

3

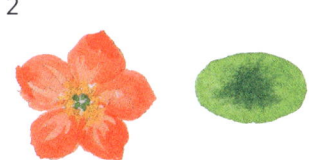

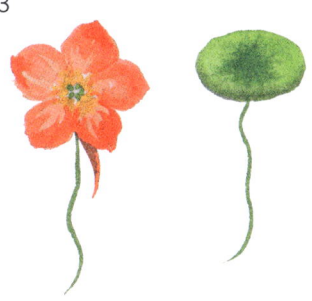

## MINIATURE NASTURTIUM

**The flowers and leaves simplify right down at this size.**

### 1.

Choose your petal colour and diluted it down. Paint five little petal blobs with a dash of cadmium orange in the centre. Allow to dry.

### 2.

Increase the concentration of your petal colour and use this to shape the petal edges and strokes towards the centre of the flower. Add dots of concentrated plant mix in the centre. For a nasturtium leaf, paint a wet, diluted oval of plant mix. While still wet, dab sap green in the centre.

### 3.

Add a tail to the leaf and a plant mix stem. For the leaf, sweep some diluted shadow mix across the bottom edge and add a stem.

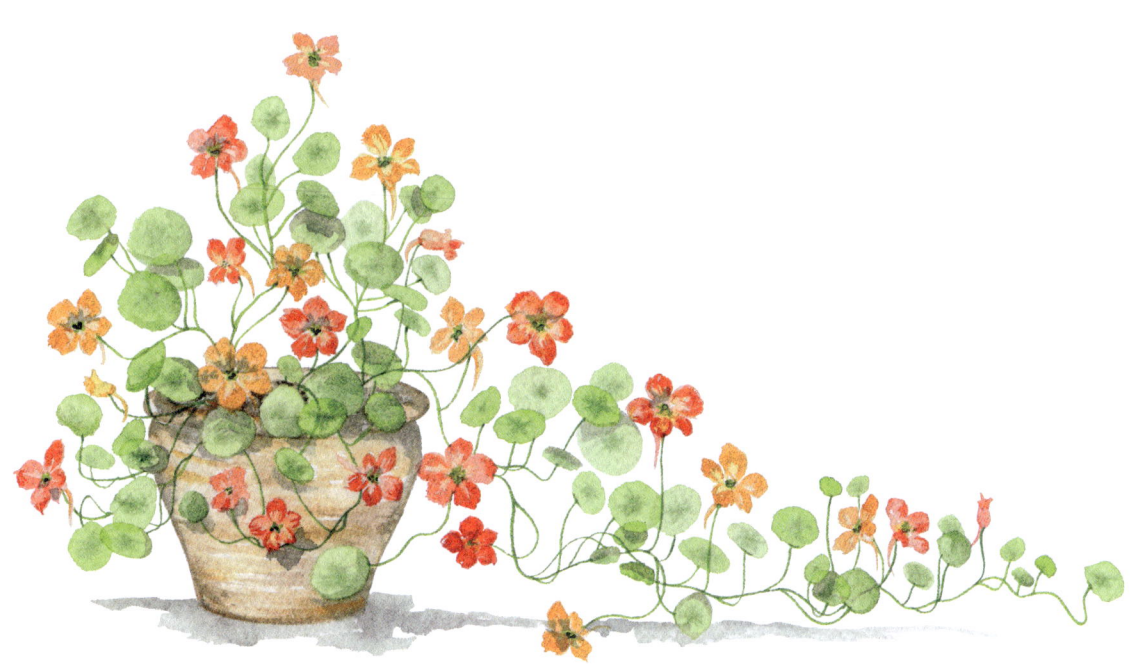

# PEACOCK BUTTERFLY

In the summer months Crumble and I are joined on our walks by a peacock butterfly at the same corner each time. The butterfly joins us for a stretch of the walk and then leaves us to carry on. The only reasonable explanation I can come up with is that this butterfly is great friends with Crumble and they take the opportunity to catch up with each other every day. Crumble would be pleased to see his friend immortalized in this book.

## WHAT YOU WILL NEED

**Brushes**
Pointed round size 4, 2, 0, ⅔, ⅘
Rigger size 0

**Paper**
Cold pressed (textured)

**HB Pencil**
**Eraser**

Approximate size of the butterfly painting: 10 x 7cm (4 x 2½in)

## Colours

yellow ochre

cadmium yellow

cadmium red

Prussian blue

cobalt blue deep

Payne's grey

burnt sienna

Mars black

cadmium orange

## Mix

**Yellow mix:** yellow ochre and cadmium yellow

**Blue mix:** Prussian blue and cobalt blue deep

**Shadow mix:** burnt sienna and Payne's grey

2

1

## 1.

Follow the drawing guide to create a faint pencil body shape. Draw a 6cm (2½in) vertical line and cross it 2cm (¾in) from the top with a horizontal 10cm (4in) line. From there you can flesh out the butterfly shape.

## 2.

With your size 4 brush, dilute your yellow mix and paint a wash in the top wing sections (forewings). While still wet, edge the wing with burnt sienna. Clean your brush and paint a C-curve of blue mix and two lower dabs either side. Dab cadmium orange where the wing touches the body. Allow the top sections to dry before repeating this step, painting the lower wing sections (hindwing). Paint burnt sienna where the hindwing meets the body.

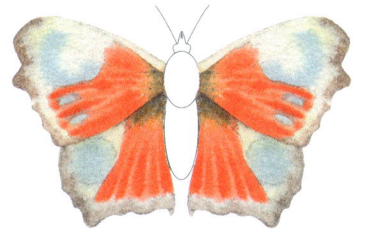 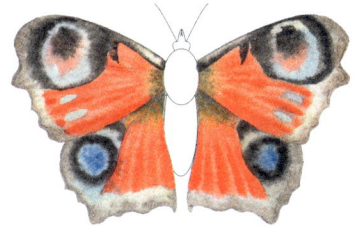 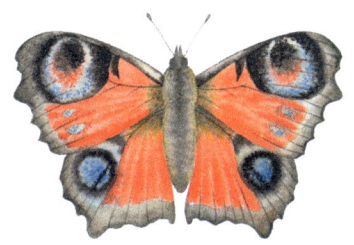

## 3.

Working on one wing section at a time; where you plan to paint red, wet the wing section with your size 4 brush. Then with a ⅔ brush, dab concentrated shadow mix dots where the wing meets the body. Switch to cadmium orange and continue your dots – these will bleed into each other on the wet page. Change to a size 2 brush and paint diluted cadmium red in long strokes out to the edge of the wet area (making space for the blue dots). While still wet, paint more concentrated cadmium red stripes along the wings creating faint channels. Allow to dry.

## 4.

In each wing section that wasn't painted red, there is a black ring. Working one wing section at a time, wet the necessary area. For the forewings, outline the top edge of the wing in Mars black with your ⅔ brush and allow the paint to bleed into the wet section. Switch to a size 2 brush and follow along the top edge of the wing until you loop down to make a large black ring. Paint a dab of cadmium red in the middle of the ring before dabbing black on top.

After wetting the necessary section on the hindwings, paint a Mars black ring with some more blue mix dabbed in the centre. Paint a C-curve of Mars black in the triangle point of this wing section. Allow to dry.

## 5.

Add dots of concentrated colour on top of the black, red and blue wing markings. With your size 0 brush, paint shadow mix along each wing outline defining the undulating edge. As you go, keep cleaning your brush and blending this outline inwards. Once dry, use your rigger brush to paint fine line shadow mix wing veins from the edge inwards. Allow them to fade as they cross the wing. Using the original horizontal pencil wingspan line as a reference, paint a wing vein from the body outwards that forks as it reaches the black ring detail. I choose not to paint in every vein to avoid too many heavy lines. This suggestion of the vein structure does what's needed.

Wet the butterfly body and paint a yellow ochre outline. Fill the body and paint the antennae with shadow mix.

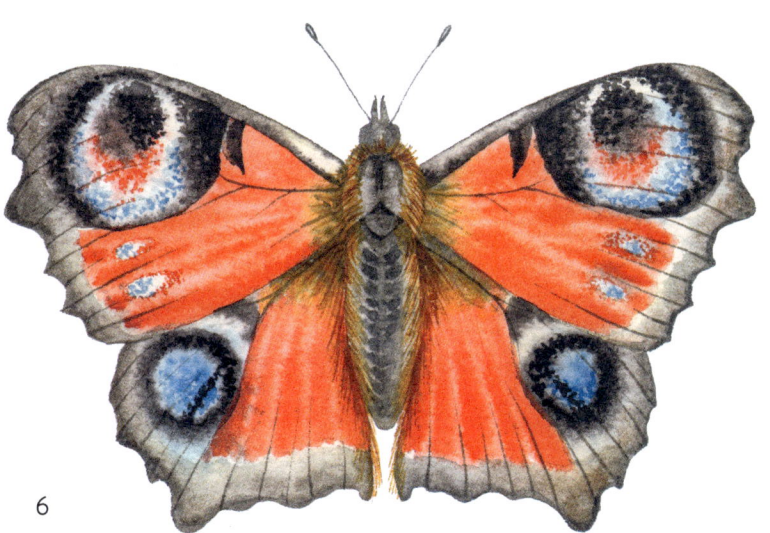

6

## 6.

With your size ⅙ brush, paint fine line hairs in cadmium orange and burnt sienna around the edge of the body and onto the wings. Paint in shadow mix contour detail down the body.

Once fully dry, rub out any visible pencil.

# WILDFLOWER BOUQUET

Summer wildflowers are dainty and plentiful. Because they don't have large, complicated flowers, you can often paint the whole plant in a single step. These little wildflowers are also a perfect starting point if you're new to putting a composition together: keeping the shapes and details simple results in a delightful arrangement that avoids overwhelming the painter with multiple layers and heavy colours.

## WHAT YOU WILL NEED

**Brushes**
Pointed round size 4, 2, 0, ⁴⁄₀
Rigger size 0

**Paper**
Cold pressed (textured)

**HB Pencil**
**Eraser**

Approximate size of each individual stem painting: 16 x 6cm (6 x 2½in)

## Colours

green gold

sap green

permanent rose

alizarin crimson

cadmium yellow

cadmium orange

French ultramarine blue

cobalt blue deep

## Mix

**Plant mix:** sap green and green gold

**Harebell mix:** cobalt blue deep and permanent rose

**Dark campion mix:** alizarin crimson and French ultramarine blue

**Campion stem mix:** sap green and French ultramarine blue

## ST JOHN'S WORT

Start by drawing a faint pencil stem with parallel curving branches. With your size 4 brush, paint five cadmium yellow petals for each flower or two mirrored C-curves for buds. With your size 0 brush, paint a fine line plant mix stem (two parallel lines if you can) and leaves with your size 4 brush. The flowers should now be dry; paint cadmium orange fine line filaments from the centre and dotted anthers with your size ⁴⁄₀ brush. Add a sweep of sap green on the leaves, buds and stem with your size 0 brush.

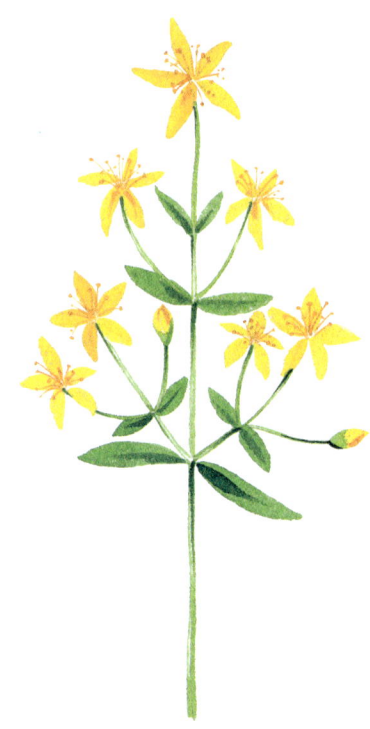

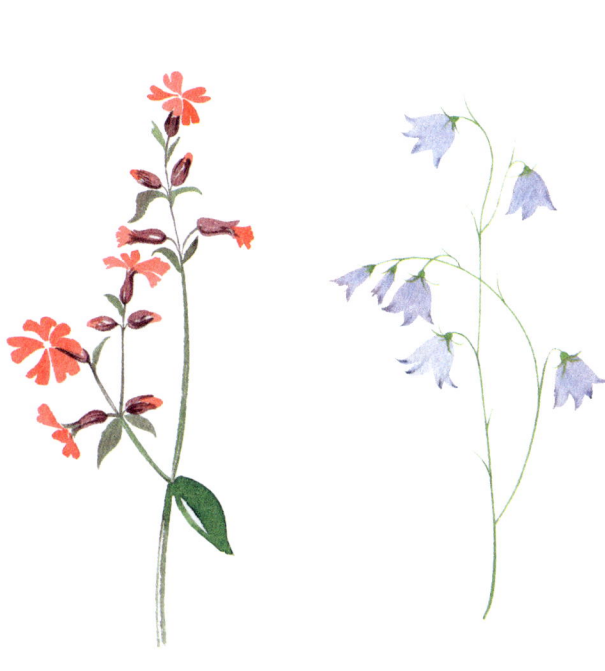

## RED CAMPION

Start by drawing a faint pencil stem with forked branches. With your size 2 brush, paint five alizarin crimson forked petals for each flower or two mirrored C-curves for buds. Paint a lobe (the long curve shape between the stem and the petals on each flower) in diluted dark campion mix on the back of each flower with your size 0 brush and continue down with a fine line stem. Switch to campion stem mix and paint in the rest of the stem. Use two parallel lines as it thickens. Paint in campion stem mix leaves with your size 2 brush.

The flowers should now be dry. Paint concentrated dark campion mix fine line detail on the lobes with your size ⁴⁄₀ brush.

## HAREBELL

Start by drawing a long slender forked faint pencil stem. For each bell flower, paint diluted C- and S-curves of harebell mix from the top central point with your size 4 brush. Bring it to a fine point at the end of the petal. Don't strive for perfection, there are five petals but you rarely see them all at once. While still wet, paint a dab of concentrated harebell mix at each petal tip with your size ⁴⁄₀ brush.

Paint the plant mix stem with your rigger brush, adding a few fine line leaves here and there on the stem. The flowers should now be dry. Paint a plant mix cup on top of each flower and fine line curling sepals with your size ⁴⁄₀ brush.

## WILDFLOWER BOUQUET

Plan your arrangement with faint pencil stems. It's important to curve the stems and weave them in and out of each other for an organic appearance. Plan where each flower will go so it has enough space around it. In this instance, the harebell flowers are the lightest colour, so paint those in first, followed by St John's wort and finally red campion.

# FIELD POPPY

The field poppy was the first splash of colour in our newly planted wildflower meadow, so I could track its growth as it burst into bloom.

## WHAT YOU WILL NEED

**Brushes**
Pointed round size 8, 2, ²⁄₀, ⁴⁄₀
Rigger size 0

**Paper**
Cold pressed (textured)

**HB Pencil**
**Eraser**

### Colours

green gold

sap green

Payne's grey

burnt sienna

cadmium red

alizarin crimson

Mars black

### Mix

**Plant mix:** sap green and green gold

**Shadow mix:** burnt sienna and Payne's grey

**Dark petal mix:** cadmium red and Payne's grey

**Detail mix:** cadmium red and alizarin crimson

## 1.

Start by drawing a faint pencil stem with lines for leaves. At the top, draw an oval to mark the base of the open flower. Paint a plant mix stem with your size 2 brush. Keep the same brush to paint a slender tapered line for a plant mix central leaf line. While still wet, add fine points of sap green with your size ²⁄₀ brush. Paint C- and S-curves off the central leaf and repeat the sap green points. Paint a plant mix seedpod in the middle of the oval at the top of the stem. Allow to dry.

1

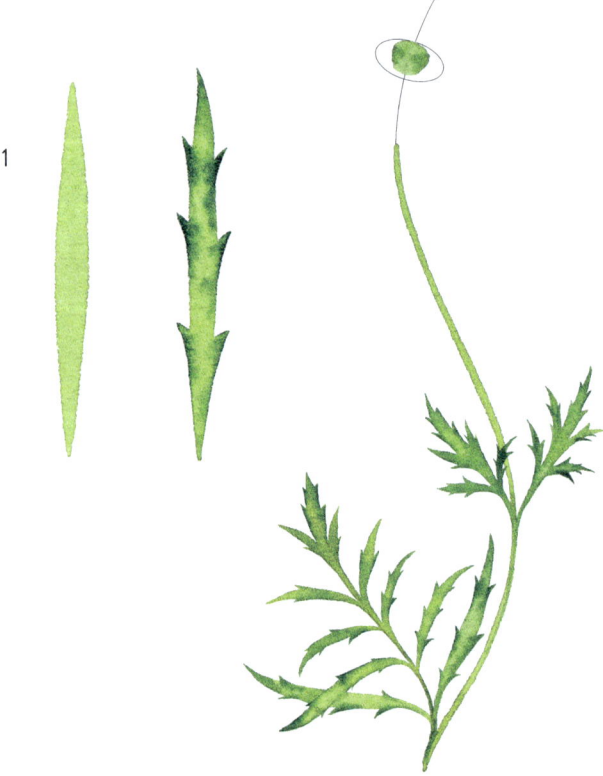

Approximate size of the field poppy painting: 16 x 7cm (6 x 2½in)

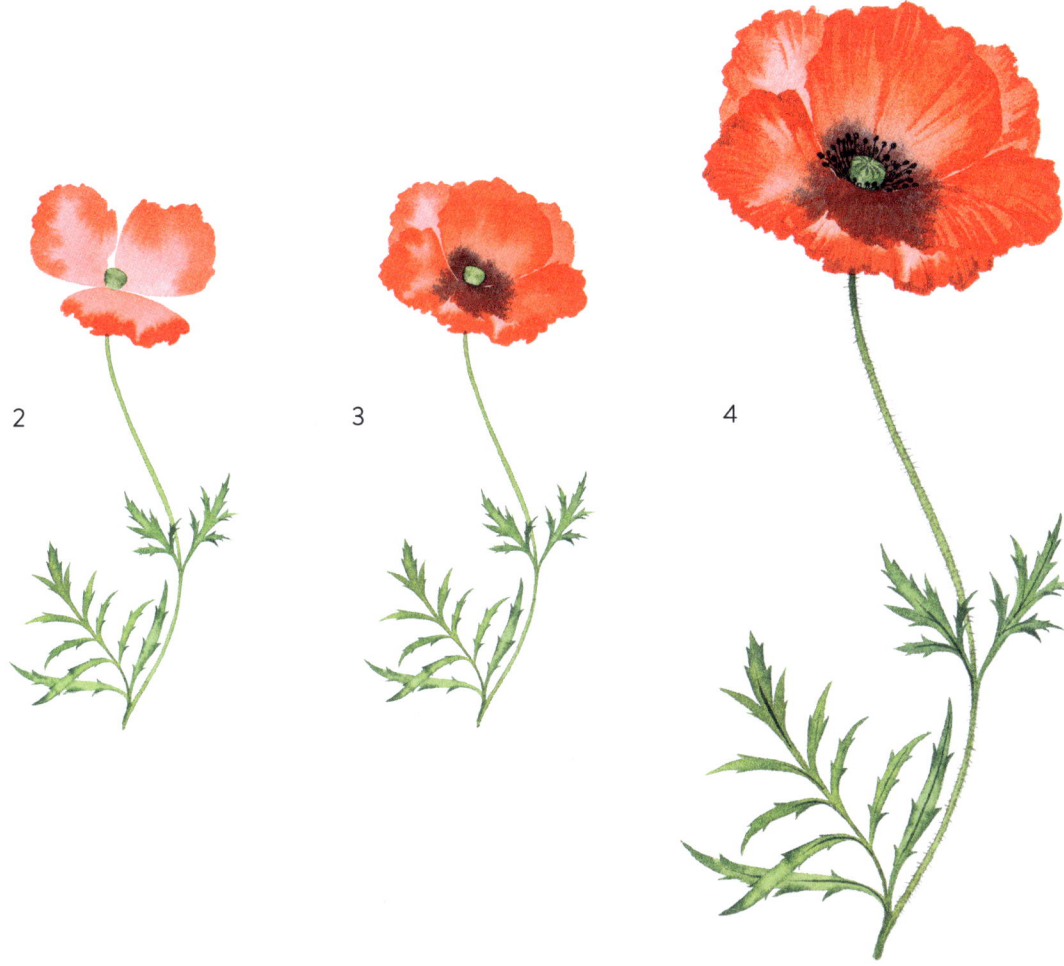

## 2.

With your size 8 brush, paint diluted cadmium red petals anchored from the central point beneath the seedpod: start with the fine point of your brush and press down to fan out the bristles as you paint outwards – leave the edges rough and frilled. You will need a few brush strokes to create each petal. While still wet, add concentrated cadmium red to the edge and allow it to bleed down. Allow to dry fully.

## 3.

Repeat step 2 to paint in all the remaining petals but add a dab of dark petal mix to the centre of each petal while still wet. Allow to dry fully and rub out any visible pencil.

## 4.

With a size 2 brush, paint scribbles of concentrated detail mix from the edge of the petals inwards. While that is drying, paint sap green central lines along the leaves with your rigger brush and diluted shadow mix hairs up the stem with your ⁴⁄₀ brush.

With your size ⁴⁄₀ brush paint a star of sap green tapered lines on top of the seedpod. Paint a cluster of Mars black dots (anthers) and join them up with fine lines (filaments) that disappear down beneath the seedpod among the petals.

# BARN OWL

I've only ever seen a barn owl once; ghost-like, perched on my mum's roof on a summer's evening.

A barn owl's appearance is undeniably impressive: their facial disc like a Tudor ruff and their feathers a luxurious patterned eiderdown. I've thought about painting them a number of times, but not known where to begin. It was on finding a single barn owl feather the morning after this rare sighting that I unlocked the secret…

## WHAT YOU WILL NEED

**Brushes**
Pointed round size 4, 2, 0, ²⁄₀, ⁴⁄₀
Rigger size 0

**Paper**
Cold pressed (textured)

**HB Pencil**
**Eraser**

## Colours

 yellow ochre

 cadmium yellow

 raw umber

 Payne's grey

 burnt sienna

 Mars black

## Mix

 **White feather mix:** raw umber, yellow ochre, Payne's grey, cadmium yellow

 **Brown feather mix:** yellow ochre and raw umber

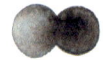 **Shadow mix:** burnt sienna and Payne's grey

Approximate size of the feather painting: 13 x 4cm (5 x 1½in)

## FEATHER

The pattern of black-ringed white spots on the feather demystifies the seemingly random markings on the barn owl's body. Once you've had a go at the feather, you will have a better understanding before attempting to paint the whole bird.

## 1.

Begin with the central quill, the stiff thin line up the middle of the feather, and follow the drawing guide to create a faint pencil feather. Mark out the patterned sections.

1

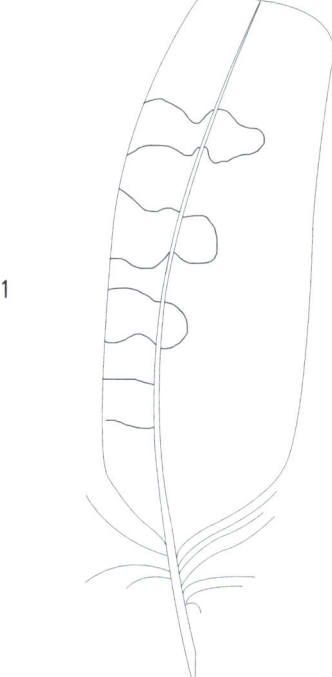

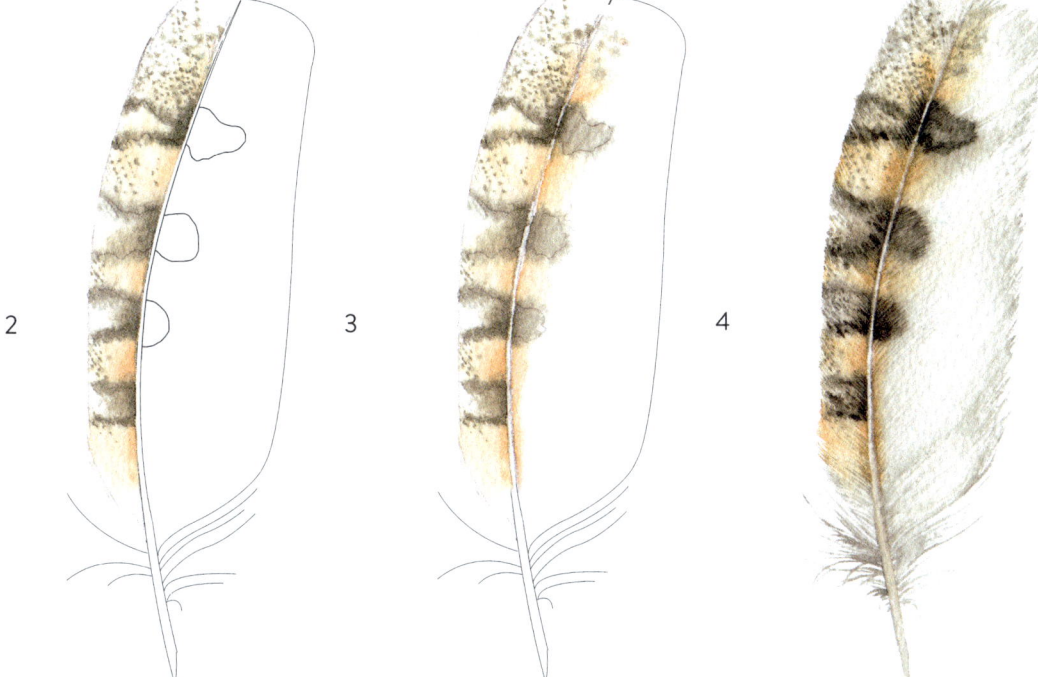

2

3

4

## 2.

With your largest brush wet one side of the feather up to but not including the central quill. Use your size 2 brush to dab yellow ochre three quarters of the way up the left-hand side (next to the quill). As it starts to dry, dab diagonal dashes of wet shadow mix along the pattern outlines and more spaced-out dabs on the yellow ochre sections.

## 3.

Wet the other side, sweep a stroke of yellow ochre up the side and dab shadow mix into the pattern sections while still damp.

## 4.

Dilute your shadow mix to a faint grey and, starting on the right-hand section, use the rigger brush to paint fine S-curves from the central quill. Keep your paint really diluted to avoid heavy lines. In fact, it's best if the paint fades out entirely before it reaches the edge of the feather. Use a ⁴⁄₀ brush to paint short tufts along the outline of the feather and then, after painting a section of these lines sweep a clean wet size 4 brush over the area in the S-curve shape, to smooth and blend these lines together. Paint more wayward C- and S-curve lines for the fluffy feathers at the bottom of the quill.

Once dry, add fine lines of more concentrated yellow ochre and shadow mix over the corresponding washes with your size ⁴⁄₀ brush. Repeat on the other side. Finally, add a tiny bit of yellow ochre to your diluted shadow mix and paint the central quill.

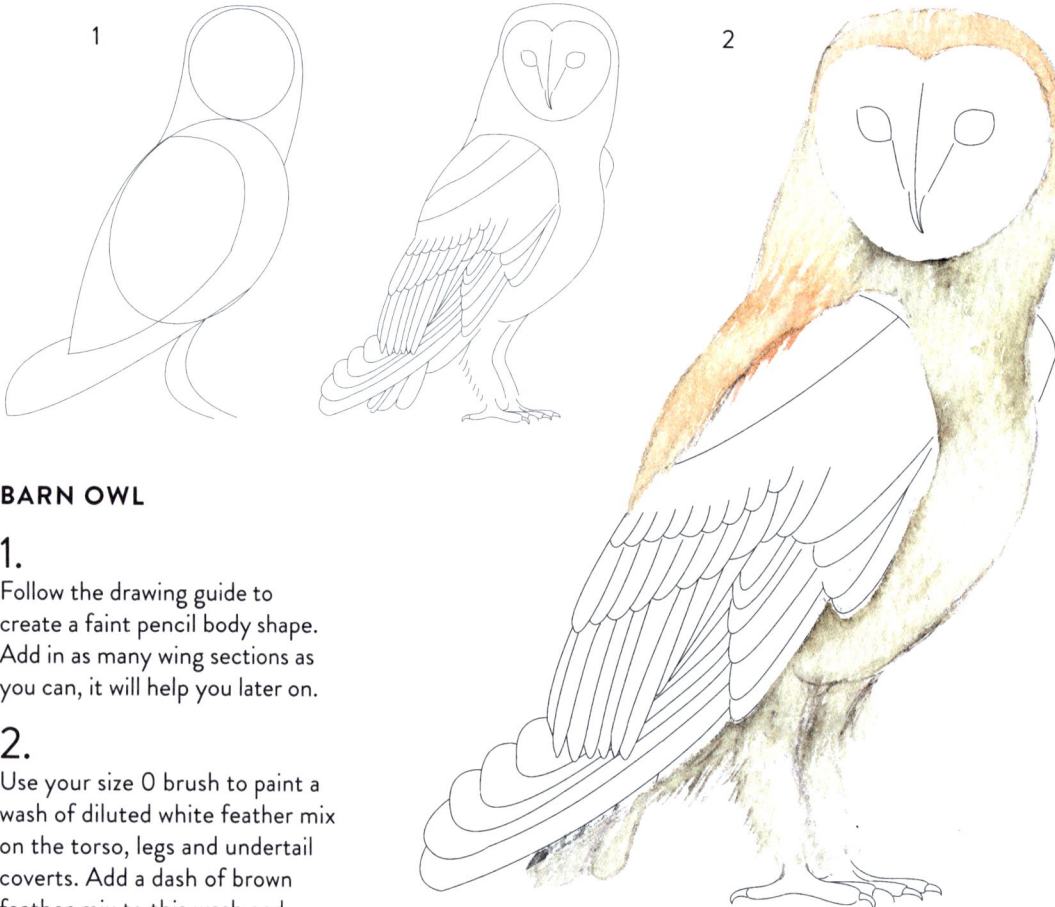

## BARN OWL

### 1.
Follow the drawing guide to create a faint pencil body shape. Add in as many wing sections as you can, it will help you later on.

### 2.
Use your size 0 brush to paint a wash of diluted white feather mix on the torso, legs and undertail coverts. Add a dash of brown feather mix to this wash and paint up around the face and down the back. While still wet add diluted shadow mix beneath the face and wings.

### 3.
Add diluted feather strokes of brown feather mix onto the wing and tail feathers with your size 0 brush. Leaving tiny gaps of unpainted space will help with the pattern later on.

Approximate size of the barn owl painting: 11 x 8cm (4½ x 3in)

Dilute some Mars black and paint tiny oval shapes and specks in as many unpainted spaces down the back and on the upper wing section (the mantle, scapulars and lesser coverts). As the feathers become more defined down the wing, add sprinklings of fine dots along the wing tips and in bands down the primaries and secondaries. Then use your ⁰⁄₀ brush to paint fine line feather tufts of concentrated burnt sienna that follows the contour of the wing sections. Switch to yellow ochre for the primaries, secondaries and tail feathers.

## 4.

Wet the area around the eyes and with your size ⅔ brush, paint diluted white feather mix streaks from the eyes out to the edge of the facial disc. Dab some burnt sienna at the eye ducts and down the side of the cere (the feathery nose) to the bill. Paint a yellow ochre scalloped edge around the facial disc. Dab the legs and feet with burnt sienna and add a tiny talon of shadow mix on the feet.

Add small lowlights of concentrated Mars black to the diluted black marks on the wing patterns. Then add tiny specks of concentrated Mars black to the head, neck and torso.

With your smallest brush, outline the eye in Mars black. Clean your brush and use the wet bristles to draw the colour inwards, leaving an unpainted 'shine'. Paint the bill in shadow mix and add some diluted shadow to the underside of the tail feathers, wings and torso and to the legs.

Once dry rub out any visible pencil marks.

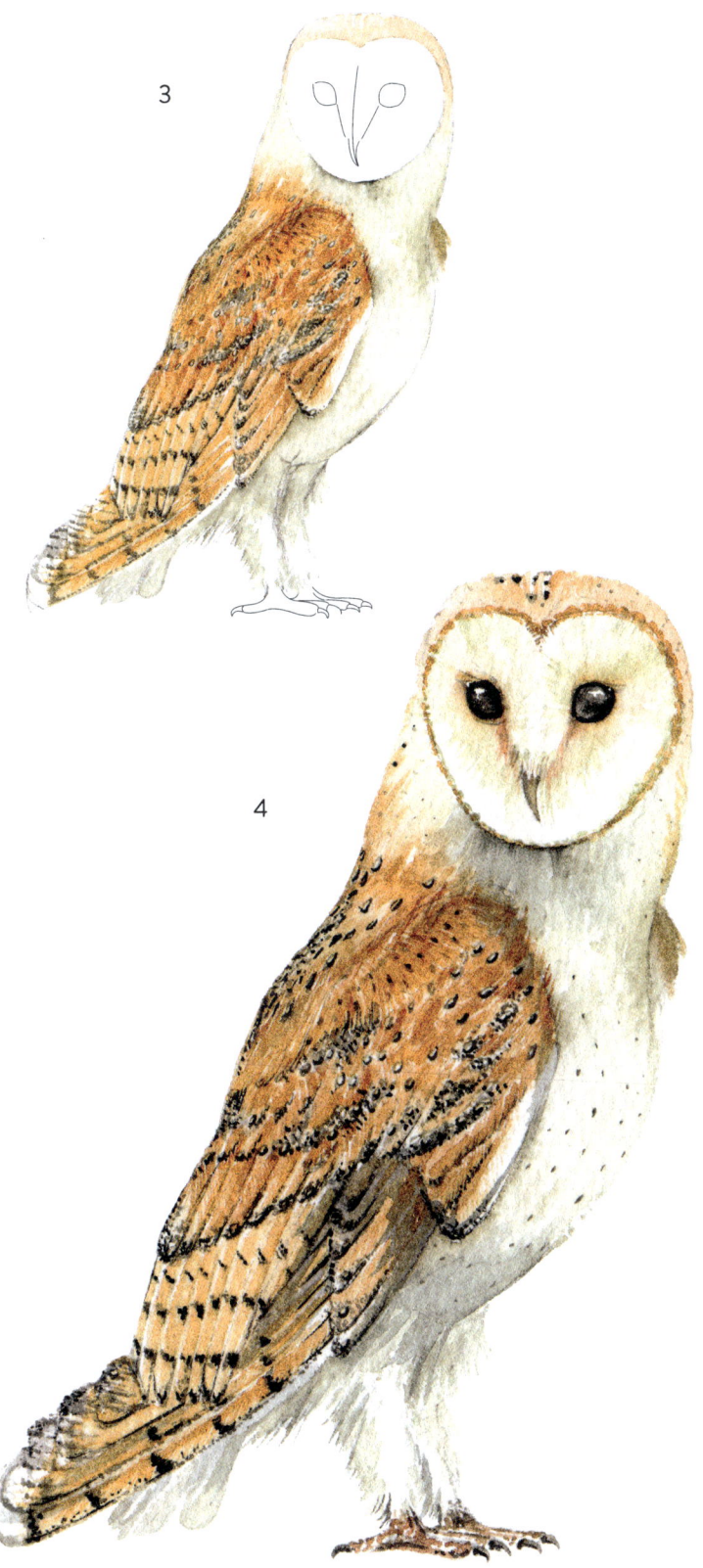

3

4

# DOG ROSE

I love the wild dog roses that tangle through the hedgerows in summer months. This project is particularly interesting to paint in the height of summer as the harsh sunlight captures the crisp shadow of each individual anther and filament in the centre of the flower.

## WHAT YOU WILL NEED

**Brushes**
Pointed round size 6, 2, 0, ⅖, ⁴⁄₀
Rigger size 0

**Paper**
Cold pressed (textured)

**HB Pencil**
**Eraser**

Approximate size of the dog rose painting:
17 x 11cm (6½ x 4⅓in)

### Colours

green gold

sap green

Payne's grey

burnt sienna

permanent rose

cadmium yellow

French ultramarine blue

yellow ochre

### Mix

**Plant mix:** sap green and green gold

**Shadow mix:** burnt sienna and Payne's grey

**Leaf mix:** sap green and French ultramarine blue

1

## 1.

Start by drawing a faint pencil stem with lines for leaves. Draw an oval at the centre of each open flower and a curve for the base of each bud. At the top, draw an oval to mark the base of the open flower.

## 2.

Dilute your permanent rose right down to almost clear water and with your size 6 brush, paint a heart-shaped petal anchored from the central oval: start with the fine point of your brush and press down to fan out the bristles as you paint outwards. While still wet, edge the petal with more concentrated permanent rose and a dab of cadmium yellow at the central point. There are five petals in total, but allow each one to dry fully before painting another that touches or overlaps. For the closed bud, paint a tear-drop shape with a few strokes to show the petals beginning to unfurl. For the partially open flower, paint smaller heart-shaped petals and a few strokes to show the petals behind.

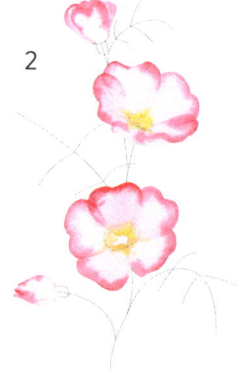

2

## 3.

Use the serrated-edge leaf technique (see page 14) to create the leaf mix leaves with your size 2 brush. Once dry, paint in the plant mix stem with your size 2 brush. For the finer branches and sepals go down to a size 0 brush. Allow to dry fully and rub out any visible pencil.

## 4.

Paint diluted permanent rose petal veins with your rigger brush. Then with your size ⁴⁄₀ brush, paint a cluster of plant mix dots in the centre of each open flower. While that dries, paint in extra plant mix leaves at each branch junction with your size 2 brush. Add some Payne's grey to your sap green and paint fine leaf lines with your rigger brush. Add sap green lowlights to all stems and sepals with your size ²⁄₀ brush.

Back to the flower, paint a cluster of concentrated cadmium yellow dots (anthers) around the centre and join them up with fine lines (filaments) that disappear down beneath the seedpod. Add a yellow ochre lowlight to the underside of the anthers.

## 5.

Dilute your shadow mix and paint fine lines with your ⁴⁄₀ brush from underneath the yellow filaments on each flower. Add dots for each anther and your flowers are now basking in the midday summer sun. Add a sweep of diluted shadow mix along the edge of petals, leaves and any shadowy corners you can find.

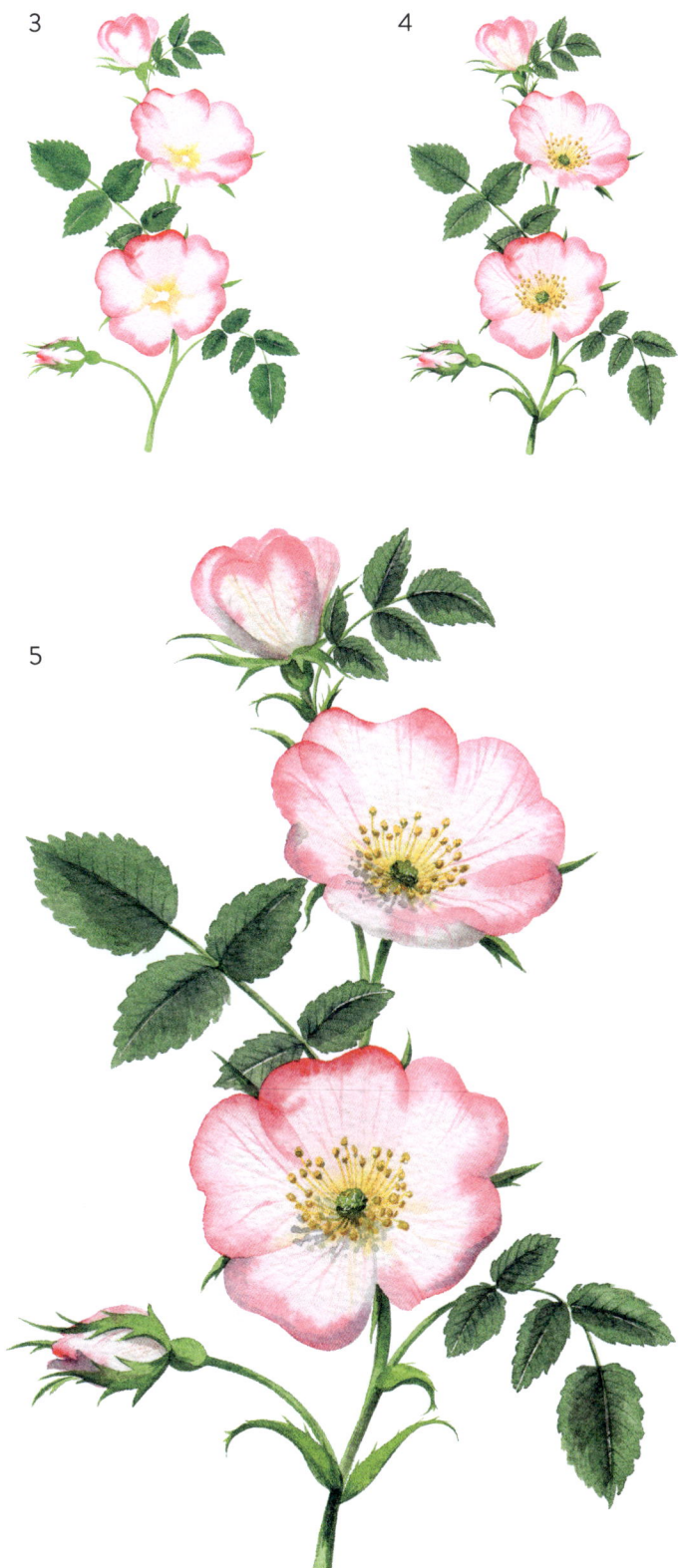

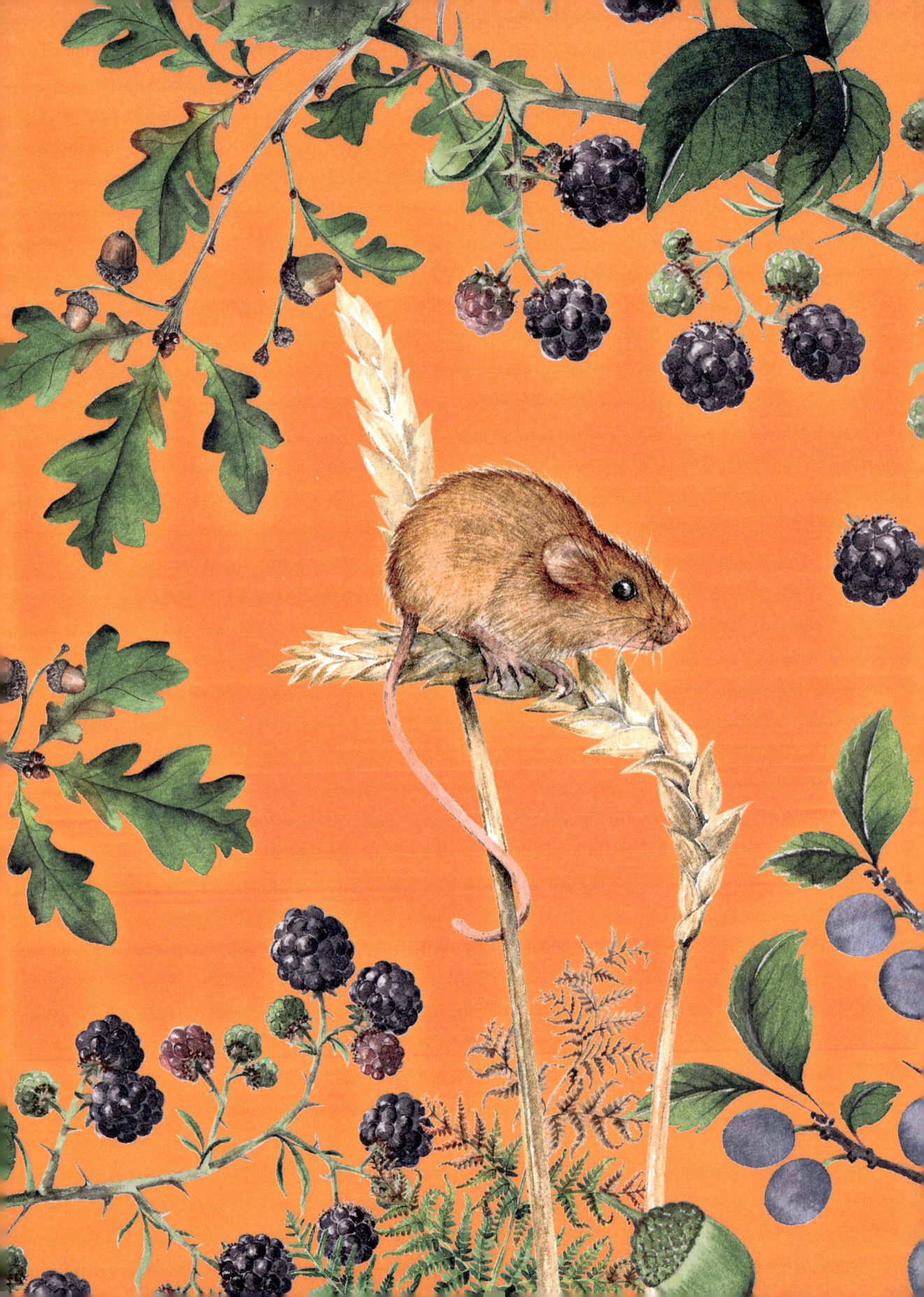

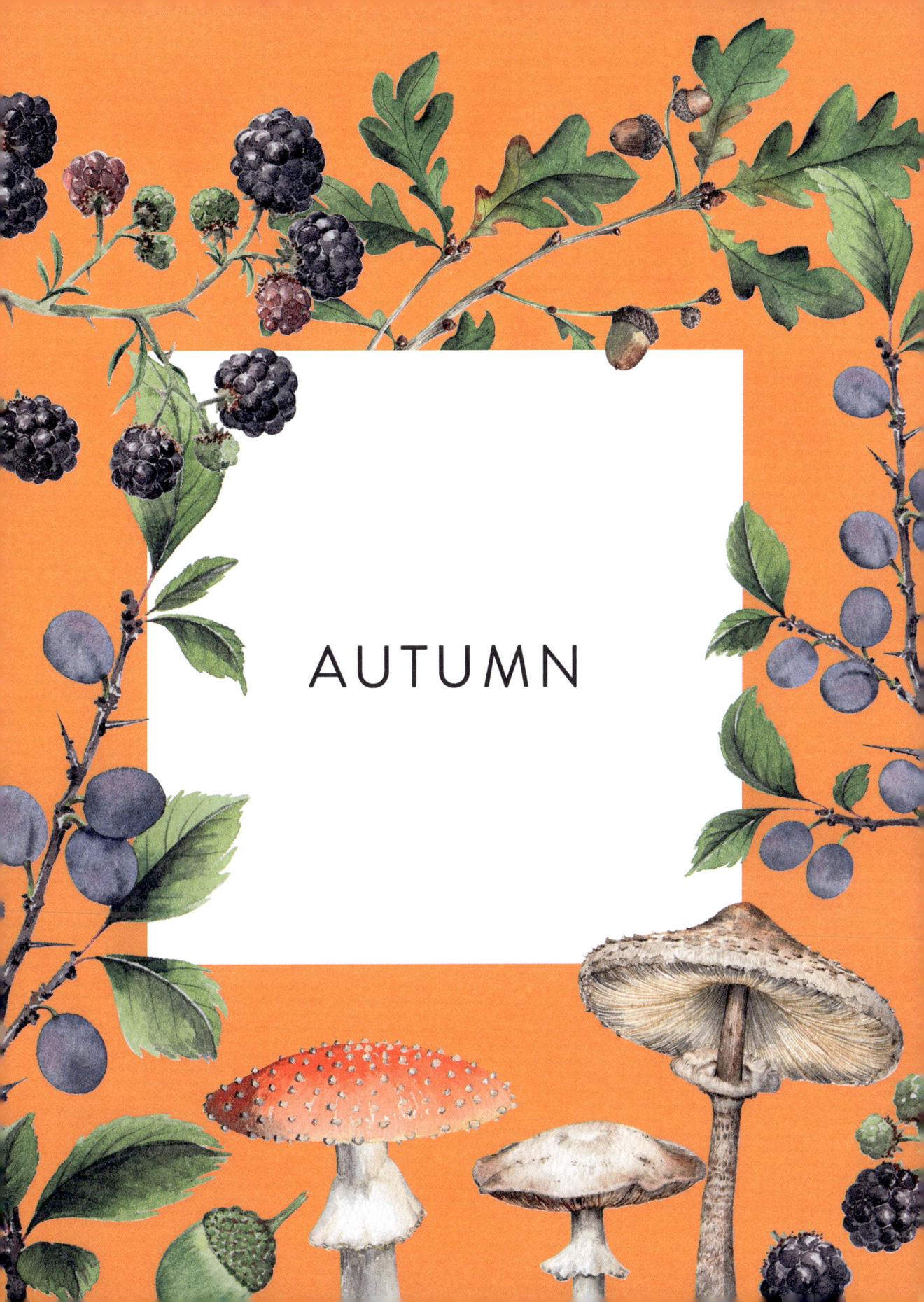

# AUTUMN

# HARVEST MOUSE

The tiny harvest mouse is the only British mammal to have a prehensile tail, which it uses to grip and balance like a fifth limb.

## WHAT YOU WILL NEED

**Brushes**
Pointed round size 2, ⁴/₀
Rigger size 0

**Paper**
Cold pressed (textured)

**HB Pencil**
Eraser

## Colours

yellow ochre

cadmium yellow

raw umber

Payne's grey

burnt sienna

Mars black

alizarin crimson

permanent rose

## Mix

**White fur mix:** yellow ochre and Payne's grey

**Yellow mix:** yellow ochre, Payne's grey, cadmium yellow

**Tail mix:** yellow ochre, Payne's grey, alizarin crimson

**Shadow mix:** burnt sienna and Payne's grey

### 1.
Follow the drawing guide to create a faint pencil body shape and ear of wheat.

### 2.
Use your size 2 brush to paint a wash of diluted white fur mix from the chin, along the bottom half of the body. While still wet, use your size ⁴/₀ brush to paint the rest of the body (except the ear) with yellow ochre and add raw umber hair texture around the edge of the shape. Add diluted permanent rose to the nose and feet.

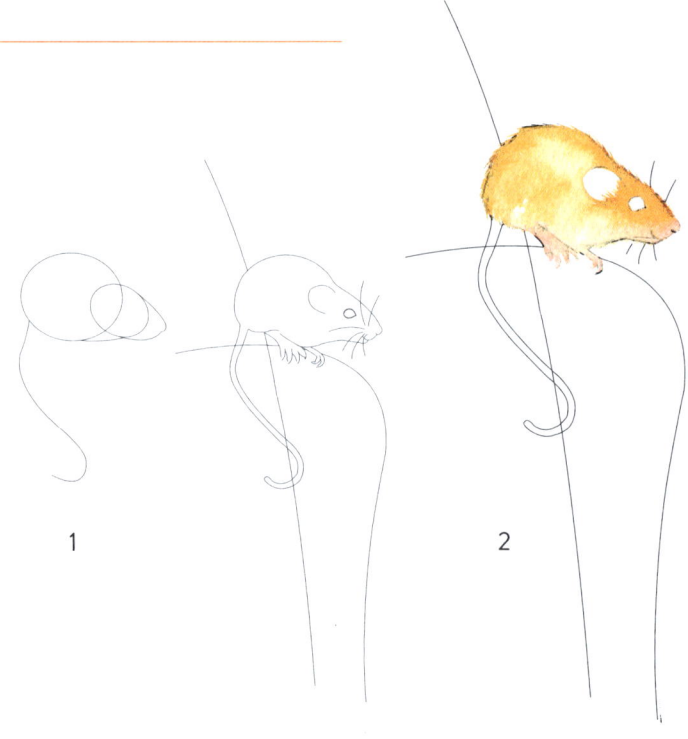

1

2

Approximate size of the mouse and wheat painting: 15 x 8cm (6 x 3in)

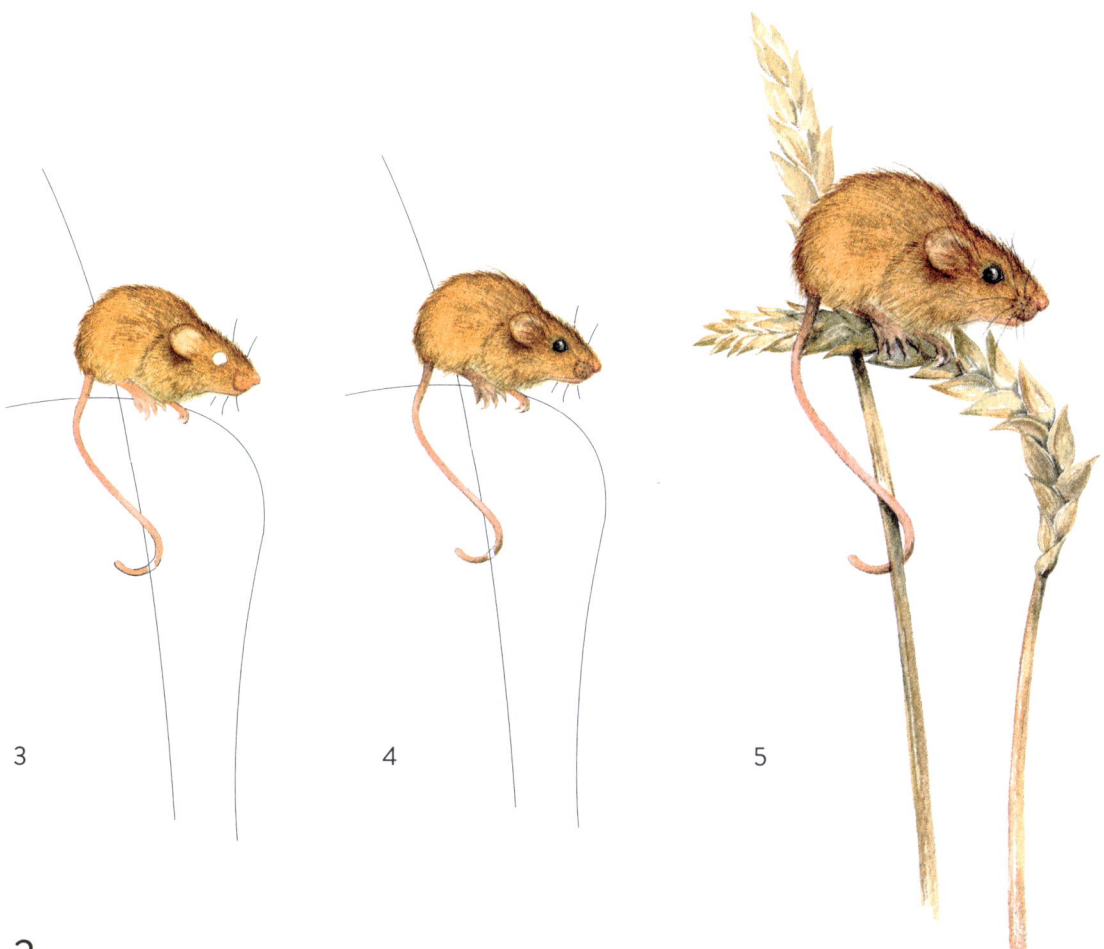

3

4

5

### 3.

Still using your size ⅜ brush, wet the ear area and outline with burnt sienna. The colour will bleed down and fade into the ear area. Once dry, paint fine line hairs of more concentrated colours that correspond with the washes over the fur. Add some tail mix lowlights to the feet and nose and paint the tail.

### 4.

Paint diluted shadow mix around the eye and allow to dry. Add some shadow mix to the tail mix and paint a few lowlights to the tail, feet and muzzle. Add further longer strands of hair to the ear and around the edge of the body in concentrated burnt sienna

and raw umber. Add raw umber claws to the feet and Mars black whisker dots.

With your smallest brush, outline the eye in Mars black. Clean your brush and use the wet bristles to draw the colour inwards, leaving an unpainted 'shine'.

### 5.

With your size 2 brush, paint the wheat stems in diluted lines of yellow mix. While still wet, add some shadow mix and burnt sienna streaks to create a rounded shape. To paint the wheat, start at the base and paint yellow mix mirrored C- and S-curves to create tear-drop shapes sprouting from a

central line. Drop in some shadow mix at the base of each one. Add further detail to the wheat in the foreground: curves of raw umber and yellow ochre as well as some shadow mix underneath where the mouse is sitting.

Finish the mouse with Mars black whiskers with your rigger brush.

# MUSHROOMS

In late autumn it's common for me to begin each dog walk with a foot-dragging reluctance. Crumble has never been deterred by the nights drawing in; his enthusiasm is infectious and it's not long before nature administers its therapeutic dose. It hushes the noise in my mind and makes space for new discoveries. Never was this truer than the fortnight in early autumn where we spotted a new species of mushroom every day.

## WHAT YOU WILL NEED

**Brushes**
Pointed round size 2, ⅙
Rigger size 0

**Paper**
Cold pressed (textured)

**HB Pencil**
Eraser

**Colour**

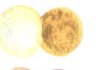 yellow ochre

 burnt sienna

 burnt umber

 raw umber

 Payne's grey

**Mix**

 Mushroom mix: raw umber, yellow ochre, Payne's grey

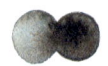 Shadow mix: burnt sienna and Payne's grey

Approximate size of the main mushroom painting: 6 x 6cm (2½ x 2½in)

## FIELD MUSHROOM

The life cycle of a mushroom is brilliant to track day-to-day, from button stage through to the curling cap of the mature mushroom.

### 1.
Follow the drawing guide to create a faint pencil mature field mushroom.

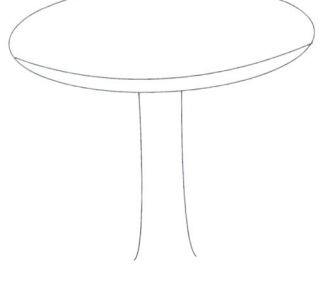

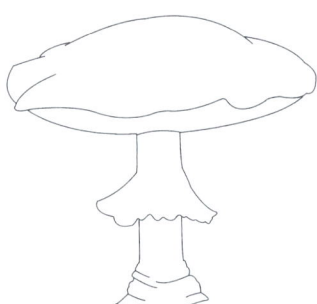

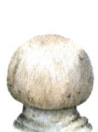
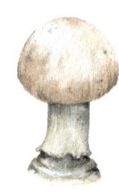
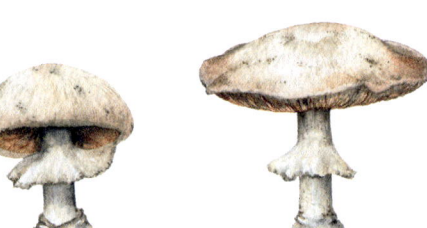
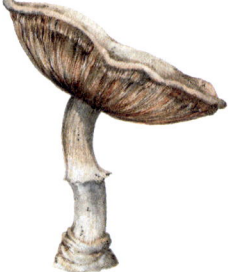

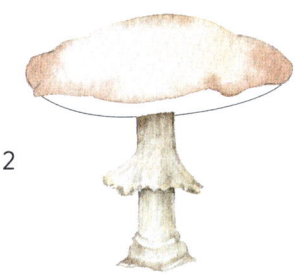

2

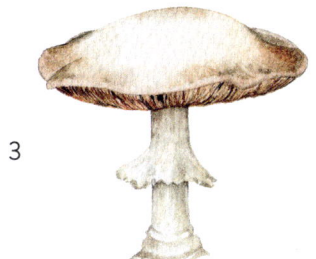

3

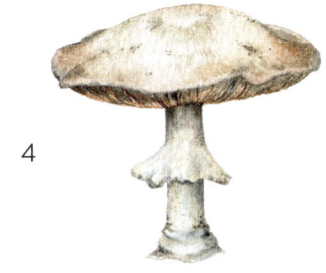

4

## 2.

With your size 2 brush, paint the cap in diluted mushroom mix and while still wet, dab diluted burnt umber around the edge and allow to bleed in. While that dries, you can paint the stem: start with the bottom, outlining the creases in mushroom mix, leaving unpainted highlights. Work your way up the stem, painting the outer edges then cleaning your brush and drawing the colour inwards with the clean wet bristles. Add some shadow mix beneath the ring.

Allow to dry, then work from the top of the stem downwards with some shadow mix at the top. Fan out your mushroom mix brushstrokes onto the skirt-like ring. Allow for some unpainted space here and there and dab the edge of the skirt with some more concentrated mushroom mix.

## 3.

Paint a wash of diluted burnt umber in the gill section underneath the cap. While that dries, use a variety of diluted burnt sienna, raw umber and shadow mix to paint faint strokes of texture around the cap a few millimetres from the edge with your ⁴⁄₀ brush. Once the gill wash is dry, use your rigger brush to paint concentrated burnt sienna fine lines curving up and out from the stem. These gills should be a bit wobbly and imperfect in places. Add a few concentrated shadow mix gills.

## 4.

Add diluted shadow mix to the edges and undersides of the stem. Sweep a line of diluted shadow mix across the top the gills and on the edges of the cap. Once dry, use your smallest brush to add mushroom mix dashes in a ring around the centre of the cap, along with a few speckles here and there. Paint a few mushroom mix streaks down the stem and some concentrated shadow mix speckles.

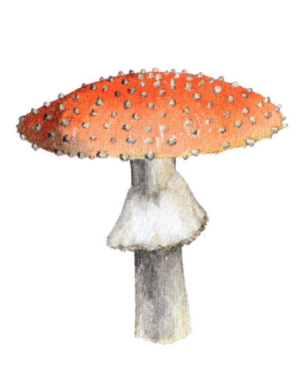

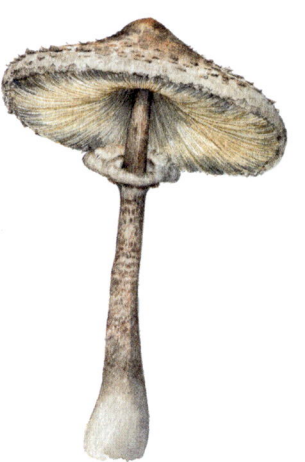

## OTHER MUSHROOMS

You can apply these steps to paint all shapes and sizes of mushroom. For the fly agaric mushroom, I used masking fluid to cover the white dots on the cap before painting the red wash over the top. This allowed for a smoother coverage and a speedier result.

# BRACKEN FERN

Bracken ferns cover the forest floor where we walk each day. They are deciduous, losing their fronds in autumn and regrowing in spring, so they provide a wonderful colour change as good as any other autumn leaf.

Be careful when handling as they are known to be carcinogenic.

A bracken fern is comprised of pinnate leaflets: the arrangement of the feather-like leaves that grow either side of a common axis. We are painting a tri-pinnate bracken as we see this arrangement of branches arranged symmetrically on the stalk first, then on the fronds growing symmetrically from one branch and then focusing in on a single frond and the tiny symmetrical leaves growing from it; the pinnation is replicated each time.

This is not a quick painting project but embrace the slow therapeutic process of painting repetitive branches and leaves, gradually changing your colours as autumn takes hold.

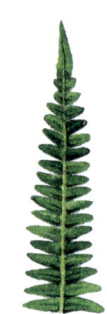

## GREEN FROND

Fresh green fronds grow straight. Paint a stem mix central line in your size 0 brush, then paint softened, elongated sap green triangles up each side, gradually tapering off to one central triangular point. Use your size ⁴⁄₀ brush to add a little dark leaf mix between each leaf and a little leaf vein.

## WHAT YOU WILL NEED

**Brushes**
Pointed round size 0, ²⁄₀, ⁴⁄₀,
Rigger size 0

**Paper**
Cold pressed (textured)

**HB Pencil**
**Eraser**

### Colour

- yellow ochre
- green gold
- sap green
- Payne's grey
- burnt sienna
- cadmium yellow

### Mix

 **Stem mix:** sap green and green gold

 **Dark leaf mix:** sap green and Payne's grey

## COLOUR CHANGE FROND

Early autumn sees the fronds starting to curl and yellow. Draw a slightly curved central line and paint it with stem mix with your size 0 brush. The leaves up either side can be a little more curved and wobbly. Begin with stem mix leaves, gradually adding some cadmium yellow to your mix. Halfway up transition to painting them in yellow ochre and finally in burnt sienna. Once dry, add burnt sienna leaf veins.

Approximate size of the bracken fern painting: 17 x 11cm (6½ x 4½ in)

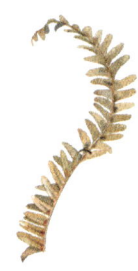

## BROWN FROND

Draw a curled and twisted pencil line for the dried-out frond. Paint yellow ochre leaves that have folded over and gradually open them back out to their correct side with a size ⅔ brush. While still wet, dab them with burnt sienna and Payne's grey. Once dry, paint in the visible leaves behind those that are folded over, with a little more burnt sienna and Payne's grey for contrast.

Where you can see the stalk, paint two fine burnt sienna parallel lines in your rigger brush. Add a few burnt sienna leaf lines with your size ⁴⁄₀ brush.

## BRACKEN FERN

### 1.
Draw a central pencil stem with branches either side that angle up and taper up to a point. Because we are painting a bracken fern in autumn, the top third has dried and is starting to curl. Add pencil fronds along each branch.

### 2.
Begin at the bottom with lush green branches that gradually yellow and finally dry out towards the top.

1

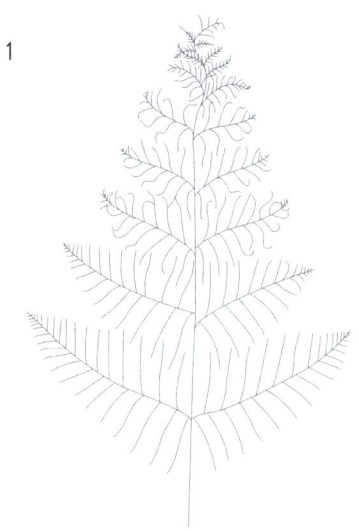

2

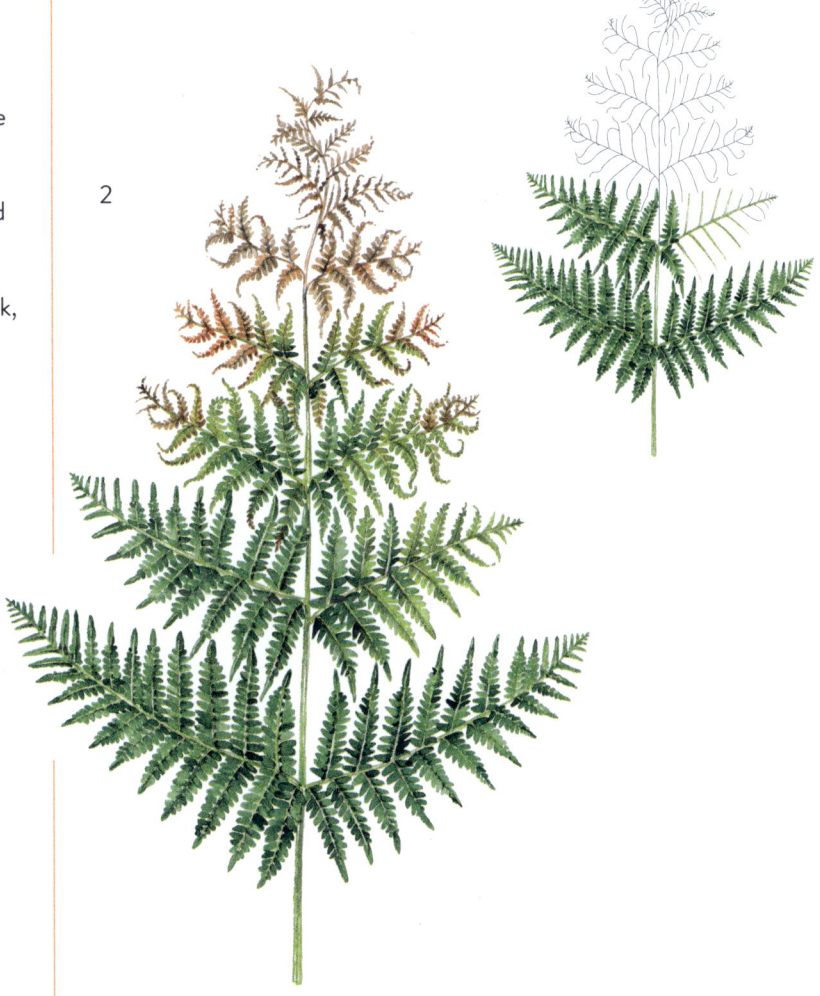

# FALLOW DEER

The annual rut – the loud displays of strength between competing male deer – takes place each year in the estate across from our house. It's not unusual for these noisy neighbours to cross the road at inopportune moments when we're driving down the country lanes. It's preferable to encounter the female herds grazing in the forest on our daily dog walks (Crumble's woeful hunting ability means we've never lost him in hot pursuit). I've twice encountered an albino deer, ghostly white in the forest: yet another reminder of how quiet observation in nature can be richly rewarded.

## WHAT YOU WILL NEED

**Brushes**
Pointed round size 2, ⅔, ⅙

**Paper**
Cold pressed (textured)

**HB Pencil**
**Eraser**
Masking fluid

Approximate size of the fallow deer painting: 14 x 8cm (5½ x 3in)

### Colour

Payne's grey

burnt sienna

Mars black

cadmium orange

sap green

green gold

cadmium red

yellow ochre

### Mix

**White coat mix:** majority Payne's grey and yellow ochre

**Orange coat mix:** cadmium orange, cadmium red, burnt sienna

**Shadow mix:** burnt sienna and Payne's grey

## 1.

Follow the drawing guides to create a faint pencil body shape. Dab dots of masking fluid on all the white spots of the deer's coat. Allow to dry fully.

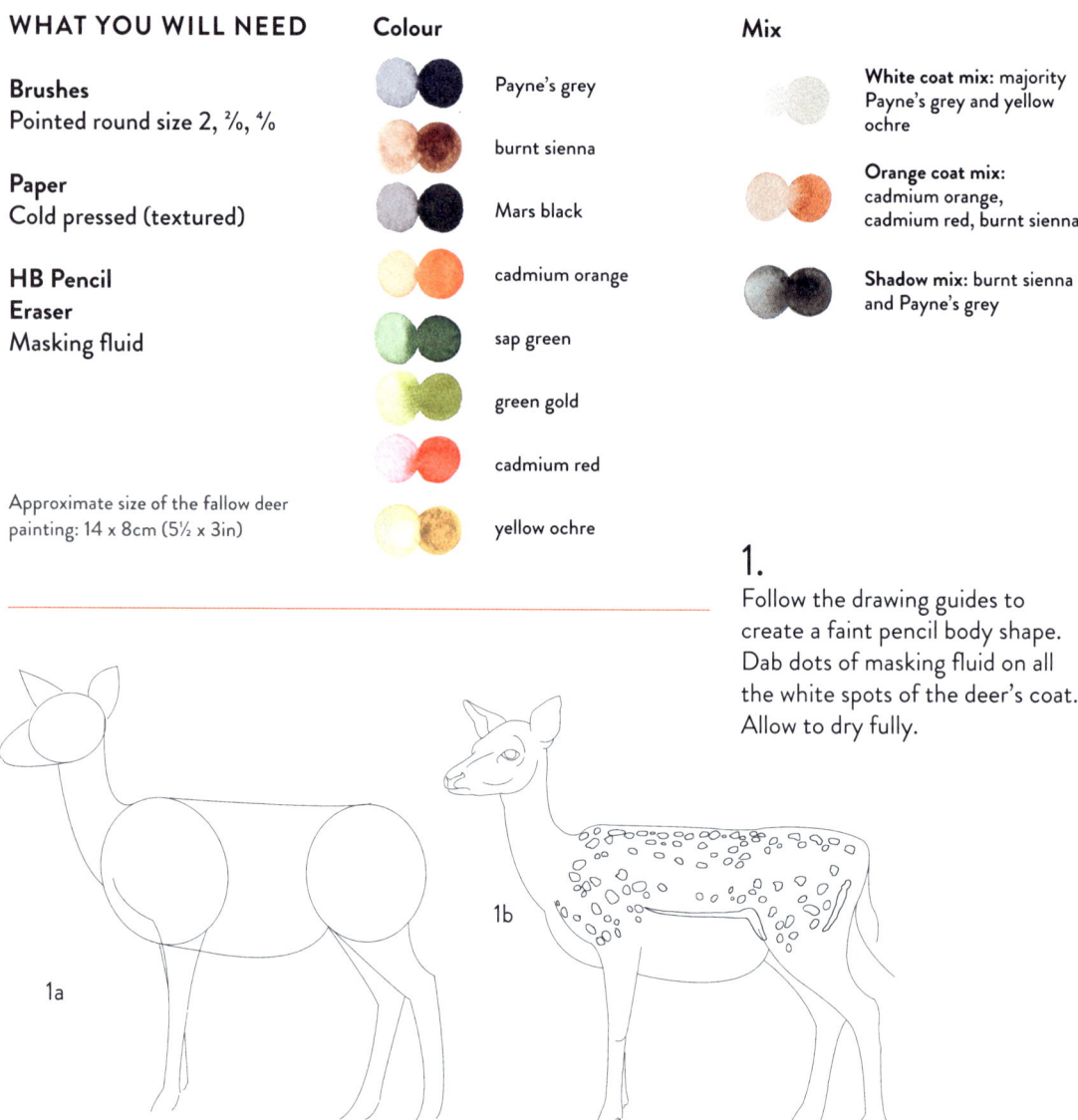

1a

1b

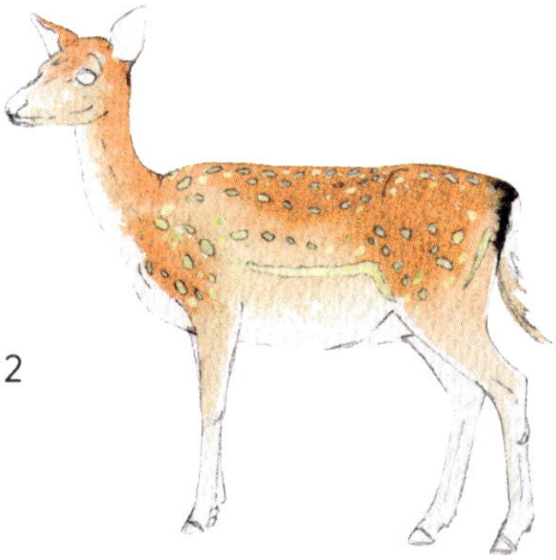

2

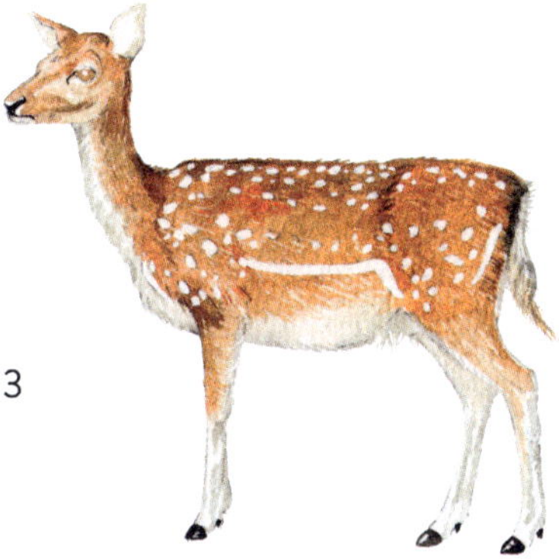

3

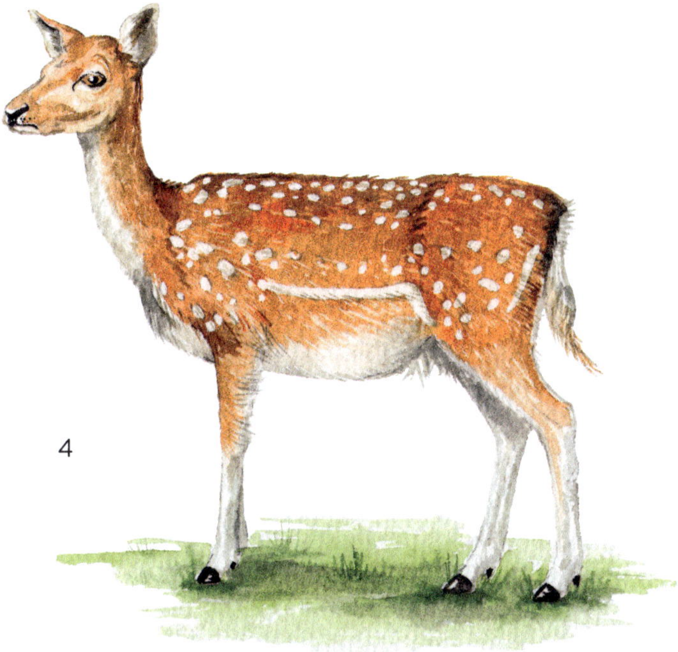

4

## 2.

Use your size 2 brush to paint a wash of diluted orange coat mix over the head and down the back of the neck. Clean your brush and use the wet bristles to blend the colour to clear on the neck and torso. Paint the rest of the body with orange coat mix, fading to clear down the legs. Add some extra burnt sienna on the head, along the back and around the tops of the legs. Finish with a sweep of Mars black just before the tail.

## 3.

With your size 4/0 brush, paint fine line hairs of more concentrated colours that correspond with the washes over the fur. Paint white coat mix in the unpainted section down the neck, torso, legs, tail and in the ears. Once dry, paint in the contours of the face and irises in diluted burnt sienna with your size 2/0 brush.

Once dry, remove the masking fluid and rub out any visible pencil. With your size 4/0 brush, follow the pencil lines in Mars black to paint the muzzle. Outline the hooves in Mars black, clean off your brush and draw the colour in with a wet brush leaving a tiny unpainted 'shine'.

## 4.

With your size 4/0 brush, outline the eye in Mars black and add a few whisker dots around the muzzle. Paint diluted Mars black hairs in the ears. Paint shadow mix hairs lightly over the unpainted dots on the coat.

With your size 2 brush, paint a mossy ground with diluted green gold. While still wet, paint in sap green grass with your size 4/0 brush. Allow to dry.

With your size 2 brush paint sweeps of diluted shadow mix down the torso, the background legs, under the tail and on the ground.

# OAK LEAVES & ACORNS

There's an ancient white oak tree right outside my studio window. With a quick turn of the head I can check on a number of busy nests in spring and the changing colours in autumn.

## WHAT YOU WILL NEED

**Brushes**
Pointed round size 4, 2, 0, ⅖, ⅘
Rigger size 0

**Paper**
Cold pressed (textured)

**HB Pencil**
**Eraser**

Approximate size of the oak leaf painting:
11 x 17cm (4¼ x 6¾in)

## Colour

- yellow ochre
- sap green
- Payne's grey
- burnt sienna
- cadmium yellow
- cadmium orange
- cadmium red
- green gold

## Mix

**Green leaf mix:** sap green and yellow ochre

**Brown shadow mix:** majority burnt sienna and Payne's grey

**Dark leaf mix:** sap green and Payne's grey

**Shadow mix:** burnt sienna and Payne's grey

## LEAVES OF WHITE OAK

The painting techniques to turn an oak leaf autumnal can be replicated for all sorts of leaves.

**Green oak leaf**

### 1.

First draw a pencil curved line that will be the central vein of the leaf. I would encourage you to paint the shape without creating a pencil outline as it allows for a more organic leaf shape. With your size 4 brush loaded with wet green leaf mix, start at the top of the pencil line creating the leaf tip (these lumpy tips down the leaf are called lobes), swiftly pick up more wet paint and repeat this technique to create the lobes down the leaf, drawing the excess colour in to fill the body of the leaf. The points will finally taper inwards at the bottom of the leaf.

### 2.

While still wet, use a size 4 brush to paint sweeps of sap green along the underside of each lobe and up the central line, followed by a few lowlights of dark leaf mix in the same places.

1
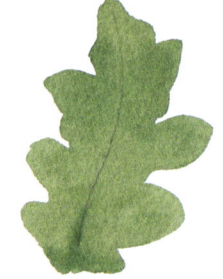

2
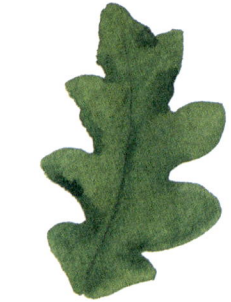

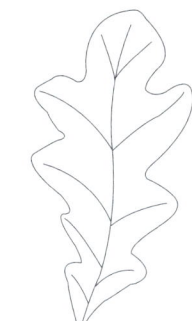
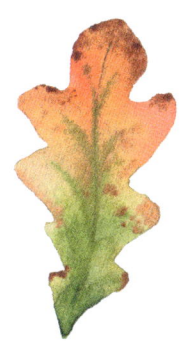
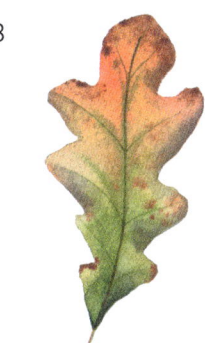

## Colour-changing leaf

### 1.
When painting a multicoloured leaf, it is helpful to have drawn a vague outline of the whole leaf, as well as the central line and veins.

### 2.
Starting at the top with your size 4 brush, paint the top third in wet cadmium orange. While still wet, add sweeps of cadmium red and burnt sienna. Quickly clean your brush and paint the next section in cadmium yellow, then green gold. Finish the bottom section with sap green and burnt sienna dabs to create leaf spots. While still wet, you can also paint green gold leaf veins along the pencil lines. Allow to dry.

### 3.
Paint diluted shadow mix on the underside of each point. Allow to dry and then paint sap green leaf veins with your rigger brush. Turn that into a burnt sienna leaf line and stalk at the bottom of the leaf. Once dry, rub out any visible pencil.

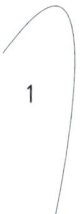
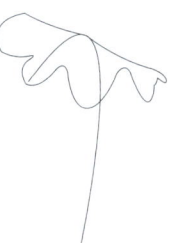
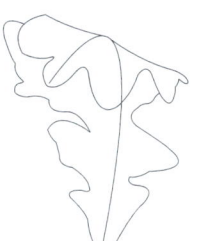
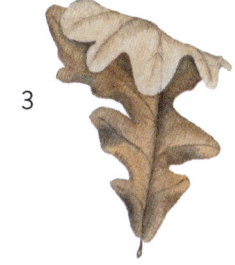

## Dried oak leaf

### 1.
Dried leaves are gnarly and curled; start with a central pencil line for the leaf vein. If your leaf is folded over, find the top edges of the leaf and draw in the curled-over shape first. Then fill in the rest of the shape.

### 2.
With a size 2 brush, paint the top section in diluted yellow ochre with a faint dab of burnt sienna bled into the top outline. Allow to dry fully. Paint the remaining section in wet burnt sienna. Sweep some brown shadow mix up the central vein and on the underside of the lobes.

### 3.
Allow to dry fully before painting brown shadow mix leaf veins with the rigger brush. For the top half, paint fine parallel leaf outlines.

# ACORN

These go through a similar colour change to the leaves.

**Green acorn**

## 1.

Paint the nut in diluted green gold with your size 0 brush. While still wet, paint streaks of sap green down the body of the nut. The lines should bleed but remain faintly visible. Paint the stalk and cap in green leaf mix diamond shapes with a size 4/0 brush. The shapes shrink as they reach down to the nut.

## 2.

Dab burnt sienna between the diamonds and at the bottom of the nut with your size 4/0 brush. Paint shadow mix lowlights on the bottom point of each diamond and down the side of the nut.

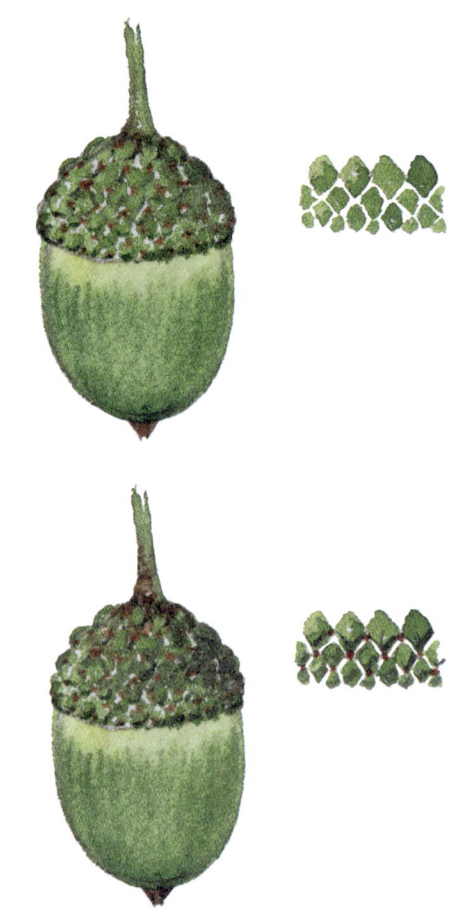

**Brown acorn**
Follow the same steps for a brown acorn but first washing half of the nut in green leaf mix and the other side in burnt sienna, then add brown shadow mix streaks. Paint the diamonds, stalk and base point of the nut in brown shadow mix and then the dabs on the cap in shadow mix.

Now you've learnt the many oak components we can put it together on a branch.

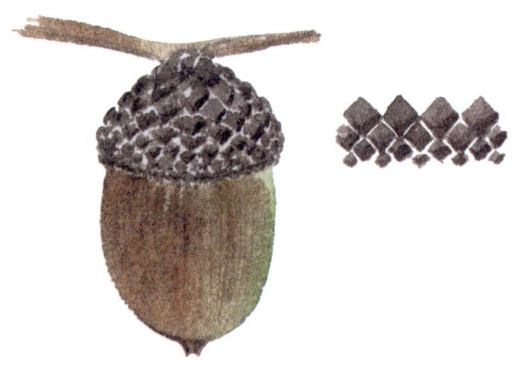

# OAK LEAF BRANCH

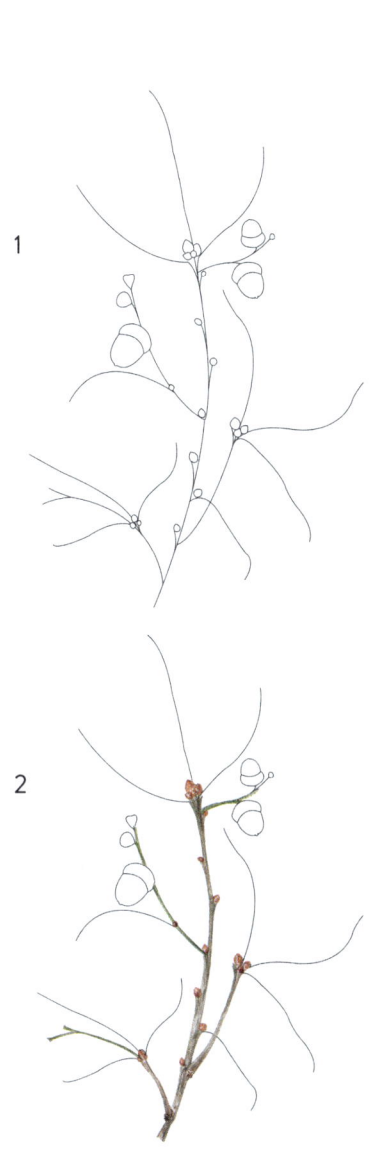

1

2

3

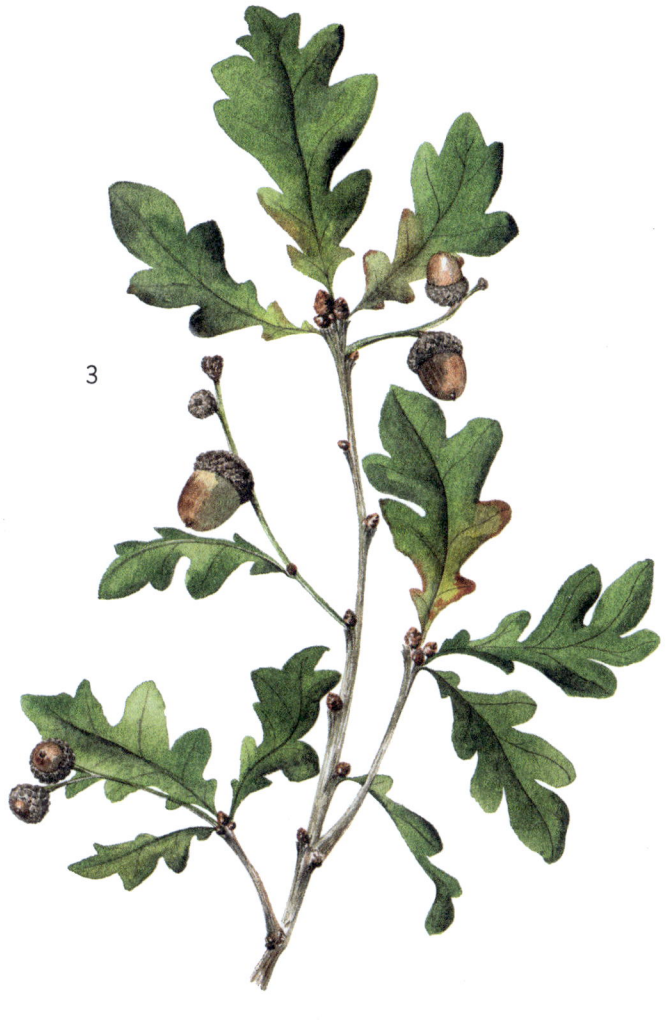

## 1.
Draw a pencil branch with space for acorns and just the central line for each leaf. The slender branch gradually swells to house a little bud nestled in along the way, as well as buds forming just above each leaf stalk (known as the petiole).

## 2.
Starting at the bottom, using your size ⅔ brush, paint the branch in a series of fine lines of brown shadow mix, allowing for slivers of unpainted space to create a ridged texture. Add gnarly sections and buds at each new branch in burnt sienna and shadow mix. Paint the young, thinner branches in green leaf mix.

## 3.
Follow the various steps for each item to complete your piece.

# AUTUMN HEDGEROW

Blackberry picking is a key childhood memory that I love to repeat every year. I've never been organized enough to pick sloes from the blackthorn bush, however, I do love to paint them. These two berry sprigs present contrasting approaches to painting texture and shape with watercolour.

## WHAT YOU WILL NEED

**Brushes**
Pointed round size 6, 4, 2, 0, ²⁄₀ ⁴⁄₀
Rigger size 0

**Paper**
Cold pressed (textured)

**HB Pencil**
**Eraser**

Approximate size of the blackberries painting: 17 x 9cm (6¾ x 3½in)

Approximate size of the blackthorn painting: 15 x 8cm (6 x 3in)

**Colour:** Blackberries

 Payne's grey

 alizarin crimson

 sap green

 green gold

 cadmium red

 burnt sienna

 yellow ochre

**Colour:** Blackthorn

 permanent rose

 cobalt blue deep

 Payne's grey

 burnt sienna

 green gold

 sap green

 alizarin crimson

**Mix:** Blackberries

 **Stem mix:** sap green and green gold

 **Blackberry mix:** Payne's grey and alizarin crimson

 **Red berry mix:** alizarin crimson and cadmium red

 **Green berry mix:** majority green gold and sap green

 **Shadow mix:** burnt sienna and Payne's grey

**Mix:** Blackthorn

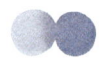 **Sloe mix:** cobalt blue deep and Payne's grey

 **Brown shadow mix:** majority burnt sienna and Payne's grey

 **Shadow mix:** burnt sienna and Payne's grey

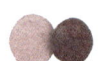 **Leaf mix:** burnt sienna, Payne's grey, alizarin crimson

## BLACKBERRY

### 1.

Follow the drawing guide to create a faint pencil stem with plenty of berries and room for some leaves. First paint in a diluted stem mix branch with your size 2 brush, leaving space for the overlapping leaves. Paint in thorns with a stem mix fine line from your ⁴⁄₀ brush and then sharpen up the shape with some burnt sienna. The branches should be thinner than the main stem with smaller thorns. Once dry, add tiny sap green leaves at the juncture of each branch.

Use the serrated leaf technique with your size 6 brush and wet sap green. While still wet, drop in a dab of Payne's grey at the base of each leaf.

### Berries

Draw a pencil outline berry shape and then draw a small circle somewhere in the middle; this is the point of the berry nearest to you if imagining it as a 3D shape. Then draw further round sections, ballooning out from that central circle until you are drawing kidney-bean shapes barely visible round the sides. The blackberry is fully formed, the red berry is a little smaller, so the small shapes will take up more room. The green berry is the smallest, so the little shapes will take up the most room.

Heavily dilute your berry mixes until they are barely visible. With your size 0 brush, outline each section leaving a tiny patch of unpainted 'shine'. Allow to dry.

Gradually increase the concentration and paint a second layer, still leaving tiny bits of unpainted space on each section as well as in-between. This is fiddly work but it's worth it!

Add stem mix sepals and burnt sienna dots for dried filaments around the base of the berry with your size ⅔ brush. Allow to dry.

Finish the green and red berries by adding some shadow mix to the berry mixes and painting dabs of shadow to the underside of some of the berry shapes with your size ⁴⁄₀ brush. For the blackberry, paint a wash of the original black berry colour over the top of the berry leaving only a small section towards the top. It will feel like you've painted over all your hard work, but it will dry with a beautiful darkness allowing you to see the detail.

### 2.

Use your rigger brush to paint Payne's grey leaf lines and add some diluted shadow mix to the underside of the stem and branches.

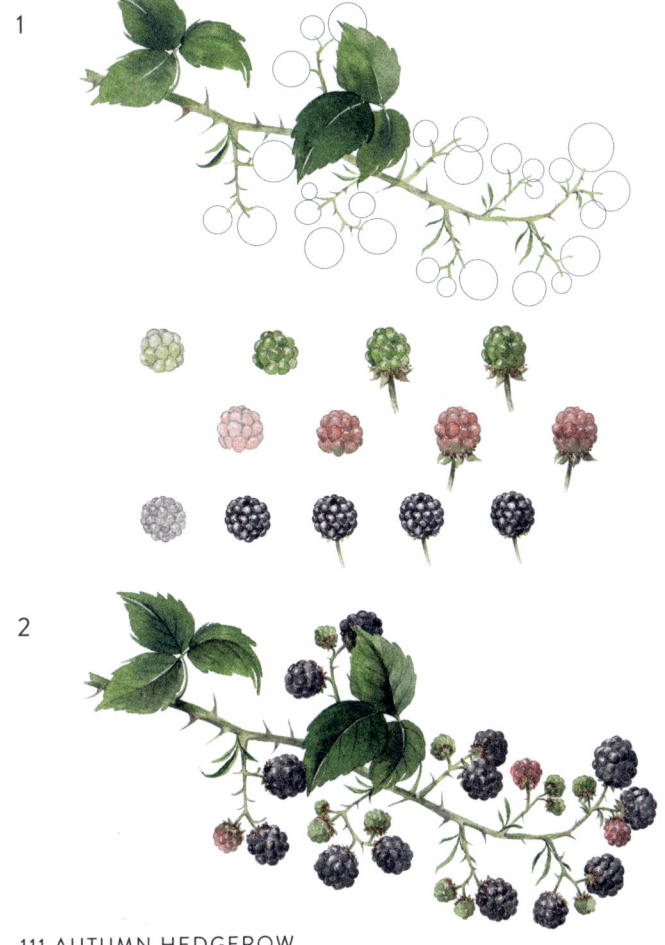

1

2

## BLACKTHORN

These berries have a velvety finish unlike the high shine of the blackberries. Instead of unpainted space, we can use different levels of concentration and smooth blends to create a rounded berry.

Draw your branch with the berries and thorns marked in. Just place a curved line for the central line of each leaf. The first thing to paint in is the sloe berries.

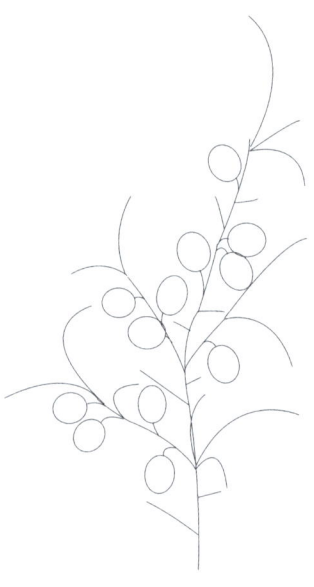

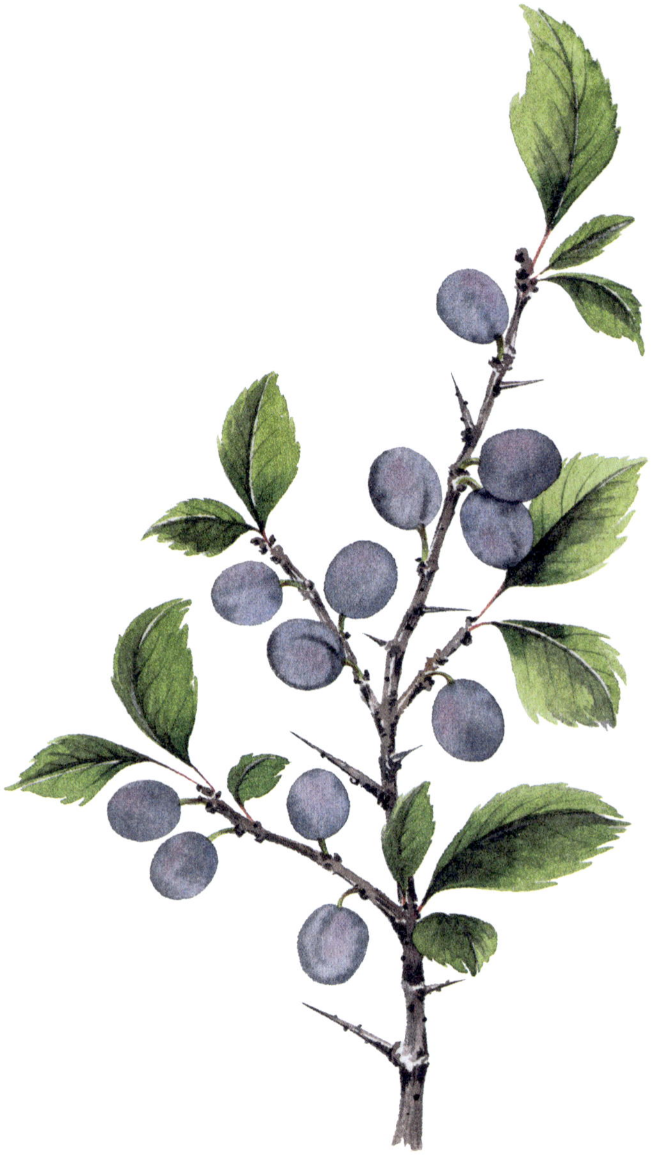

## SLOE BERRIES

With your size 2 brush, paint a diluted oval of sloe mix. While still wet, outline with some concentrated Payne's grey and a dab of permanent rose on the body of the berry. While still damp, paint a curve of Payne's grey creating the slight dimple on the berry. Paint a fine line green gold curved stalk.

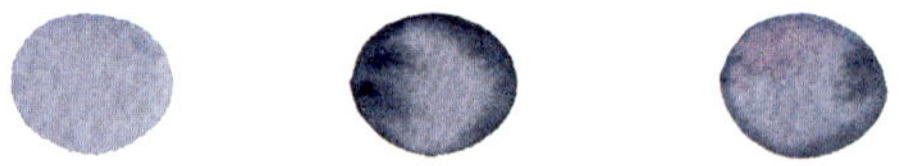

## LEAVES

With your size 4 brush paint a tapered line in wet green gold. Paint another, slightly smaller line by its side with the tip curving out but coming down into the central base point. Add another slightly smaller line and repeat until you've created one half of a serrated leaf. Drop in some sap green to the base while still wet. Repeat on the other side leaving a fine sliver of unpainted space in-between the two sides.

Once dry, add a central Payne's grey leaf line with your rigger brush, as well as leaf veins fanning out. You can also add a wash of diluted Payne's grey up the centre of the leaf and blend it out for more roundness.

Connect your leaves to the branch with a fine line of leaf mix with your rigger brush.

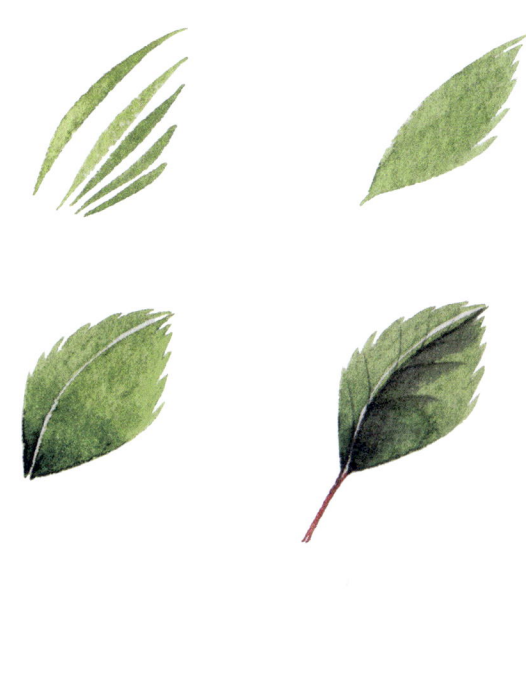

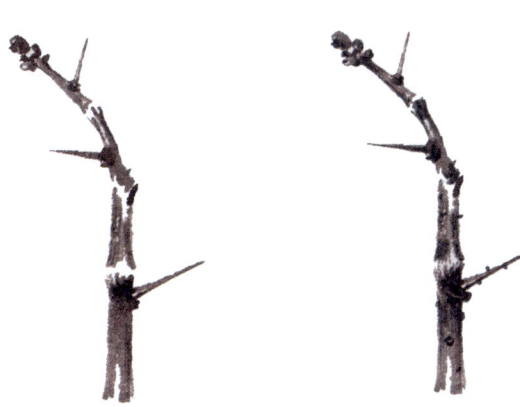

## BRANCH

The branch can be painted in the gaps between the berries and leaves but it's a strong enough colour that you could layer it up over the top of the painting if you wished. Use brown shadow mix and with your size 2 brush – starting at the bottom – paint along the branch in sections leaving a little unpainted space at each junction. Add gnarly knots and thorns with a smaller brush. Once dry, you can go back with some more concentrated shadow mix to add further detail to the branch.

# LOOSE WATERCOLOUR AUTUMN LANDSCAPE

I always wondered where to start with landscape painting but soon realized that if I looked out across a glorious vista, all I was looking at was broad brush strokes and watercolour washes.

My best bit of advice when translating a landscape into a watercolour piece is look to the horizon and notice the palest colours first. Focusing on what is faintest first mimics how we approach any watercolour painting: putting down those initial diluted washes and building up layers. With that approach, watercolour is the perfect medium to have a go at simple landscapes.

Approximate size of the autumn landscape painting: 17 x 10cm (6¾ x 4in)

## WHAT YOU WILL NEED

**Brushes**
Pointed round size 8, 2, ²⁄₀
Rigger size 0

**Paper**
Cold pressed (textured)

**HB Pencil**
**Eraser**
**Washi tape**

**Mix**

**Shadow mix:** burnt sienna and Payne's grey

**Grey green mix:** Payne's grey and sap green

### Colour

 Payne's grey

 burnt sienna

 green gold

 cadmium red

 cadmium orange

 yellow ochre

 sap green

 French ultramarine blue

## 1.

When working with washes, I like to tape my paper down around the edges with washi tape to keep it flat. It's not officially stretching the watercolour paper, but it minimizes warping while painting.

We're going to begin by painting abstract shapes of the trees, shrinking into the distance. Create plenty of diluted green gold, cadmium orange, yellow ochre and French ultramarine blue in your palette. With your size 8 brush, scribble cadmium orange and yellow ochre into two corresponding banks of 'trees' tapering away into the middle of the painting with a few broad brush strokes across the base of the piece in the foreground. Add some green gold pointy treetops. Clean off your brush and paint a French ultramarine blue sky scribble. Continue to Step 2 before it dries.

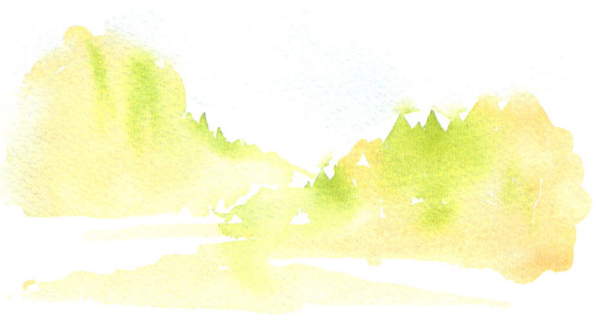

2
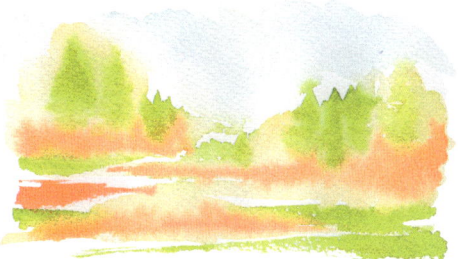

3

## 2.

While still wet, add more concentrated green gold tree shapes with your size 2 brush. Mix in some cadmium red to your cadmium orange and paint streaks of this colour along the banks of trees. Add more streaks of this and green gold in the foreground.

## 3.

In adding more concentrated layers we create a sense of perspective. Reserve your stronger colours for the items in the foreground and fade them out for items in the distance. The page will have dried considerably and you can begin the next stage even if it's not bone dry, it adds to the interest. Add some Payne's grey to the green gold and with your size ⅔ brush, paint in diagonal detail strokes on the pine trees. For the red trees, create scribbled dabs of wet cadmium red and cadmium orange with your size ⅔ brush. While still wet, sweep some wet Payne's grey along the bottom of the tree lines and sweep some burnt sienna across some of the undulating strokes in the foreground. Allow to dry.

## 4.

Use your rigger brush to paint some Payne's grey branches in any visible gaps in the red trees' foliage. Add tree trunks, making sure those in the distance are paler than those in the foreground. Mix some more Payne's grey into your green gold and add finer detail to the tops of the pine trees with your size ⅔ brush. Add more concentrated dabs of cadmium red and burnt sienna to the trees. In the foreground, paint sweeps of the grey green mix over the undulating ground with your size 2 brush and finish with some Payne's grey grasses with your rigger brush.

4
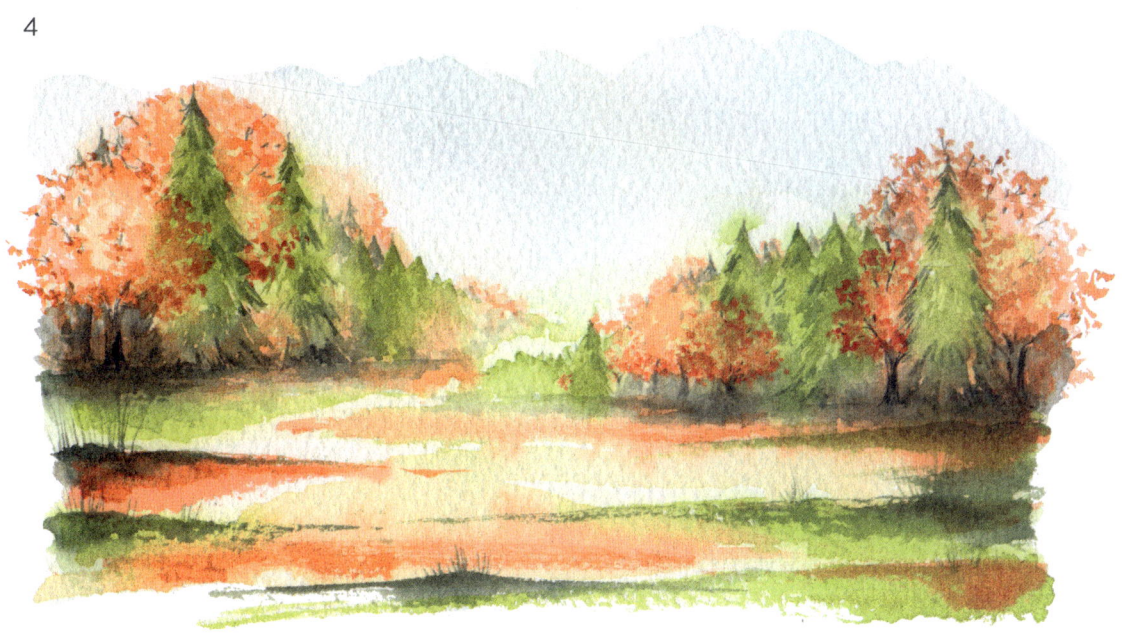

# COMMON PHEASANT (MALE & FEMALE)

The first of October marks the start of game season in England and our garden becomes a safe haven for flocks of birds. Female pheasants are slim enough to squeeze through gaps in our fence whereas the male pheasants announce themselves tumbling over our hedge with a squawking, inelegant flight.

When they aren't teetering their considerable weight on our dainty bird feeder, they can be found trampling Ant's vegetable patch. They only stay as long as Crumble will allow, but the females' brilliant camouflage allows them a longer stay than their gentlemen friends.

## WHAT YOU WILL NEED

**Brushes**
Pointed round size 8, 4, 2, 0, ⁴⁄₀

**Paper**
Cold pressed (textured)

**HB Pencil**
**Eraser**

Approximate size of each pheasant painting: 9 x 8cm (3½ x 3in)

## Colour

 yellow ochre

 green gold

 sap green

 Payne's grey

 French ultramarine blue

 alizarin crimson

 raw umber

 cadmium orange

 burnt umber

 burnt sienna

 cadmium red

## Mix

 **Red feather mix:** burnt sienna and alizarin crimson

 **Ochre feather mix:** yellow ochre and Payne's grey

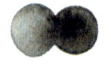 **Shadow mix:** burnt sienna and Payne's grey

 **Brown shadow mix:** majority burnt sienna to Payne's grey

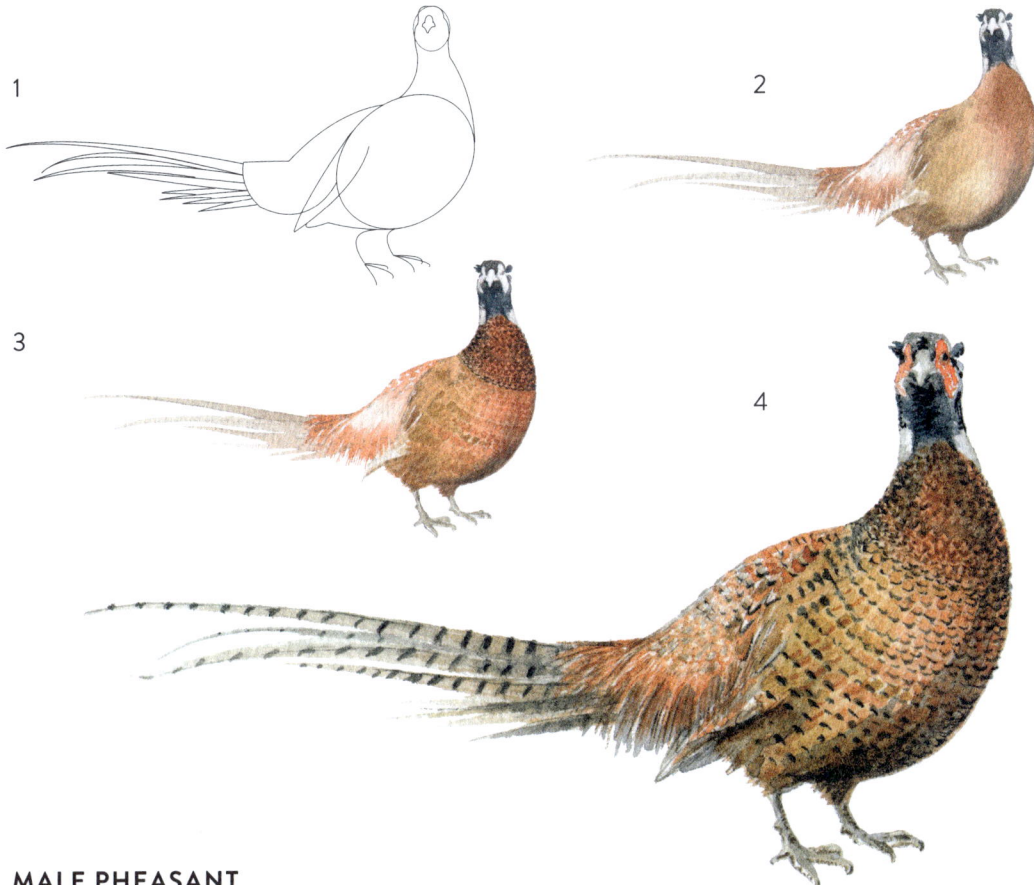

## MALE PHEASANT

### 1.
Follow the drawing guide to create a faint pencil body shape.

### 2.
The pheasant's feathers are a rich blend of red, gold and chestnut tones. Use your size 2 brush to first paint diluted ochre feather mix tail feathers and outline the legs and feet. Then paint a wash of red feather mix down the torso, blending into raw umber towards the legs and back. Paint dabs of red feather mix down the back towards the tail and create a brush of fine feathers with your ⁴/₀ brush. Dab diluted French ultramarine blue and Payne's grey up the neck and over the head.

### 3.
Using the more concentrated versions of the colours previously used and a size ⁴/₀ brush, paint little 'V's from the top of the brown neck, two thirds down into the body, making sure to follow the roundness of the torso. As the feathers get larger down the body, paint little brush stroke rectangles and all the way down to the legs.

### 4.
Once dry, add a tip of dark shadow mix to each feather with your size ⁴/₀ brush. Add dabs of concentrated colour to the back and add dark shadow lowlights. Stripe the tail feathers with shadow mix and add a few fine lines to the legs, feet and fine line feathers curving over the back. Define the slightly concealed wing with some diluted shadow mix feathers. Paint the cadmium red comb around each eye.

Once the painting is dry, rub out any visible pencil. Use Payne's grey to dot the eyes and add a few lowlights to the navy-blue neck area with your size ⁴/₀ brush. Add some diluted shadow mix to the white collar and beak. Sweep a size 4 brush of shadow mix down the torso to the legs and feet.

# FEMALE PHEASANT

## 1.

The female pheasant is smaller than the male, with shorter tail feathers, but use the same drawing structure to create your basic pencil form. Paint in a basic wash of diluted yellow ochre and add tail feathers of ochre feather mix with your size 2 brush. While still wet, edge the head, neck and torso with ochre feather mix to create a rounded shape. Once dry, use your size 4/0 brush to dab feathers from the neck down the torso to the legs, gradually increasing their size. This should only be faintly visible.

## LOOSE WATERCOLOUR PHEASANT

**Capturing a pheasant mid crow and flap calls for a looser style.**

Once you've had a go at the detailed version, now is a great time to loosen things up, pick up a slightly larger brush and simplify things. Having studied the minutiae of each feather, you've got the general knowledge of the bird to be able to paint a quick and expressive loose watercolour version.

Start with the same simple pencil drawing structure and colour palette from the detailed study, but instead of diligently colouring in each section with basic washes, sweep a size 4 brush with vigour and energy across each contour of the body and wings and fill the shape with as few brush strokes as possible.

## 2.

It's worth drawing in the placement of the wing feathers before embarking on the brown shadow mix detailing. Starting at the top of the head with tiny dabs, paint in brown shadow mix feather markings with your size 4/0 brush. Add some burnt sienna accents to help define the eye, wing and tail feathers. Add concentrated ochre feather mix lowlights on the legs and beak.

Then go down to a size 2 brush and use the fine tip to scribble in curve feathers on the wing, legs, neck and tail. All the while the page will be slowly drying, allowing you to then add dark dabs across the body for the feather markings.

Choose a size 0 brush to add the concentrated colours for the face and neck, leaving slivers on unpainted space between colours. The sight of the white page not only allows these strong colours to remain separate but also adds a little highlight to the bold piece.

## 3.

Use your smallest brush to add some fine line downy feathers around the wing in brown shadow mix. Paint a raw umber iris and once dry, dot with concentrated Payne's grey. Add a fine line and nostril to the beak and a sweep of diluted shadow under the chin and down the torso to the legs.

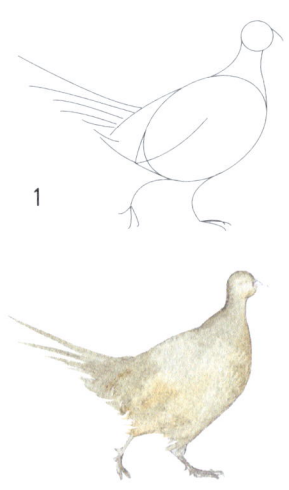

1

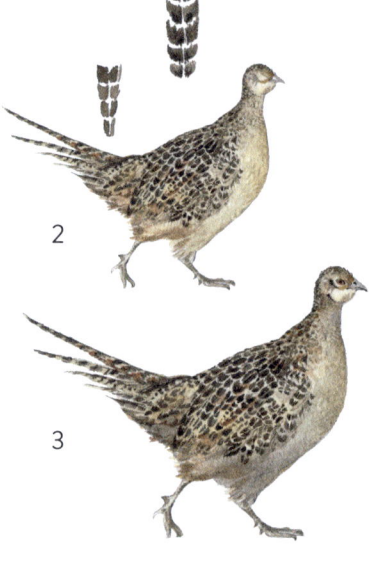

2

3

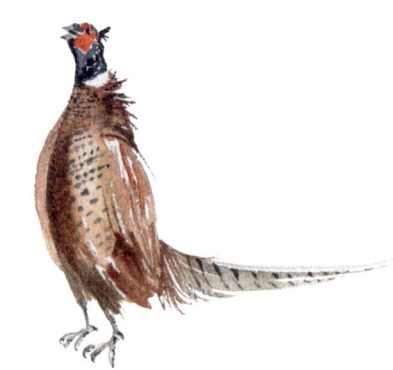

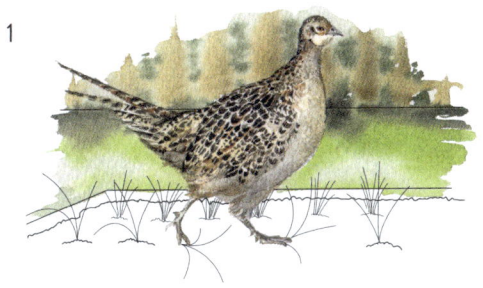

1

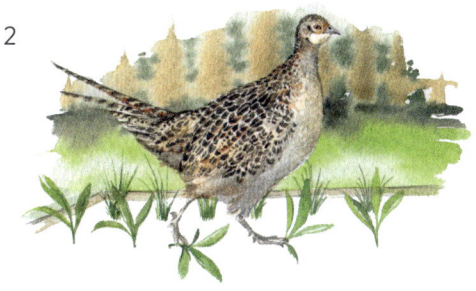

2

## VEGETABLE PATCH

The female pheasants may not have the show-stopping colours of the male but they're brilliant at camouflage. It can be hours before we spot them nestled among the veg.

While it can be easier to paint in your background first, it's not impossible to paint your subject matter and then build a scene around them afterwards.

### 1.

Draw the faint pencil surroundings. Here I have a clear distinction between the soft-focus background and a more detailed vegetable bed where the pheasant resides. With a fine-pointed round size 8 brush, wet the 'soft focus' background area, carefully painting around the edge of the bird. While still wet, use the same brush to paint green gold grass, yellow ochre fence panels and Payne's grey and sap green dabs in between. Finish with a line of Payne's grey along the ground. All of this will dry lighter. Allow to dry fully.

### 2.

With a size 0 brush, paint a diluted yellow ochre wooden frame, allow to dry and then paint sap green and green gold vegetable shoots, some of which are trampled underfoot. The plant colours should be more concentrated than the background, so they show up when layering on top.

### 3.

Paint in diluted brown shadow mix soil with your size 2 brush, leaving plenty of unpainted space for highlights. Build up shadow mix in the area underneath the bird. Now the bird is surrounded by colour and not the white page, it needs a little more shadow and definition to show up. Add concentrated lowlights of sap green to the plants with your size ⁴⁄₀ brush. Once fully dry, rub out the pencil.

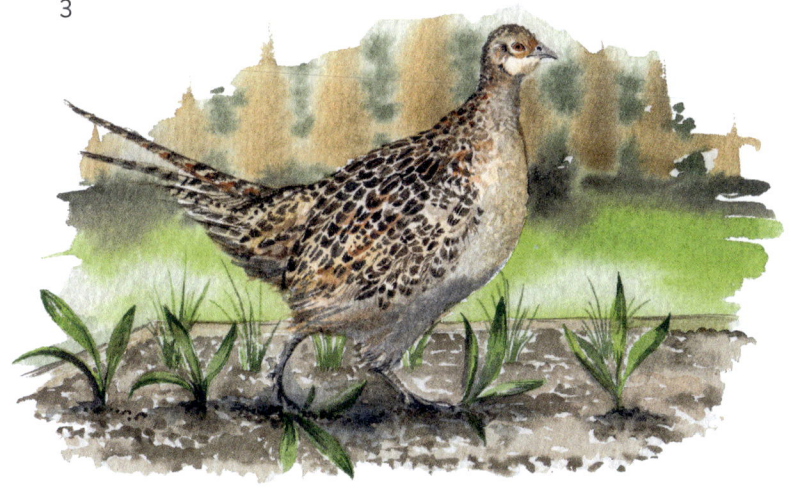

3

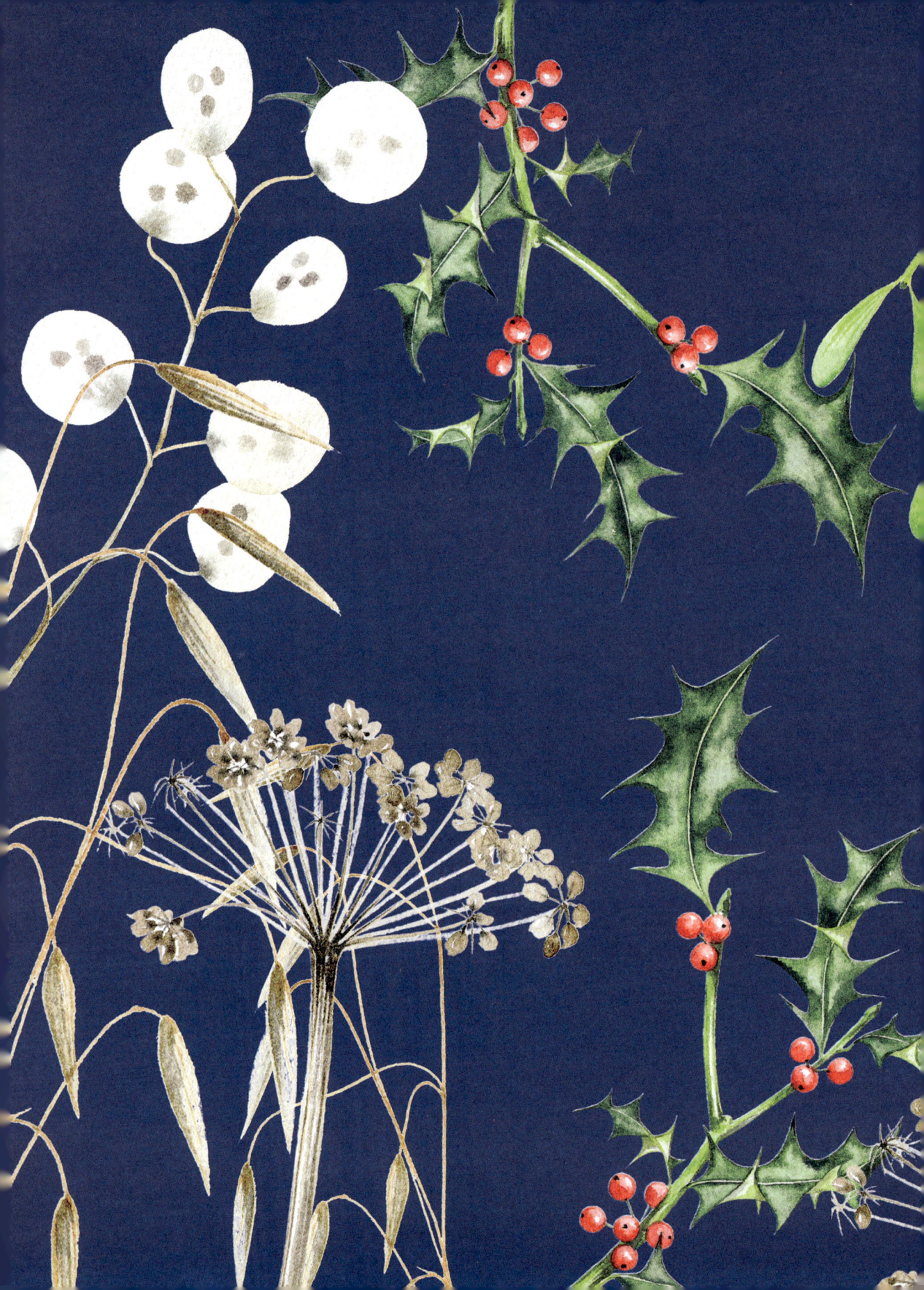

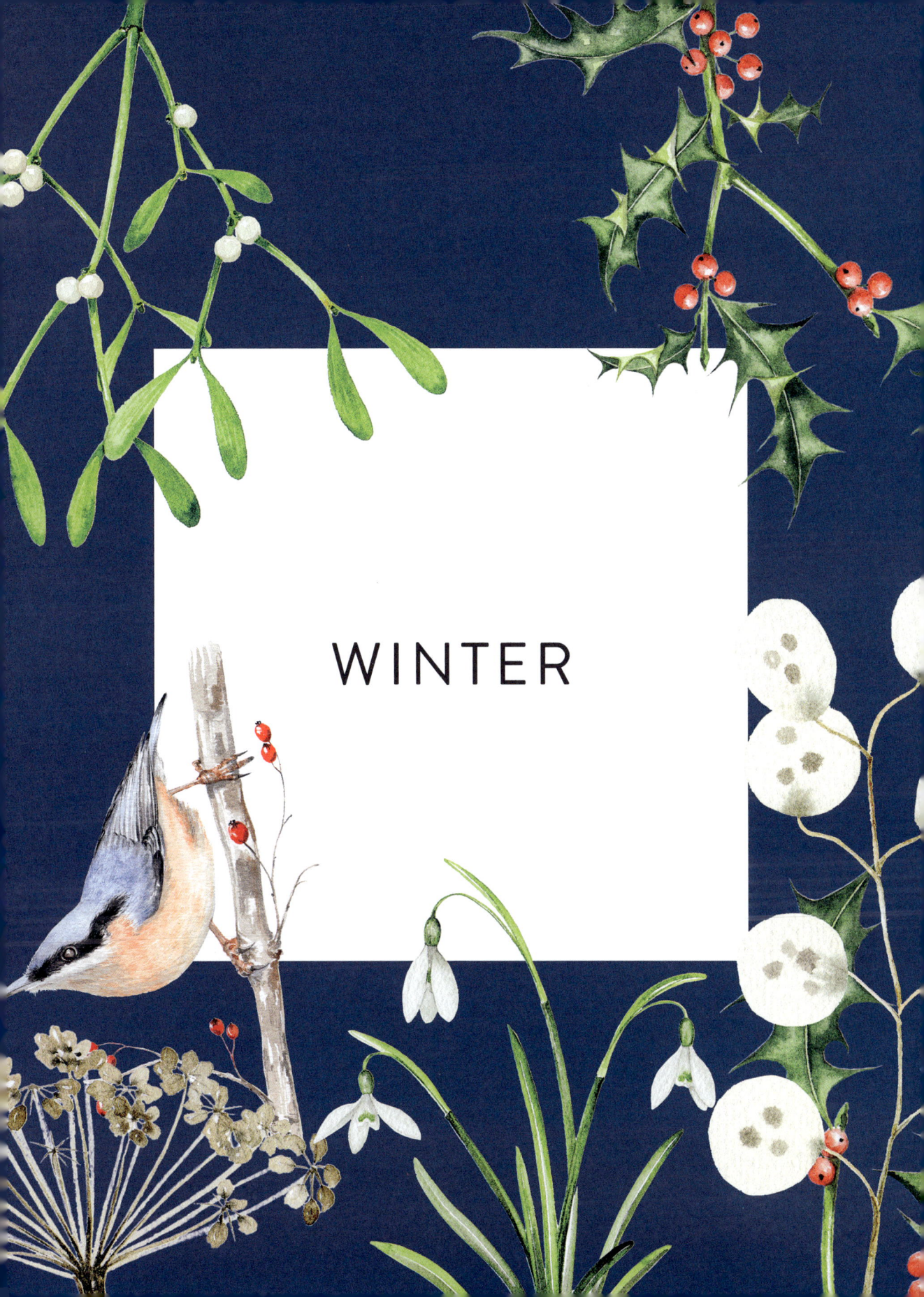

WINTER

# NUTHATCH

I try not to have favourites but... it's the nuthatch every time. Hanging upside down with a superhero mask of feathers, I just love seeing this bird in action.

## WHAT YOU WILL NEED

**Brushes**
Pointed round size 4, 2, 0, ⅖, ⁴⁄₀

**Paper**
Cold pressed (textured)

**HB Pencil**
**Eraser**

### Mix

 **White feather mix:** yellow ochre and Payne's grey

 **Orange feather mix:** cadmium orange and cadmium red

 **Shadow mix:** burnt sienna and Payne's grey

## Colour

 yellow ochre

 burnt sienna

 Payne's grey

 alizarin crimson

 cadmium orange

 cadmium red

 cobalt blue deep

 Mars black

## 1.
Follow the drawing guide to create a faint pencil body shape.

## 2.
Use your size 2 brush to paint a diluted wash of orange feather mix on the breast and stomach. Paint diluted cobalt blue deep over the head and across the back. Edge the feathers around the back with some diluted Payne's grey. Paint diluted Mars black on the strip from the beak across the eye with a size 0 brush. Paint the beak cobalt blue deep, with a dab of Mars black on the tip while still wet.

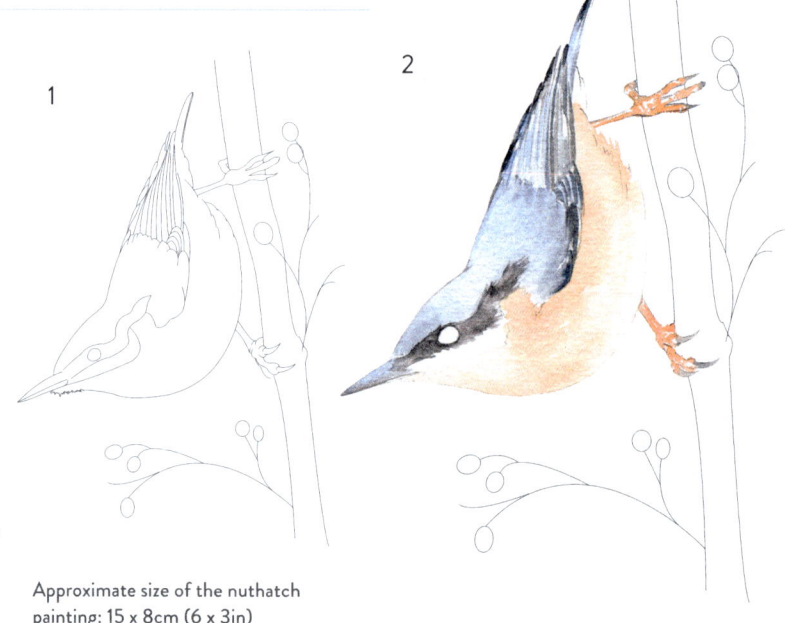

Approximate size of the nuthatch painting: 15 x 8cm (6 x 3in)

3

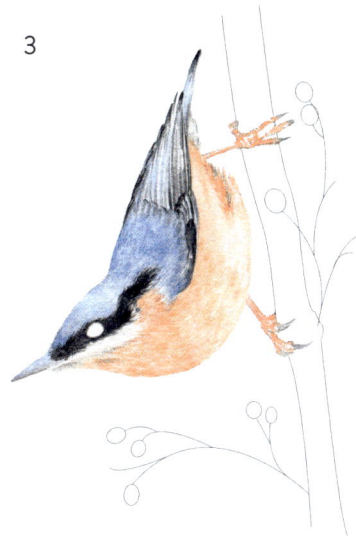

**4.**

Add dabs of gnarly texture to the feet with burnt sienna. With your size ⅙ brush paint a fine line along the beak and outline the eye in Mars black. Clean your brush and use the wet bristles to draw the colour inwards leaving an unpainted 'shine'. Add some diluted shadow to the underside of the tail, body and legs with your size 2 brush, painting strokes that give a sense of the feather texture.

To paint the branch, use your size 4 brush with some burnt sienna and shadow mix strokes up and down until the brush dries out and you get a lovely dry brush texture. Paint in the branches with a size ⅔ brush and add cadmium red berries with a little unpainted 'shine'. While still wet, dab some alizarin crimson into the berry and top with a few dabs of concentrated Mars black. With your size 2 brush, add diluted shadow where the nuthatch's feet sit on the branch, as well as on the underside of the berries.

Paint in the covert wing feathers with diluted cobalt blue deep and Payne's grey with tiny slivers of unpainted space in between with your size ⅔ brush. Drop in more concentrated Payne's grey on the tips while still wet. Paint the underside of the tail feathers with white feather mix.

Add some burnt sienna to the orange feather mix and use it to paint the legs and feet with your size ⅔ brush. Add a tiny talon of shadow mix on each foot.

**3.**

Use your size ⅙ brush to paint in fine feather tufts across the body using a more concentrated version of the wash colours. Add lowlights of more concentrated Payne's grey to the covert wing feathers. Once dry, rub out any visible pencil.

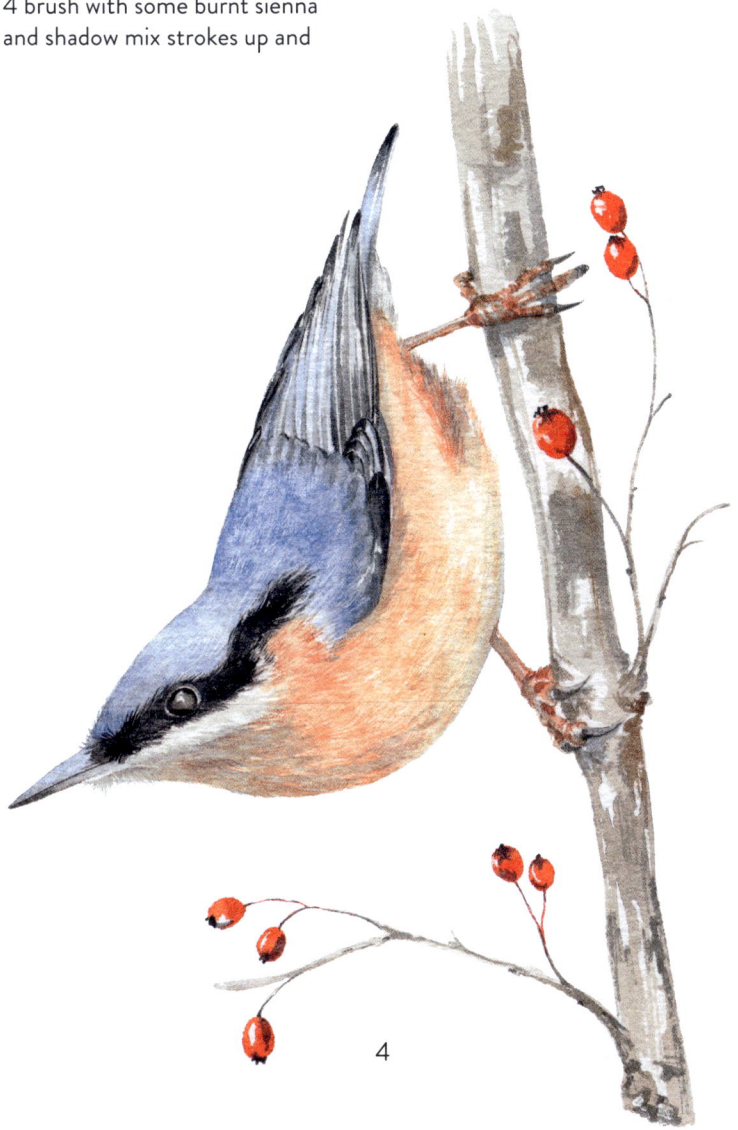

4

# SCOTS PINE

Scots pine trees are some of my favourites to paint and to hug!

## WHAT YOU WILL NEED

**Brushes**
Pointed round size 8, 2, ⅔
Mop brush size 6

**Paper**
Cold pressed (textured)

**HB Pencil**
**Eraser**

## Colour

Payne's grey

burnt sienna

raw umber

cadmium orange

cobalt blue deep

green gold

sap green

## Mix

**Green mix:** sap green and green gold

**Shadow mix:** burnt sienna and Payne's grey

**Brown shadow mix:** majority burnt sienna to Payne's grey

## 1.

Draw a horizontal horizon line then draw a tall straight trunk in the foreground. Add gnarly branches either side. Then with your mop brush wet the entire area. Use your pointed round size 8 brush to paint streaks of diluted cobalt blue deep sky above the horizon line. Then paint a diluted wash of green mix on the area below the horizon line, avoiding the tree trunk (it's inevitable there will be a little bleed into the tree). Sweep a little diluted sap green beneath the tree. Finally, create distant trees along the horizon line with dabs of concentrate cadmium orange, green gold and finally some shadow mix. Allow to dry fully.

Approximate size of the Scots pine painting: 20 x 15cm (8 x 6in)

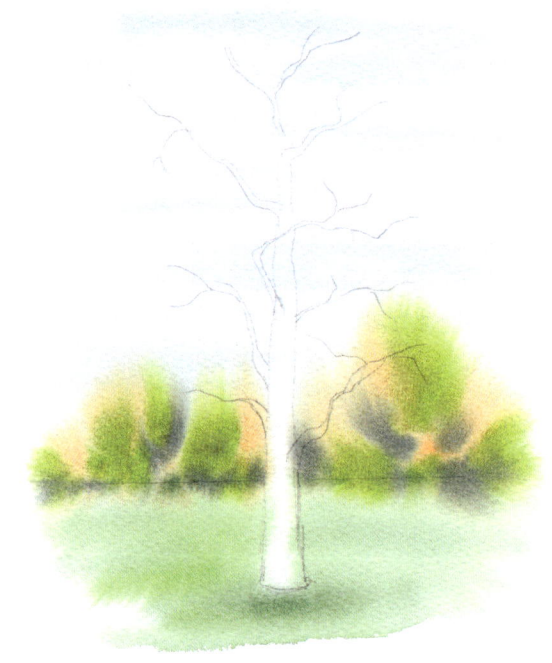

1

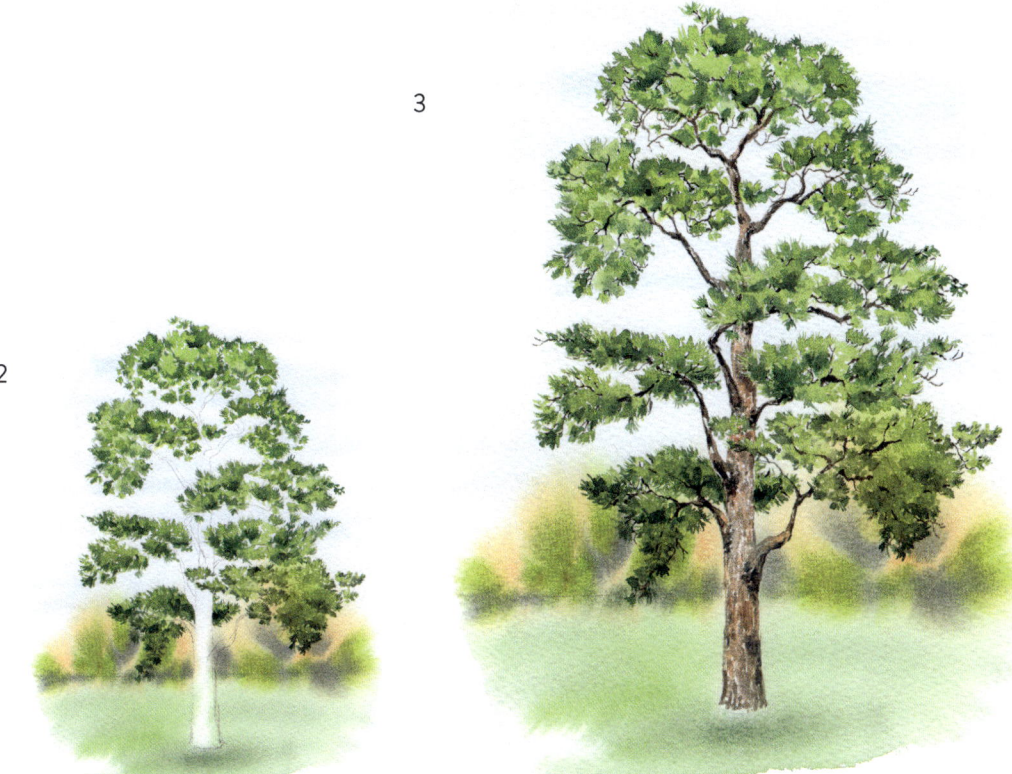

## 2.

To paint the busy boughs of pine needles, work on filling out the area around each branch, one by one. Paint lots of little C-curves of green mix into a messy cloud of colour with your size 2 brush. While still wet, add sap green flicks with your size ⅔ brush around the edges and in the body of the green area to give the effect of pine needles. Add extra little spiky clouds floating around the edges of the main boughs of pine needles.

## 3.

Wake up your burnt sienna, raw umber and brown shadow mix and with your size 2 brush, paint dabs of these diluted colours on the trunk, working your way upwards. Leave tiny slivers of unpainted space here and there to create the bark texture. Increase the brown shadow mix on the branches. Once you meet the green pine needles, swap down to a size ⅔ brush and increase the concentration of your brown shadow mix. Now carefully paint in the branches in any visible gaps through the clouds of pine needles. You can also paint some branches on top of the green areas too. Once fully dry, rub out any visible pencil.

## 4.

With your size 2 brush, paint sweeps of diluted sap green from the base of the trunk outward, fading into the green wash.

Go back over the trunk with your size ⅖ brush and your concentrated brown shadow mix, adding gnarly texture and knots. If you painted new bare branches, add little clusters of pine needles in sap green.

Once the green texture around the base of the trunk has dried, add little grass shoots of concentrated sap green with your size ⅖ brush. Allow to dry fully.

## 5.

Mix up some diluted shadow mix and choose which side of the tree will be in shadow. With your size 2 brush, paint a diluted sweep of shadow up one side of the trunk and in all the shadowy nooks, the undersides of the branches and boughs. Then with your size 8 brush, paint a line across the grass from the base of the trunk. Angle your brush low to the page and paint a few sweeps of colour to create the shadow of the tree on the ground. Angling the brush low like this will dry out the colour and give you a rough, organic edge to the shadow, looking just like the pine needle boughs above.

4

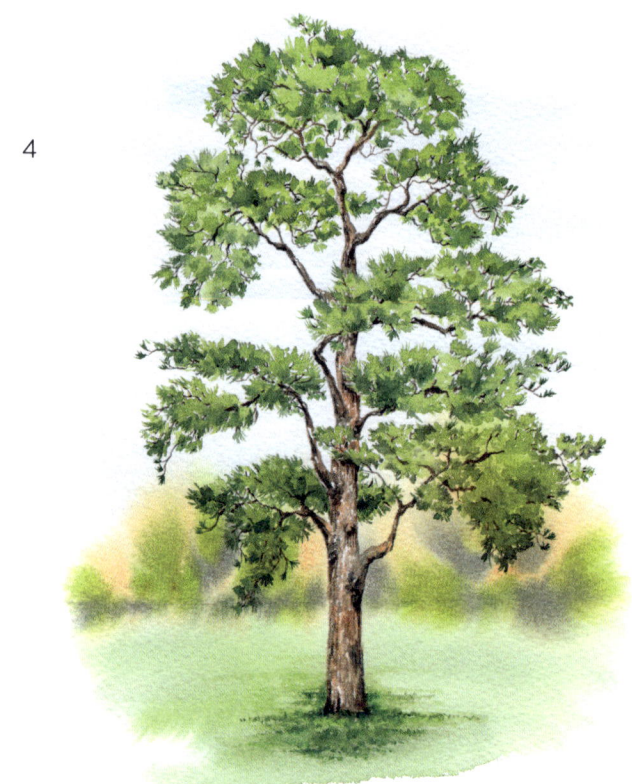

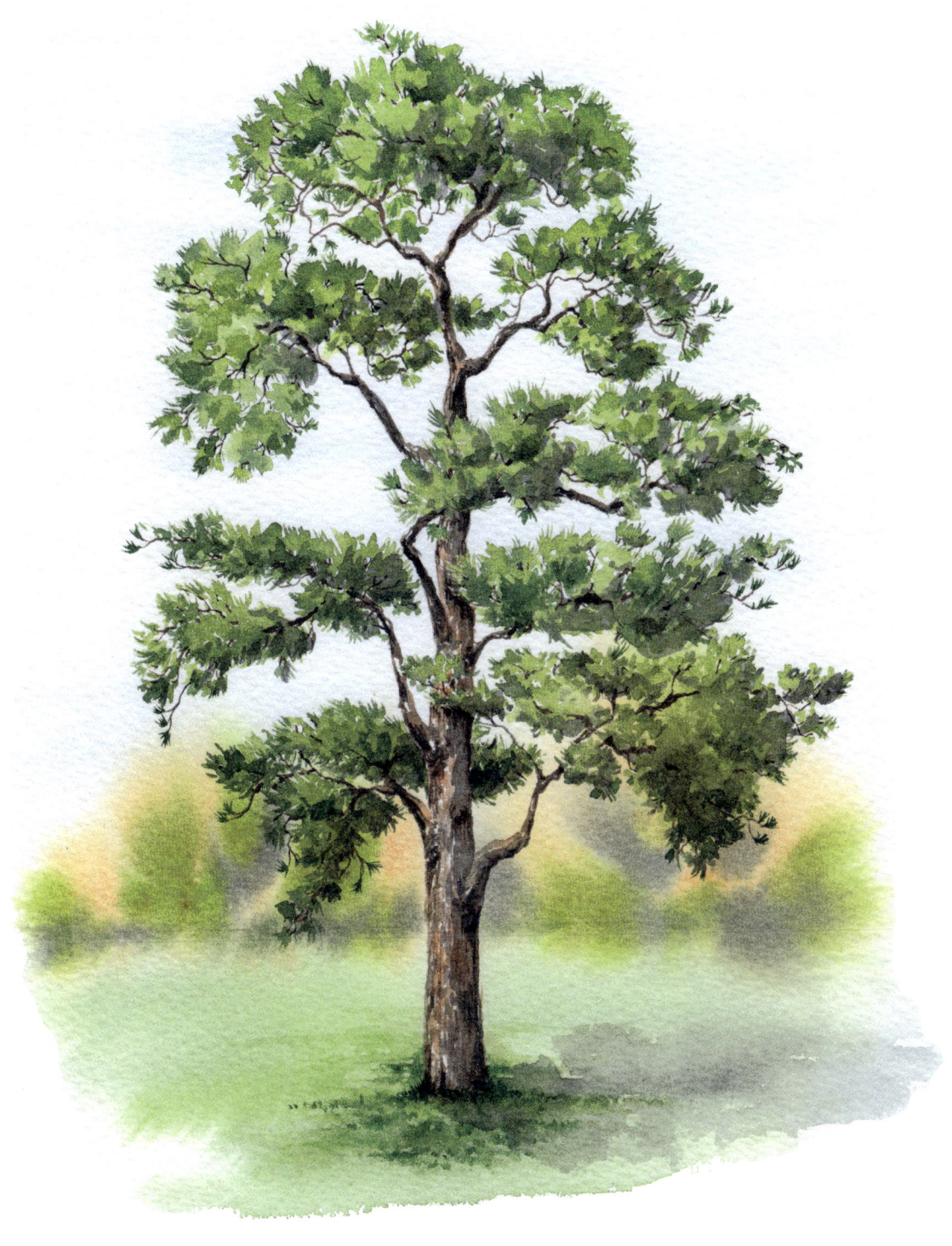

127 SCOTS PINE

# WINTER WREATH

Holly and mistletoe are undisputed winter classics, but the plants that thrived in summer are now all dried out and living a ghostly second existence. Try mixing dried cow parsley, honesty and other seed heads with your fresh winter foliage for a wonderful contrast.

## WHAT YOU WILL NEED

**Brushes**
Pointed round size 4, 2, 0, ²⁄₀, ⁴⁄₀
Rigger size 0

**Paper**
Cold pressed (textured)

**HB Pencil**
**Eraser**
**Compass**

Approximate size of all detail plant paintings: 14 x 7cm (5½ x 2¾in)

Approximate size of wreath painting: 11 x 11cm (4¼ x 4¼in)

## Colour

Payne's grey

alizarin crimson

sap green

green gold

cadmium red

burnt sienna

yellow ochre

French ultramarine blue

cadmium yellow

## Mix

**Plant mix:** sap green and green gold

**Shadow mix:** burnt sienna and Payne's grey

**Gold mix:** yellow ochre and Payne's grey

**Dry mix:** yellow ochre, Payne's grey, burnt sienna

## DRIED FOLIAGE

### Wheat

### 1.

Draw a faint pencil stem with lots of branches curling over to one side. Paint a tapered line of gold mix with your size 4 brush to create each seed pod.

### 2.

With your rigger brush, paint fine lines of yellow ochre down each seed pod, then paint the stem and branches with the same brush and colour. Once dry, add a sweep of diluted shadow mix on each pod with your size 2 brush.

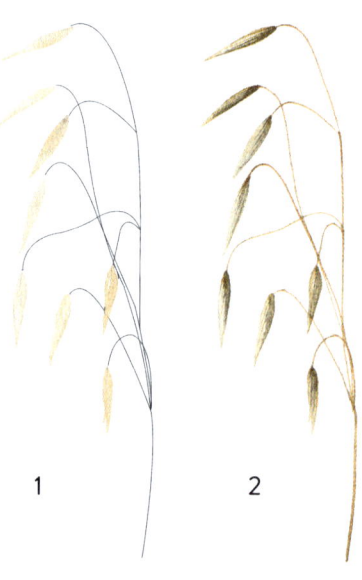

1          2

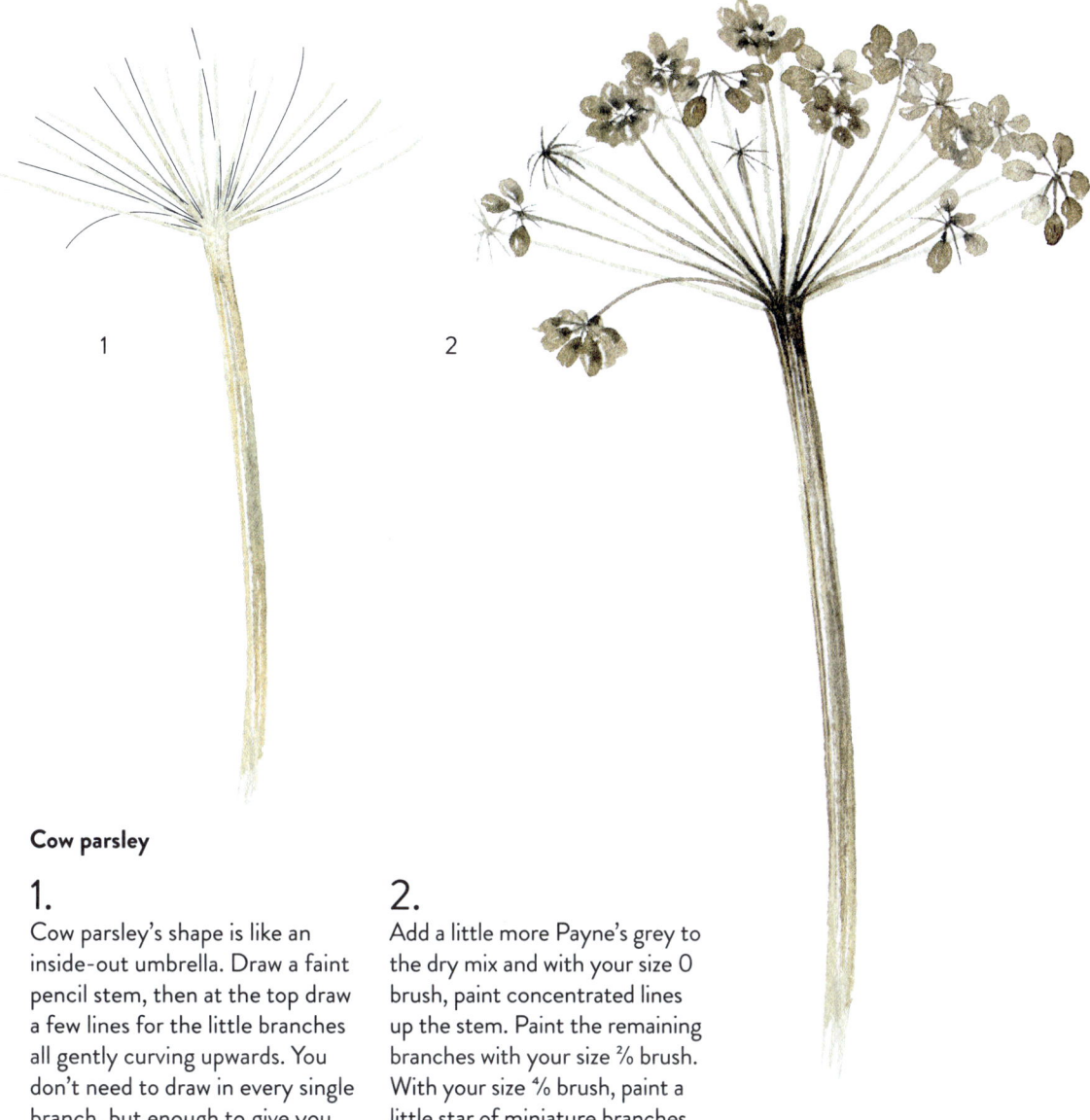

1

2

## Cow parsley

### 1.

Cow parsley's shape is like an inside-out umbrella. Draw a faint pencil stem, then at the top draw a few lines for the little branches all gently curving upwards. You don't need to draw in every single branch, but enough to give you a rough framework. With your size 2 brush, paint lines of dry mix with slivers of unpainted space in between for the thick, ridged stem. Paint diluted dry mix branches with your size ⅖ brush, these will be the background fronds, so space them out as you will be painting another batch next. Allow to dry.

### 2.

Add a little more Payne's grey to the dry mix and with your size 0 brush, paint concentrated lines up the stem. Paint the remaining branches with your size ⅖ brush. With your size ⅘ brush, paint a little star of miniature branches at the top of these concentrated stems. Add a little loop of diluted dry mix to most of the tiny star branches to create the dried seeds.

**Honesty**

## 1.

Draw a faint pencil stem with parallel branches. Starting at the bottom, paint a dry mix stem with your rigger brush and curve it out to the first branch. Paint a diluted dry mix disc with your size 4 brush and add a dab of shadow mix where the branch meets the seed pod. Work your way up the stem, painting stem and seed pod respectively. If you have any overlapping seed pods, allow the previous one to have dried fully before painting the next one.

## 2.

Paint a clear wash onto the first three seed pods, allow them to partially dry for about ten seconds then paint three 'seeds' of diluted shadow mix with your size 2 brush. If the surface is too wet and the colour spreads too far, don't panic, blot it with some tissue and repeat the three dots and they should stay put.

1

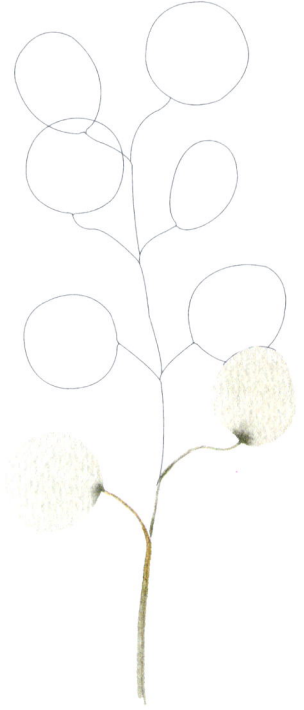

2

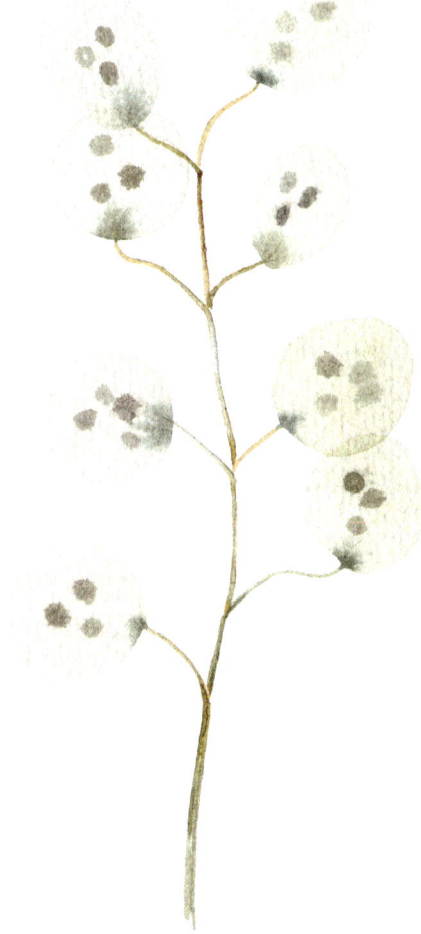

# FRESH FOLIAGE

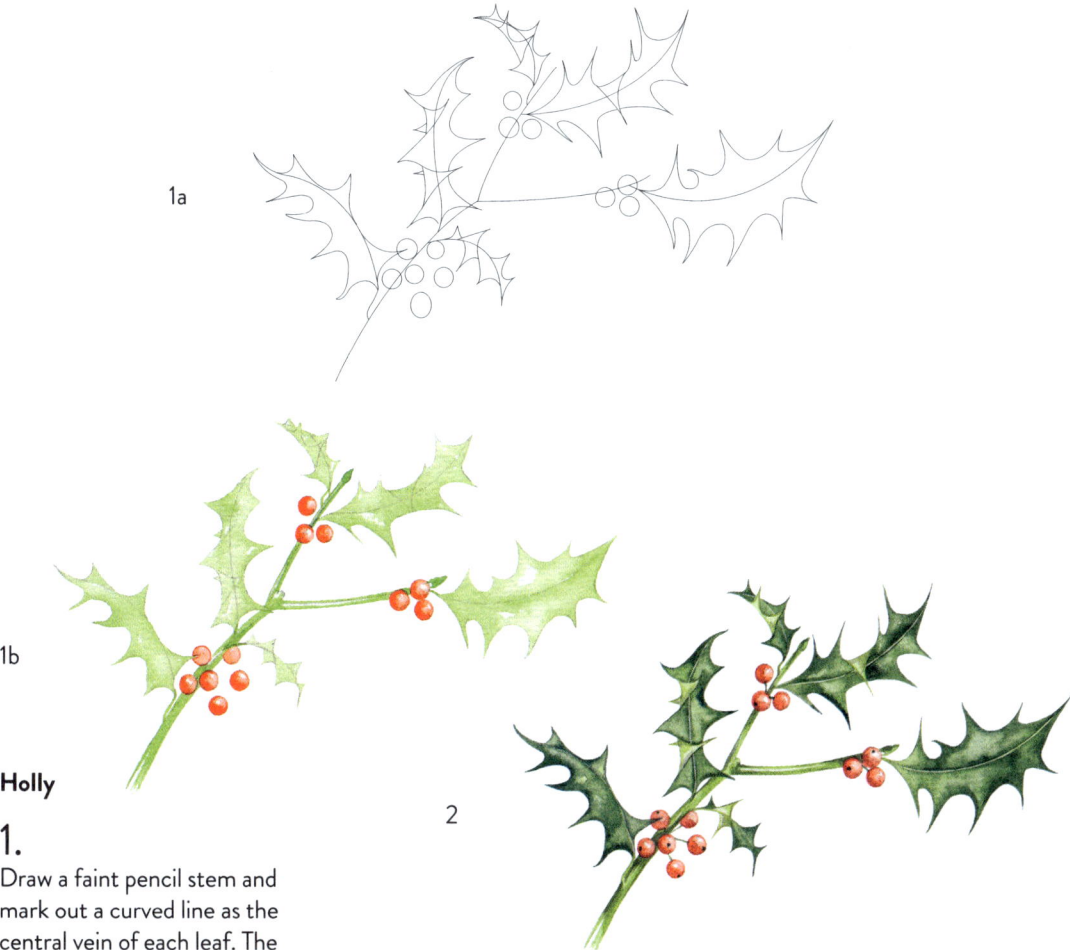

1a

1b

**Holly**

## 1.

Draw a faint pencil stem and
mark out a curved line as the
central vein of each leaf. The
spikes undulate up and down along
the edge of the leaf, so follow
the drawing guide to create the
different leaf shapes. Draw in
clusters of berries too. Your size
2 brush is large enough to create
a wash, but to have control at the
fine points, use it to paint each leaf
in diluted plant mix and the stem
in slightly more concentrated
plant mix. Use your size 0 brush
to paint the outline of each berry
in cadmium red. Clean your brush
and use the wet bristles to draw
the colour inwards, leaving some
unpainted 'shine'.

## 2.

Leaving a tiny unpainted line
down the middle of each leaf, use
a ⅔ brush to outline the leaves
in sap green. Then wet the brush
and draw the colour in. Add a
little French ultramarine blue to
your sap green and add a dab of
this darker colour in places to
highlight the shiny surface of the
leaves. Leave the underside of
the leaves unpainted but outline
these sections with a fine line of
green gold. Add a few streaks
of sap green down the stem and

paint tiny branches connecting
the stem to the berries.

Add a sweep of alizarin crimson
to the berries and dot each
one with a concentrated dab of
Payne's grey. Finish with a sweep
of diluted shadow mix on any
shadowy undersides of leaves
and stems.

1a

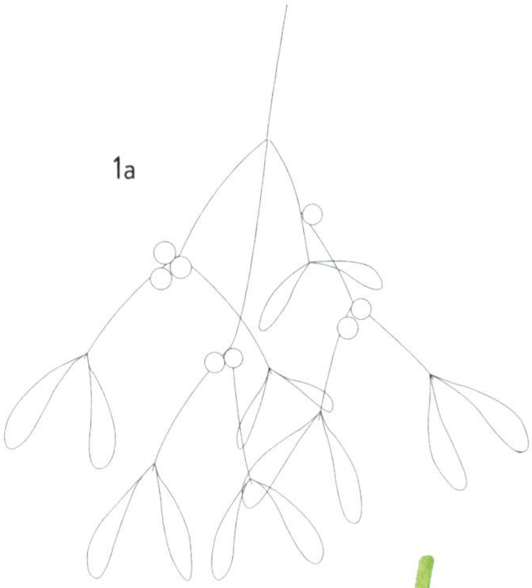

2

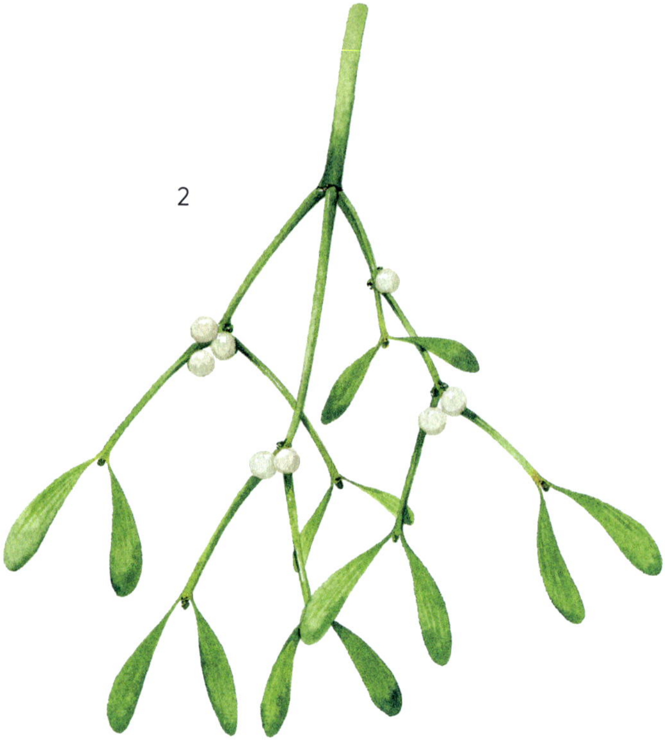

1b

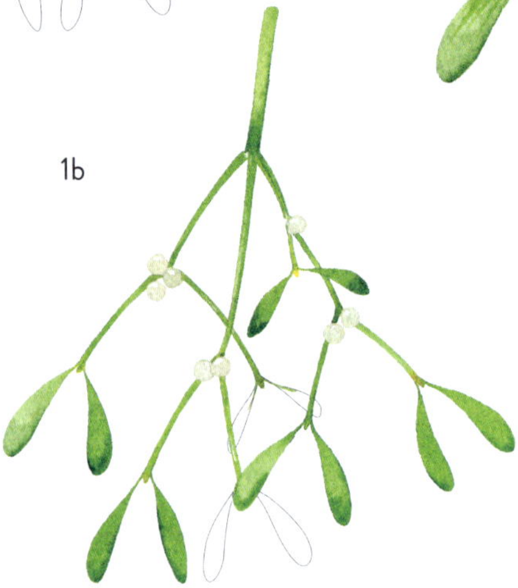

## WINTER SPRIG

If you enjoy painting these more detailed, large-scale plants, arrange three together in a sprig. Choose the palest plant to paint first in the background, like honesty, then build up your stronger colours.

**Mistletoe**

## 1.

Draw a faint pencil stem with branches, berries and leaves. Starting at the top, paint green gold down each stem, branch and leaf with your size 0 brush. Finish each branch with a dab of cadmium yellow as the bract between each pair of leaves. Add a little sap green to the end of each wet leaf and allow it to blend. Once fully dry, you can paint the overlapped leaves. Also paint the berries in diluted gold mix with a tiny bit of unpainted space for shine.

## 2.

Paint diluted lines of green gold on each leaf with your size 0 brush. At each branch junction, use some sap green to add some knobbly extra bracts (the tiny buds that sit at the ends of the branches). Paint concentrated shadow mix at the growth where the three main branches grow from the central stem, then dilute your shadow mix and paint a little sweep around the underside of each berry.

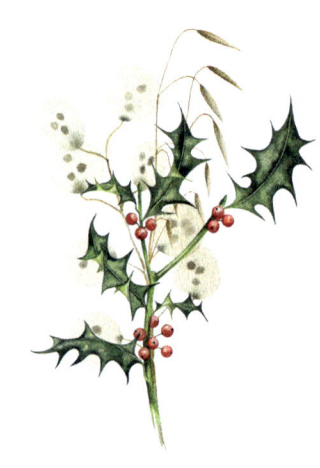

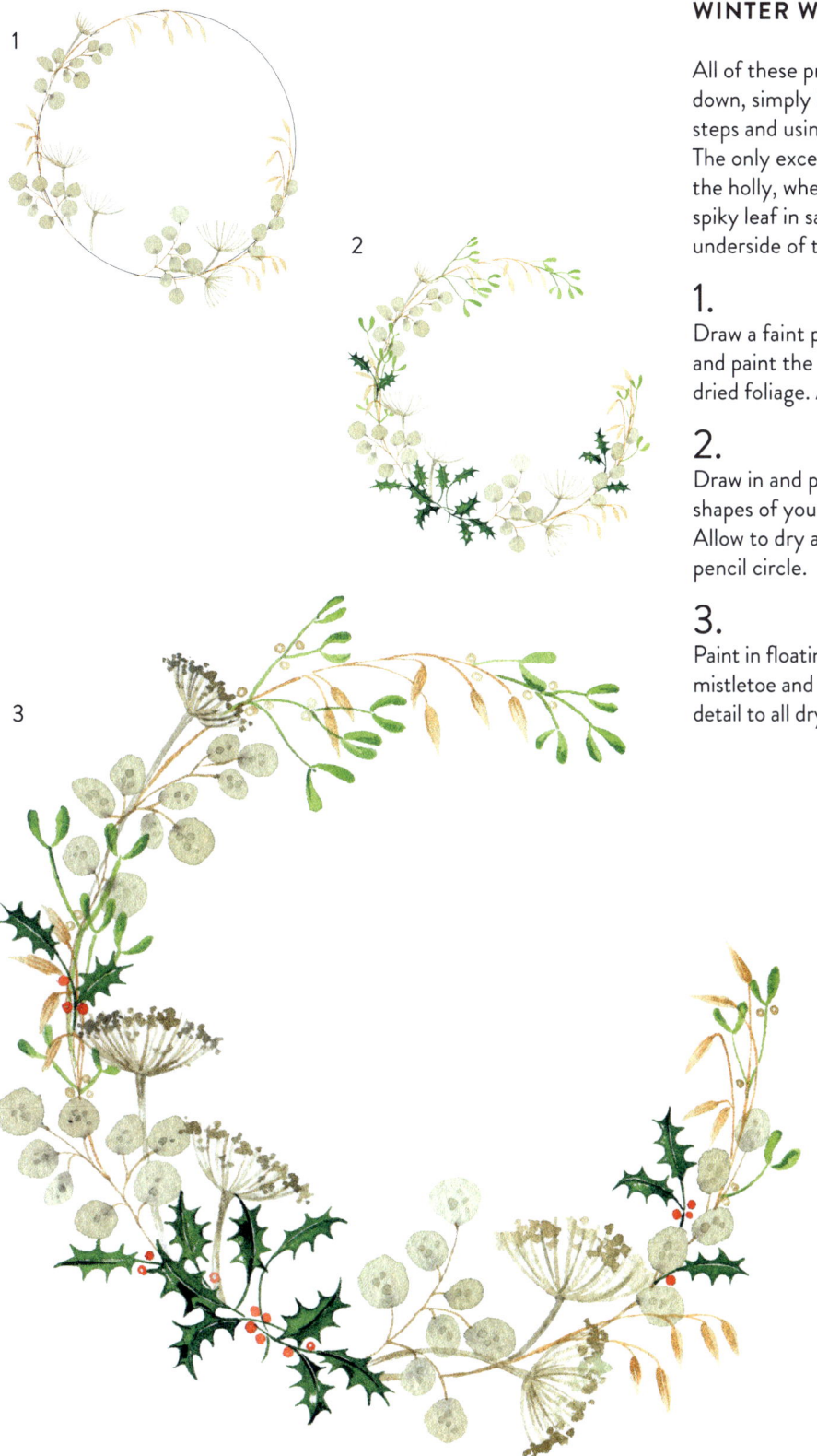

## WINTER WREATH

All of these projects can be scaled down, simply by following the steps and using smaller brushes. The only exception to this rule is the holly, where I paint a simpler spiky leaf in sap green with no underside of the leaf showing.

### 1.

Draw a faint pencil circle. Draw in and paint the basic shapes of your dried foliage. Allow to dry.

### 2.

Draw in and paint the basic shapes of your fresh foliage. Allow to dry and rub out the pencil circle.

### 3.

Paint in floating berries around the mistletoe and holly branches. Add detail to all dry and fresh foliage.

# RED FOX

The red fox's fiery coat lights up the dark winter days with a festive feel. If only it snowed a bit more – the sight of a fox in a snowy field would make a perfect Christmas card!

## WHAT YOU WILL NEED

**Brushes**
Pointed round size 2, 0, ⁴⁄₀

**Paper**
Cold pressed (textured)

**HB Pencil**
Eraser

Approximate size of the fox painting:
14 x 8cm (5½ x 3in)

## Colour

Payne's grey

burnt sienna

Mars black

cadmium orange

cadmium red

sap green

green gold

yellow ochre

## Mix

**White fur mix:** majority Payne's grey to yellow ochre

**Orange fur mix:** cadmium orange and cadmium red

**Shadow mix:** burnt sienna and Payne's grey

## 1.

Follow the drawing guide to create a faint pencil body shape.

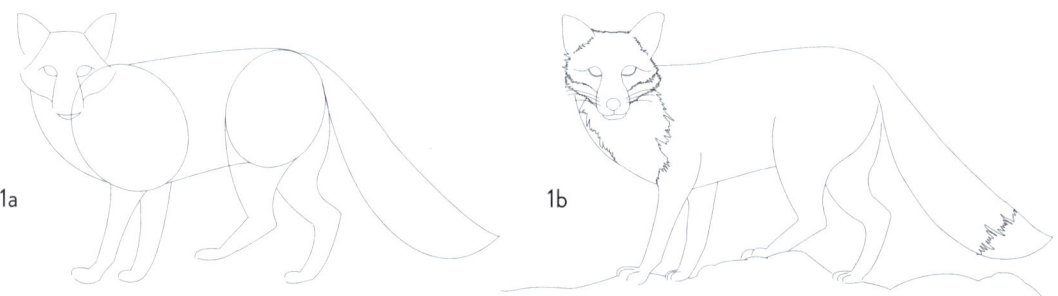

1a

1b

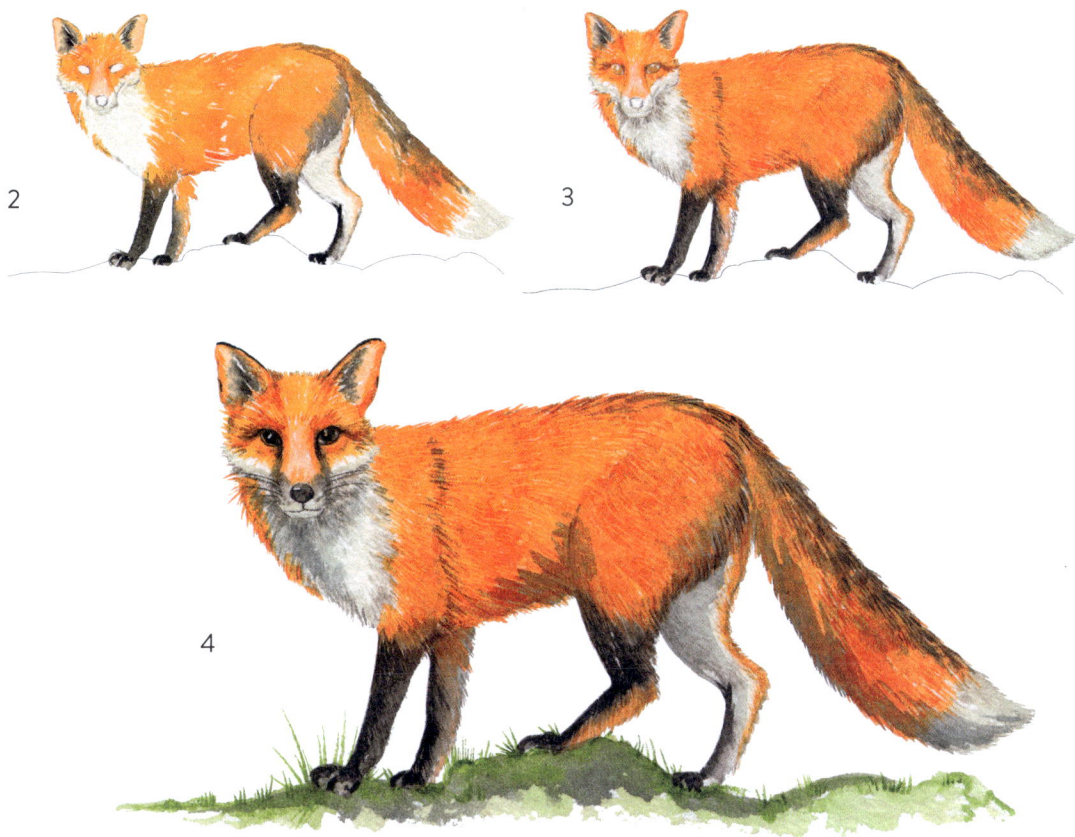

## 2.

Use your size 2 brush to paint a wash of diluted white fur mix from the chin down the torso, the inside back leg and tail tip. Paint the rest of the body with orange fur mix strokes. Switch to diluted Mars black down the foreground legs. Add a little burnt sienna to the orange fur mix for the hind leg and tail section and edge the haunches and tail with diluted Mars black strokes.

With your size 0 brush, paint the face with similar loose strokes of orange fur mix. Outline the ears in diluted orange fur mix and add strokes of diluted Mars black inside.

If you like this loose, scribbly style you could skip Step 3 and go straight to facial detail.

## 3.

With your size ⅙ brush, paint fine line hairs of more concentrated colours that correspond with the washes over the fur. Use shadow mix to add fine line contours to the fur. Paint diluted burnt sienna irises in the eyes.

## 4.

With your size ⅙ brush, outline the eye in Mars black and bring the line down either side of the nose. Clean your brush and blend the colour into the fur with a few whisker dots on the muzzle. Once dry, paint a Mars black nose, mouth, whiskers and ear tips. Allow to dry fully and rub out any visible pencil.

With your size 2 brush, paint a mossy ground with diluted green gold. While still wet, paint in sap green grass with your size ⅙ brush. Allow to dry.

With your size 2 brush, paint sweeps of diluted shadow mix down the torso, the background legs, under the tail and on the ground.

# HELLEBORE

When looking for something seasonal to paint at Christmas time that isn't red or green, hellebores are a real breath of fresh air.

## WHAT YOU WILL NEED

**Brushes**
Pointed round size 4, 2, 0
Rigger size 0

**Paper**
Cold pressed (textured)

**HB Pencil**
**Eraser**

### Colour

sap green

green gold

Payne's grey

burnt sienna

permanent rose

alizarin crimson

### Mix

**Green mix:** sap green and green gold

**Petal mix:** sap green, green gold, permanent rose

**Dark mix:** alizarin crimson, Payne's grey, burnt sienna

**Shadow mix:** burnt sienna and Payne's grey

## 1.

Follow the drawing guide to create a faint pencil hellebore plant. This is one of the rare occasions that I draw the petals in before painting them, but the leaves can just be marked with the central leaf vein line. Make sure to draw a small circle in the centre of an open-faced flower or an oval for angled flowers.

1

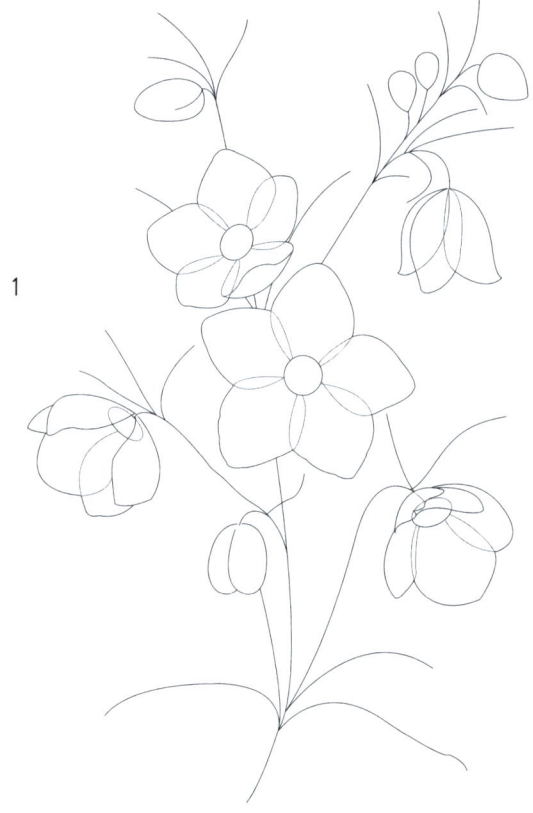

Approximate size of the hellebore painting: 17 x 10cm (6½ x 4in)

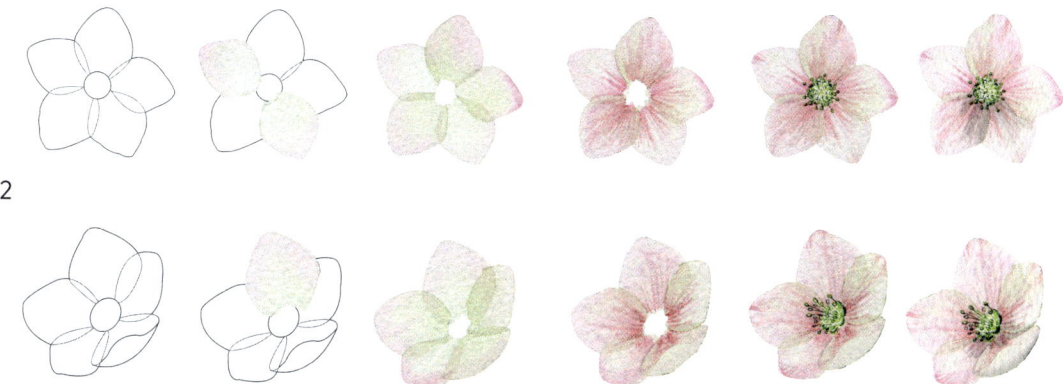

2

## 2.

Dilute your petal mix right down and paint as many petals that don't touch each other as possible with your size 4 brush (hellebore petals are actually sepals). As you paint each petal, dab some diluted permanent rose at the tip and let it blend in. Once those are completely dry, repeat the process until all petals are painted. Make sure to leave the central circle/oval unpainted.

## 3.

With your flowers painted, you can see where the stem and leaves are still visible. First paint the serrated-edge leaves (see page 14) in green mix with your size 4 brush. Once those have dried, begin at the bottom of the plant and paint in the stem with your size 2 brush. As the stems get more slender up the plant, add a little alizarin crimson to your green mix and paint with your size 0 brush.

3

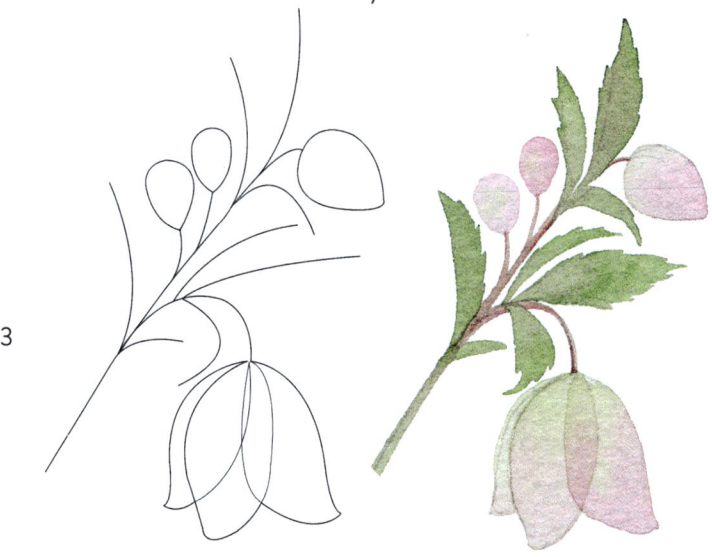

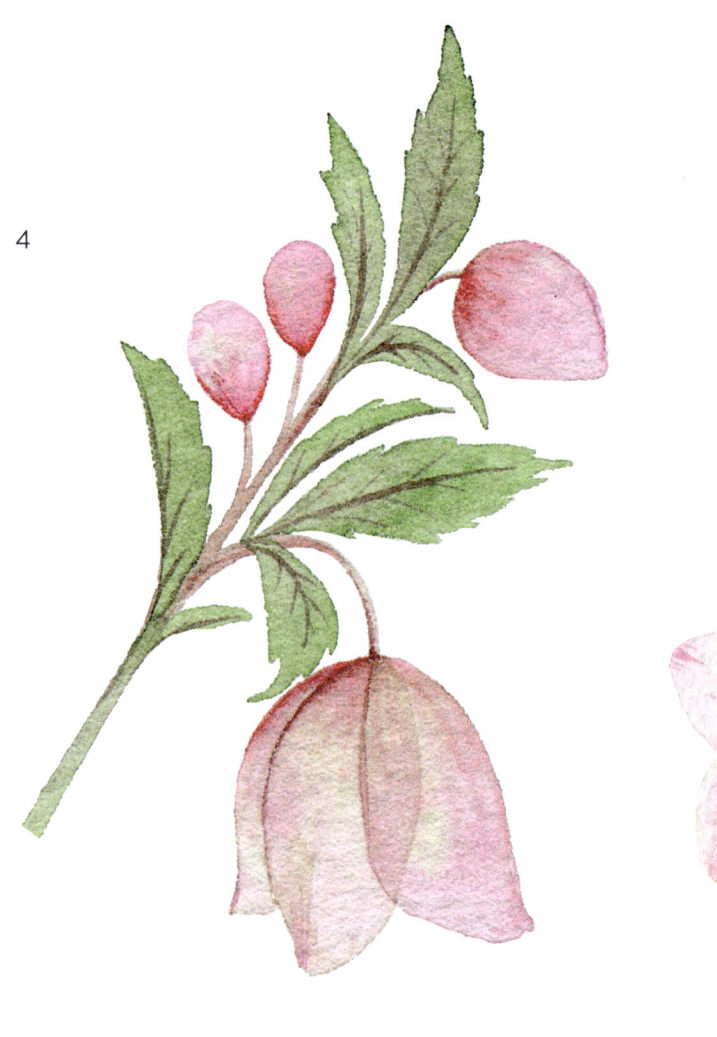

4

**4.**

With all the basic shapes painted in, it's time to add some detail. Paint an alizarin crimson central leaf line and leaf veins with your rigger brush. Hellebore petals are streaked with delicate pink veins. The best way to keep these lines from being too heavy is to lightly wet the petal you're working on with a damp brush, then paint diluted lines of permanent rose from the flower centre outwards. Then paint a few diluted lines of alizarin crimson.

**5.**

With your smallest brush, paint small diluted C-curves around the edge of the central area then paint the anthers with tiny circles of concentrated green gold in and around the central area. Paint fine lines back into the centre and add sap green lowlights.

5

## 6.

Add dark mix lowlights to the slender ends of the stems and allow to dry. Add diluted shadow to any shady underside you can find as well as a few streaks on the petals below the central stamen. Add concentrated shadow mix lowlights to the filaments and anthers in the middle of the flowers and at the base of the buds.

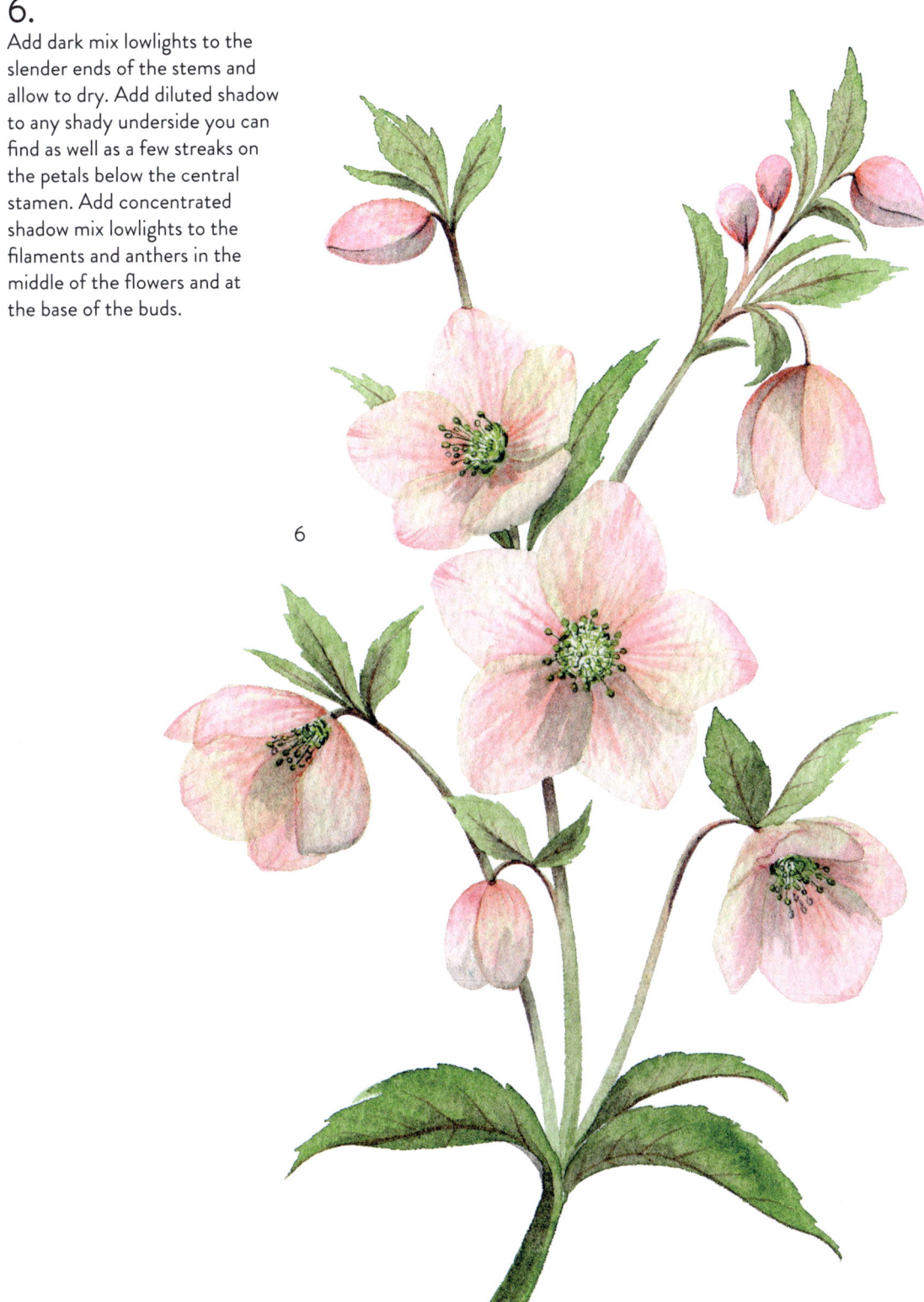

6

# EVERGREEN LANDSCAPE

Evergreen forests provide such atmospheric inspiration for what can otherwise be seen as a cold and dark time of year. We collect bits and pieces of fallen greenery on our winter walks: fir and pine branches make great additions to any winter wreath (see page 128)

## WHAT YOU WILL NEED

**Brushes**
Pointed round size 8, 2, ⅖
Mop brush size 6

**Paper**
Cold pressed (textured)

**HB Pencil**
**Eraser**

## Colour

 Payne's grey

 burnt sienna

 Mars black

 sap green

## Mix

 **Tree mix:** sap green, Mars black, Payne's grey

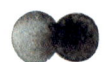 **Shadow mix:** burnt sienna and Payne's grey

Approximate size of the landscape painting: 15 x 15cm (6 x 6in)

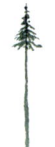 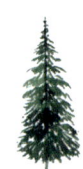

## 1.

Draw a series of pencil hills. Then with your mop brush, wet the area above these pencil lines. Use your pointed round size 8 brush to paint clear water right up to the pencil lines. While still wet, paint some curves of diluted shadow mix into the sky area with your size 8 brush. To paint the first layer of trees, you want the page to still be significantly damp but not so wet that the paint leaves no definition at all. I find the time spent painting in the sky allows the page to dry enough. Follow the fir tree steps to paint in your trees with diluted tree mix and your size ⅖ brush.
Allow to dry.

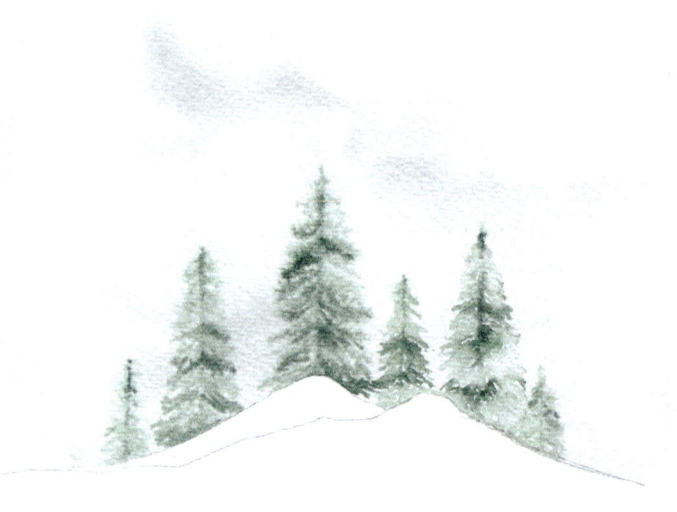

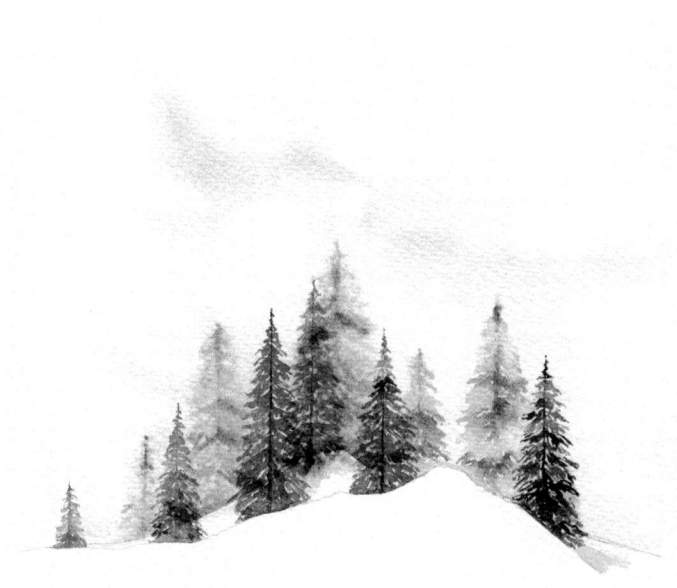

## 2.

That first layer of trees will lighten as it dries, but add a tiny bit more concentration to your tree mix and paint in a series of trees on the hill in front. If the base of the tree is visible, use a clean wet size 2 brush to sweep across the base and blend the colour into the hill. Add some diluted shadow mix and use the brush strokes to create the appearance of light and shade on the snow. Allow to dry.

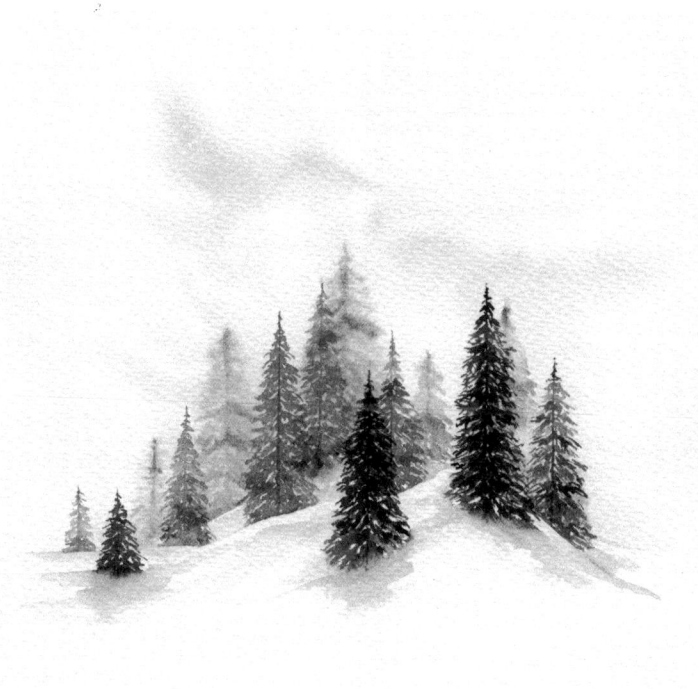

## 3.

Now with a fully concentrated tree mix, paint in a few more trees in the foreground. Repeat Step 2, smoothing out the base of the tree with a size 2 brush and some diluted shadow mix to create light and shade on the snow. Finish with a few concentrated lowlights of Payne's grey on the branches. Once dry, rub out any visible pencil.

# SNOWDROPS

What a relief it is to see a common snowdrop after a long, dark winter. Their arrival is reassurance of brighter days ahead and the start of another seasonal cycle. They're quick to droop in a vase if picked, so treat a snowdrop sighting as your first opportunity to head out into nature and draw on location.

## WHAT YOU WILL NEED

**Brushes**
Pointed round size 4, 2, 0
Rigger size 0

**Paper**
Cold pressed (textured)

**HB Pencil**
**Eraser**

**Colours**

 yellow ochre

 green gold

 sap green

 Payne's grey

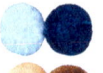 French ultramarine blue

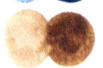 burnt sienna

**Mixes**

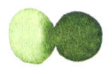 **Plant mix:** sap green and green gold

 **Petal mix:** sap green, burnt sienna, Payne's grey, yellow ochre

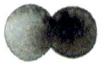 **Shadow mix:** burnt sienna and Payne's grey

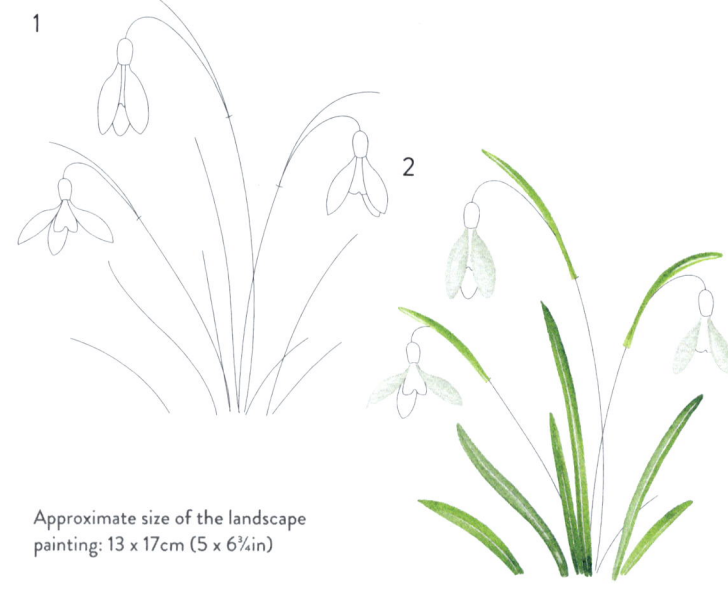

Approximate size of the landscape painting: 13 x 17cm (5 x 6¾in)

## 1.
Follow the drawing guide to create a faint pencil cluster of snowdrops.

## 2.
The flowering stem reaches a point where the weight of the flower curves over and a separate stem called the spathe continues upwards. Paint the spathe with your rigger brush in plant mix. For the various leaves shooting up around the stems, use your size 4 brush to paint sap green parallel tapered lines that come to a soft point. Leave a tiny sliver of unpainted space up the middle to create the leaf's subtle crease.

The snowdrop flower is comprised of three teardrop petals (outer perianth segments) and three shorter – usually green and white – inside petals (inner perianth segments). Mix your petal mix and add plenty of water, diluting right down to almost clear water. With a size 2 brush, paint two of the outer petals (that aren't touching each other) to each flower and allow everything to dry fully.

## 3.

With your size 2 brush, add a few more leaves in a more concentrated sap green with a dash of French ultramarine blue. Paint the rest of the stem and use your rigger brush for the slender overhanging curved stem (the peduncle) in sap green.

With a size 0 brush, paint the visible inner petals in petal mix. Allow to semi-dry and drop in some plant mix for the flash of green on this inner petal.

## 4.

Fill in any unpainted petals. With your size 4 brush, use the petal mix to paint in sweeps of snow along the base of the plant. While still wet, add a dab of shadow mix beneath the appearance of each shoot in the snow. Paint the green bulb (ovary) holding the petals together in plant mix with a size 0 brush and while still wet add a dab of concentrated sap green at the top.

Look for places among the leaves, petals and stems where you can add a bit of shadow mix to create a bit of depth.

**A few favourite snowdrop varieties spotted on my walks:**

**a** *Galanthus Pliatcus* 'Augustus'
These large, domed petals have a gorgeous seersucker fabric texture with green inner segments.

**b** *Galanthus* 'Primrose Warburg'
Yellow ovaries and yellow green inner segments. These look like gold pearl drop earrings.

**c** *Leucojum aestivum* 'Summer snowflake'
The tallest 'snowdrop' I've found with 8 pointed petals forming a bell shaped flower with multiple flowers on a single stem.

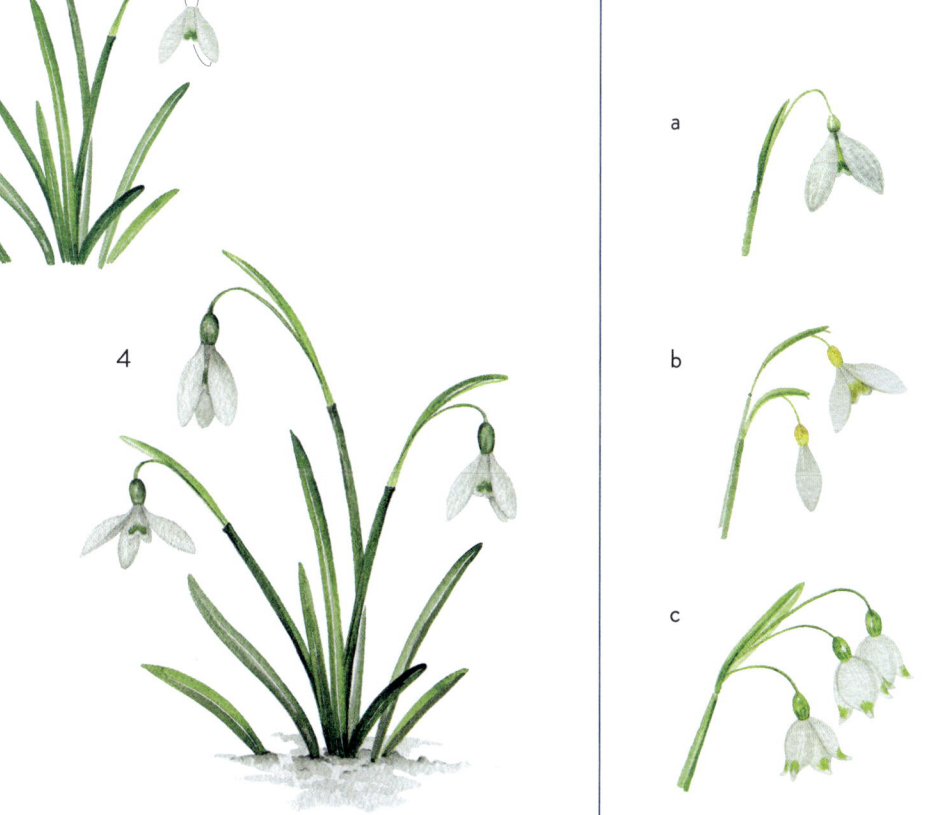

# ACKNOWLEDGEMENTS

With thanks to all our friends and family for their great support.

It's been such a pleasure to work once again with Ellie and the brilliant people at Octopus. It's wonderful to feel part of such a great team.

Thank you, Oscar, for your immediate enthusiasm for my work and brilliant guidance.

To my Patreon community, who have been my cheerleaders throughout, I love our global painting circle.

Gem and Eleanor, thank you for keeping the studio running while I buried my head in this book.

Ant – the best lockdown companion – thank you for your endless support and belief in me.

Thanks to Crumble, who got us out walking every day.

First published in the UK in 2023 by Ilex, an imprint of Octopus Publishing Group Ltd
Carmelite House
50 Victoria Embankment
London EC4Y 0DZ
www.octopusbooks.co.uk

An Hachette UK Company
www.hachette.co.uk

The authorized representative in the EEA is Hachette Ireland, 8 Castlecourt Centre, Dublin 15, D15 XTP3, Ireland (email: info@hbgi.ie)

Text and illustrations copyright © Harriet de Winton 2023
Design and layout copyright © Octopus Publishing Group Limited 2023

Distributed in the US by Hachette Book Group
1290 Avenue of the Americas
4th and 5th Floors
New York
NY 10104

Distributed in Canada by Canadian Manda Group
664 Annette St.
Toronto, Ontario
Canada M6S 2C8

Harriet de Winton has asserted her right under the Copyright, Designs and Patents Act 1988 to be identified as the author of this work.

ISBN 978-1-78157-900-8

A CIP catalogue record for this book is available from the British Library.

Printed and bound in China

10 9 8 7 6

Publisher: Alison Starling
Commissioning Editor: Ellie Corbett
Managing Editor: Rachel Silverlight
Editorial Assistant: Jeannie Stanley
Art Director: Ben Gardiner
Designer: Eleanor Ridsdale
Assistant Production Managers: Lucy Carter & Nic Jones

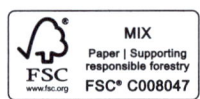

FSC
MIX
Paper | Supporting responsible forestry
FSC® C008047
www.fsc.org

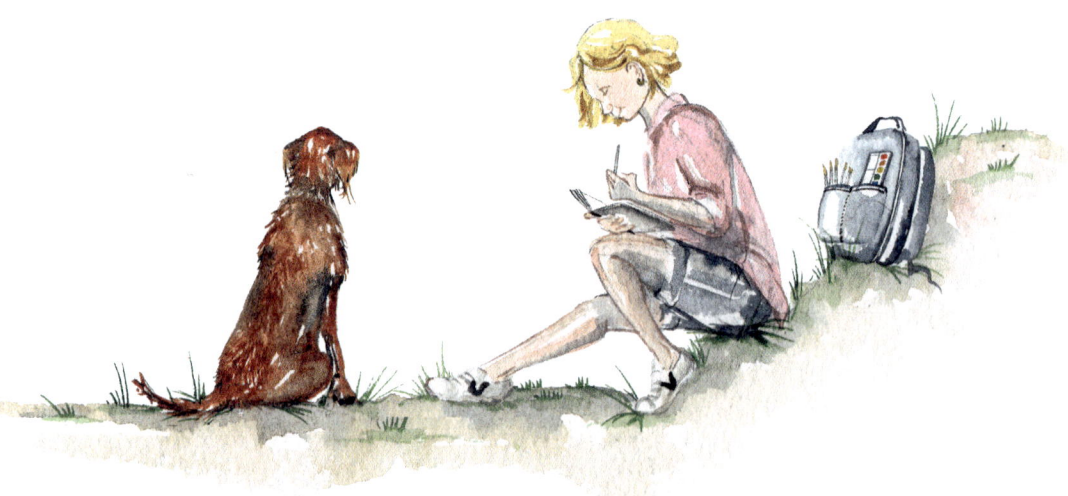